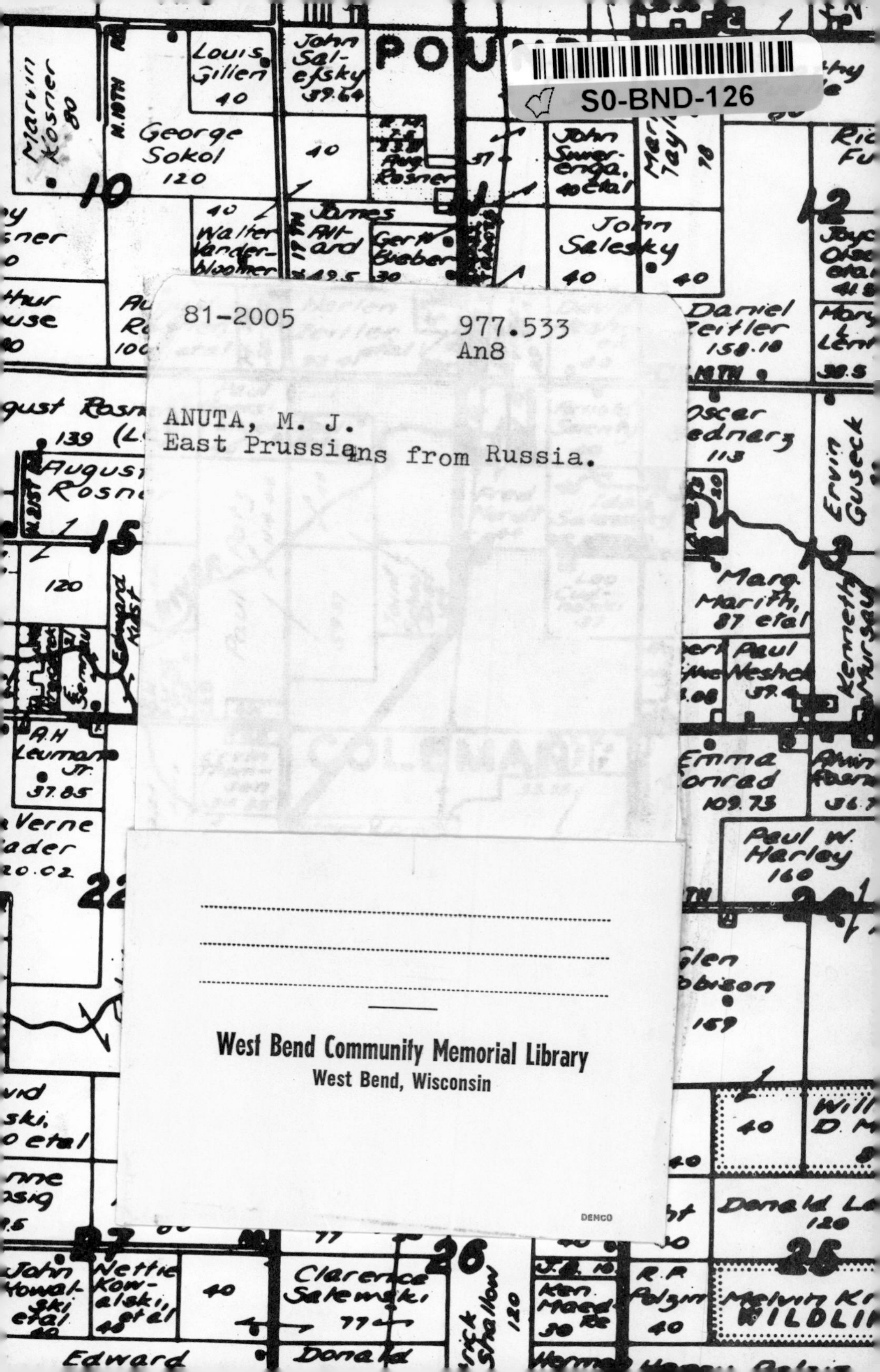

Louis Gillen 40
John Salefsky 37.64
George Sokol 120
Walter Vander-bloomer
James Altard
Gert Bieber
John Swerenga, et al
John Salesky 40
Daniel Zeitler 158.18
Oscer Bednarz 113
Ervin Guseck
Marg. Marith, 87 et al
Paul Neshek
A.H. Leuman Jr. 37.85
Emma Conrad 109.73
Paul W. Harley 160
Glen Robison 159
Donald 120
Clarence Salemski 77
John Howatski et al
Nettie Kowalski, et al
Ken. Maedke 30
R.P. Polzin 40
Edward
Donald

EAST PRUSSIANS
FROM
RUSSIA

Michael J. Anuta

EAST PRUSSIANS
FROM
RUSSIA

Michael J. Anuta

To
The Pilgrims from
East Prussia
and
Their Descendents

TABLE OF CONTENTS

ILLUSTRATIONS AND MAPS

ACKNOWLEDGMENT

I most gratefully acknowledge that most of this history has come to me through my grandparents who were born and raised, married and had children in East Prussia and then moved to the Russian Ukraine where they had more children and then came to this country. To my parents, who came here as young people, mother coming alone at age 16. She later married my father in Pound and raised a large family. Both sets of grandparents lived with us for years at a time. To my relatives and family near and far.

I express my special gratitude to Dr. Adam Giesinger, President of the American Historical Society of Germans from Russia for a complete review of this work, collating the subject matter and making many most valuable suggestions and corrections. I thank the staff of the American Historical Society of Germans from Russia especially Miss Ruth M. Amen, immediate Past President and to Mr. Herman D. Wildermuth, Mr. Arthur E. Flegel, Dr. Albert W. Wardin, Mrs. Emma S. Haynes and others who helped with some difficult documents.

The Kiev photographs taken by Mr. Dean Conger of National Georgraphic and which appeared in JOURNEY THROUGH RUSSIA by Mr. Bart McDowell are used by special permission. The pictures from OSTPREUSSEN, Band 16 der Reihe, "Die Deutschen Lande", from DAS OSTPREUSSENBLATT are used through their courtesy. Mr. Paul Patz furnished the pcitures of the Patz Company and Patz Farm. The Rev. Mr. C. V. Strelec's "Burning Bush" for a history of his life; his personal records and reports to the Northern Baptist Convention. To the American Baptist Historical Society and the Annuals of the Northern Baptist Convention as well as the Wisconsin Baptist State Convention for records and information concerning Rev. C. V. Strelec and Rev. Michael S. Anuta.

To the Historical Sketch of the First Baptist Church of Pound by Emil Will, the "SEVENTY FIVE YEARS OF BLESSINGS" a history of the Pioneer Baptist Church (formerly German) in Pound, sent me by Mrs. Albert Borkowski and the SECTION EIGHT BAPTIST CHURCH 75th ANNIVERSARY 1901-1976" booklet.

A great deal of work has been done by Orville Broderick in gathering photographs and material. I thank him and the people who cooperated with him: Mrs. Dorothy Brooks Fuelle, Jerry Maloney, C E. Maloney, Cy Maloney, Mrs. Walter Woller, Mrs. Henry Johnson, Mrs. Elizabeth Johnson, Mrs. Kinzinger, Mrs. Charlotte Gross, Mrs. Augusta Ermis Wertelewski Cobus, Mrs. Geraldine Dupuis, Mr. Ambrose Fortier, Mrs. Ann Perrault, Mrs. George Martens, the Louis Bergeron family, Mrs. Ruth Sokol, Lloyd Gissenaas, Mrs. Robert Stadlman, The Rev. Richard Reece, the Rev. Gerald Van Prooven, the Rev. F. W. Zink, the Rev. Nevin Beehler, the Rev. Samuel Kostreva Sr., Mrs. Ed Stank, Miss Ruth Heisel, Mrs. Frank Gengler, Mrs. Frank Rost, Mrs. J. E. Van Vonderen, Rene Durocher, Barbara Jane Page, Ms. Mae Murroch, Mr. & Mrs. Donald Anutta, Mrs. C. V. Strelec and her daughter Mrs. Helen Robinson, Mrs. Maria Frank, Mrs. Elisabeth Malessa, Mrs. Verne L. Batten, Mrs. Alice Wolowicz, M. L. Hanson, Patricia Rudolph.

I am most grateful to my wife Mrs. Marianne Mildred Strelec Anuta and our daughter Mrs. Janet Grace Anuta Dalquist for their assistance and suggestions.

Michael J. Anuta
RA 655 Westland
Menominee, Mi. 49858
1978

PREFACE

This is a history of a unique people about whom there has been no historic record other than in a very general manner. They first fled to East Prussia, as a land of refuge and after centuries of life there moved to the Russian Ukraine. They lived in the Ukraine for only twenty-five to thirty-five years before being compelled to leave because of developments which had not been anticipated. They came to the United States and began a new life for a third time.

Their pilgrimages are epic in their courage and heroism, their faith and endurance under the burdensome conditions under which they built a life of greatness wherever fate took them. Their sojourn in East Prussia for generations attached to them the designation of "Prusi" and they regarded themselves as such even when they arrived in the United States.

The author is a first generation American of these people. Born only eleven years after the arrival of his grandparents in the United States, he has had the opportunity of learning this history directly from his forebears from personal experiences with them, from living with them and sharing their faith and life. Greater depth has been added to this history by Elisabeth Malessa who died July 8th 1978 but was a daughter of one of the last of the Labusch family. This came from a correspondence of nearly forty years with her in East Prussia, and in visits to Germany to see her. The research for this work can be said to be the entire span of life of this writer—over seventy five years.

Michael J. Anuta

Chapter 1

East Prussia, the Land and its Early History

A substantial part of northern Europe was visited by the ice ages. As the last of the ice age glaciers retreated, the land developed a cover of grasses and trees over many thousands of years. (17) 249,446,447. Eventually northern Europe was covered by large growths of deciduous trees and coniferous forests. The retreating glaciers left many evidences of the presence of the ice age with numcrous lakes, marshes, swamps, bogs morains and eskers running in a northwesterly and southeasterly direction.

The southern and western parts of Europe adjacent to the oceans and seas developed more rapidly than the interior because of the friendly influence of better climate induced by the ocean currents. The waters of the oceans and the rivers running into them would have provided an easier means of travel for the early inhabitants of Europe for both trade and fishing. The people slowly moved northward as food sources developed until they reached the northern Germanic and Baltic coasts.

The territory with which we will be most concerned is the area between the Vistula and the Niemen Rivers and running southerly inland for a like distance. The land between these rivers remained a dense wilderness for a longer period of time than other areas of Europe.

In the course of time and political development, this territory became known for some seven centuries, as East Prussia. East Prussia for most of its history had about 14,300 square miles of land. This would be larger than Belgium but a little smaller than Switzerland. In American territory it would be about the size of Vermont and Connecticut put together.

The coastal lands of East Prussia included many lagoons and dunes. The coastal cliffs were mined for amber which is a pine resin found in alluvial soil. Amber is highly electrical and is used as the base for amber varnish. Cigarette holders, mouthpieces for pipes and beads and ornaments were made from it.

The interior of East Prussia where the forests have been removed is a rather low rolling plain merging into the glacial formations already referred to. The visitation and revisitation of the area by the glaciers left some 3,300 lakes scattered over the southerly half of this region. When cleared, a little more than half of this land was usable farm land of variable richness contributed by the long time presence of grass and forest cover. Some of it has been termed by a German historian as "gardenrich" (1), (3), (5), (17).

East Prussia was the northerly portion of the Paleazoic platform known in geology as the Polish Platform (17) and thus served as the northern part of the great gateway corridor between Europe and Asia. (31) p 30. This gateway corridor was the meeting ground and battle ground of the great population and racial migrations and invasions which surged back and forth between the East and the West for centuries (31) p 30.

Running from the Baltic to the Black Sea, this gateway contained no major natural barriers excepting the Masurian lakes left by the glaciers in southerly East Prussia. (1) (2), (17) (5), (31).

Since World War 11 the northern portion of East Prussia, including the former city of Koenigsberg, now Kaliningrad, has been located and become a part of the Soviet Russian territory while the southerly portion has been located within the Soviet Poland zone. (5)

At various times, this gateway corridor has been invaded by the Huns, Mongols, Tartars, Turks, Cossacks, Lithuanians, Scandinavian (Swedish), the Teutonic, Slavic and Frankish races. For example, in 1240 the conquest of Russia by the Tartars was complete. Half a million or more armed Asia-

1

tics swept over the land destroying everything. Only the combined efforts of Europe stopped the Tartars in Silesia and Moravia. This invasion lasted for 250 years. (18) p ix.

The Masurian Lakes with their crystal clear waters were more of a barrier in the summer. In the wintertime, when frozen over the lakes almost formed a natural highway. In any event, in military operations, they had their strategic values. Tannenberg in 1410 and again Tannenberg in World War 1, was a decisive battleground near these lakes for the peoples from the opposite sides of this corridor.

The natives living in the East Prussian area in the twelfth and thirteenth centuries were descendents of the same people who had followed the retreating glaciers of the last ice age. It is believed that the ancestors of these natives painted the pictures of large animals in the caves of southern Europe. Their language was classfied as the Baltic subdivision of the Indo-European group. (1), (2), (5),. These natives called themselves in their Baltic language "Prusi", "Prutzi", "Pruczi, or, Borussi" or some similar sounding name.

The Prusi religion was basically nature worship. The origin of the Christmas Tree and its use during the Christian festival of Christmas may have come from these original Prusi. Primitive man has been known to feel a sensitiveness and a kinship with nature and particularly with certain trees. The annual change of foliage, the decay and revival of foliage of the deciduous trees, gave the aborigines some understanding of their own birth, life and death and the possibility of revival after death. These beliefs of early men have become part of the fundamental ideas which have persisted for ages in distant parts of the earth. They have even found a place in some of the later religions.

Even the physical dependence of man upon certain trees for refuge from wild animals, for food, for materials for weapons, for medications, for fuel, for shelter and in some cases fibres for clothing, have buttressed their spiritual feelings of intuitive oneness with nature. The tall oaks of the Old Prussians, (Prusi) were said to be inhabited by gods who gave responses just as the old Hebrews had their "terebinth of the teacher" (Gen. X11, 6), and the "terebinth of the diviners" (Judges 1X, 37). The powers of tree-dieties, though often specially connected with the elements, are not necessarily so restricted. The Sacred trees can, and perhaps in the case of the Prusi, did form the center of their religious life.

It is said that the chief sanctuary of the Prusi was a holy oak around which lived priests and a high priest known as "God's mouth". Similarly, in Africa are sacred groves into which the priest alone may enter, and Syrian writers have mentioned a "King of the Forest" and a tall olive tree which Satan seduced the people to worship. (5) Britannica Tree-Cults.)

The Prusi of East Prussia fiercely resisted invasions of their lands. They were not very easily reached for they lived along the coasts, on the banks of the many rivers and among the Masurian glacial lakes of the interior. The Teutonic Knights termed this area the "Wildnis". The trees, therefore, provided the Prusi not only with the foundations for their religion, but food, shelter and many other needs together with a refuge from their enemies who sought to invade and conquer them. Their religion, culture, and inter-tribal relations apparently were such that the natives developed a character of great cohesiveness. These qualities were of such a high order that the Prusi were enabled to stand up to much more advanced civilizations and to check their advances for a very long period of time. This resistance is comparable to that given the white men by the North American Indian civilization.

The territory of East Prussia constituted a land mass, along with many natural resources which the neighboring sovereigns coveted as they sought to expand their own principalities. However, prior attempts at expansion at the expense of the Prusi were met with the most fierce resistance. Christian, Bishop of Prussia, who had received part of Kulmerland as a fief from the Polish Duke of Masovia, formed an Order of Knighthood known as the Order of Dobrzin and sought to subdue the Prusi. He met with no success. Konrad, Duke of Masovia (1) p 31 sent a message and invitation to Herman von Salza, the Hochmeister (grandmaster) of the Teutonic Order (Der Deutsche Orden) who was at Venice at the time, to come to East Prussia and conduct a crusade

The Knights of the Teutonic Order accepted the invitation and greatly influenced the course of history of the Baltic key-land region and left the imprint of its material and spiritual greatness which remained for a long time after the suppression of the Order in 1809.

ST. ADELBERT

The first attempt to Christianize the Prusi was by St. Adelbert, Bishop of Prague, who, with some of his monks, undertook a heroic mission into the wild unknown areas of East Prussia in 997. To reach the tribes he apparently entered, in ignorance, a sacred tribal area known as "Remova". He died at the hands of the Prusi at this place.

No further attempt was made to Christianize these people for over a century.

TEUTONIC ORDER

The Teutonic Order of Knighthood (Der Deutsche Orden), was formed in Jerusalem in 1198 during the Third Crusade to the Holyland, at the German church of St. Mary the Virgin. The Knights Templar also known as the Knights of St. John of Jerusalem, had been organized some ninety years earlier, but in many respects, the Teutonic Knights were a greater order than the Templars. In the view of some of the Sovereigns and Knights, the Crusades to the Holyland were largely over when the Teutonic Knights received the invitation. The invitation addressed to Hochmeister Hermann von Salza read as follows

> "What is the use of crusading in the far East, Illustrious Hochmeister, when heathenism and the Kingdom of Satan hangs over our borders? Come to Preussen, head a Crusade there. The land is fruitful. It really flows with milk and honey, not to speak of amber, and was once called the "Terrestrial Paradise" — by whom I forget. In fact, it is clear that the land should belong to Christ and if the Christian Teutisch Ritterdom could conquer it from Satan for themselves, it would be well for all parties."

> (1), (2) (Frederick the Great, Carlyle Works Vol. 1 p 94.)

The Teutonic Knights did come to East Prussia in 1229-1230. They began to establish the order by building forts and other necessary structures in which to live and from which to conduct their crusade. The greatest castle and the headquarters of the order was eventually built at Marienburg in the northwestern part of East Prussia not far from the mouth of the Vistula.

The Prusi, as already indicated, were a remarkable people in many respects. Although being out of the stream of European history, they nevertheless so fiercely and capably resisted the Crusade of the Teutonic Order that for the first fifty years, very little was achieved by the Knights.

The Prusi fought to a standstill the best armed and trained fighting men of the known world. They often chased the invaders back into their forts and, like the American Indians, they burned, pillaged, captured weapons, materials, food and other supplies along with men and women so that the Knights were eventually constrained to call for help from other orders of Knighthood of Europe. The Teutonic Knights also invited the Brothers of the Sword (Schwertbrueder) from Lithuania to assist them. Mighty Ottokar, King of Bohemia, and his own Knights came and helped the Teutonic Knights in their crusade in the year 1255. Ottokar conquered Samland in the northern part of East Prussia in about a month and "tore up" Remova (where St. Adelbert had been massacred) and generally "burned up the face of the earth" in the northern lands of the Prusi. (1), (2). A fortress was built on the Baltic in honor of King Ottokar and called the King's Fort, that is, Koenigsberg. (1), (2), (3).

Johann, also King of Bohemia, came with his Knights a century later and once again conducted a crusade against the fierce Prusi. Other Knights and Sovereigns from all over Europe helped or participated in this Crusade against the native Prusi over a period of more than two centuries. (1), (2).

With the fighting there was preaching. As in other areas of the world where the Cross followed the sword, the missionary followed the soldier. Then came the political forces, administrators and colonizers. (1), (2), (3).

The invitation to the Teutonic Knights to crusade in East Prussia implied that what they conquered would belong to the "Order". This was duly confirmed by treaties and agreements. The Order did eventually conquer the Baltic coast from the Vistula to the Niemen.

The Brothers of the Sword conquered the rest of the Baltic including the area north of the Niemen, and the Finns and Lithuanians. None of the Orders of Knighthood were able to conquer the Lithuanians on the Upper reaches of the Niemen River nor the Samogitians on the other side of the upper reaches of the Niemen. The Lithuanians later recovered from this conquest and re-entered history in a most remarkable way when, through the marriage of Duke Jagiello of Lithuania with Queen Hedwig (Jadwiga) of Poland, Lithuania and Poland formed one of the most powerful nations in Eastern Europe stretching from the Baltic to the Black Sea.

The conquest by the Teutonic Order included the coast of the Baltic basically between the Vistula and Niemen Rivers and far inland. Under the terms of their invitation and treaty agreements, they claimed sovereignty over the conquered areas. Their material contributions to the development of Teutonic East Prussia were great and influenced the neighboring regions.

The purpose of the crusades was to rescue the Prusi from paganism, either by conquest or by extermination. From a practial point of view, the surrounding rulers wanted to get rid of the Prusi and the christianizing of them was only an excuse for that conquest. Then when the Knights did conquer a goodly portion of East Prussia, the neighboring sovereigns and nations became concerned for their own safety from the Knights. Eventually, in 1410, at Tannenberg Grunewald, Lithuania and Poland with the remaining unconquered Prusi and some Tartars and Russians joined forces to check the power of the Knights. The defeat of the Knights was decisive. (1), (2). The Order gradually declined in influence but continued as a vital and influential force for several more centuries.

Those Prusi, who had been conquered by the Teutonic Knights and had become Christian, were given allotments of land and were considered as settlers along with the other peoples whom the Order had invited in to settle the vacant lands. Some of the Prusi were given the status of nobility and were given large grants of land. Thus, the Prusi who had submitted to the Knights of the Teutonic Order were not only allowed to remain as settlers and subjects of the Order, but they in turn became assistants to the invaders and conquerors. (1) (2). It is interesting that the defeat of the Teutonic Order took place in the same locality (Tannenberg) where Von Hindenberg defeated the Russians in World War 1. Weakened by Tannenberg, the Order finally became a vassal dukedom under Poland when Albrecht, the last Grandmaster, became duke under the suzerainty of Poland.

In the course of later developments, Frederick William, the Great Elector who was the ruler of Brandenberg, the core of the later Kingdom of Prussia, from 1640 to 1648, in the last years of the Thirty Years War (1618-1648) by aiding Sweden in a war with Poland, prevailed on the King of Poland to renounce his rights over East Prussia and himself assumed the title Duke of Prussia. Frederick III, son of the Great Elector, ruler of Brandenburg-Prussia from 1688 to 1713 in 1701 had himself crowned King of Prussia and as such he was Frederick I. The crowning took place in Koenigsberg and thus East Prussia was then known as the Kingdom of East Prussia for some time. (31) p 35. With what was formerly Ermeland which had been held by Poland, East Prussia retained substantially the same form and area until World War I. From 1815 the name of East Prussia was given the easternmost province of Germany, formerly known as Prussia.

Re-population and resettlement continued almost uninterrupted from the time of the Teutonic Knights through the rule of the Prussian sovereigns into the eighteenth century.

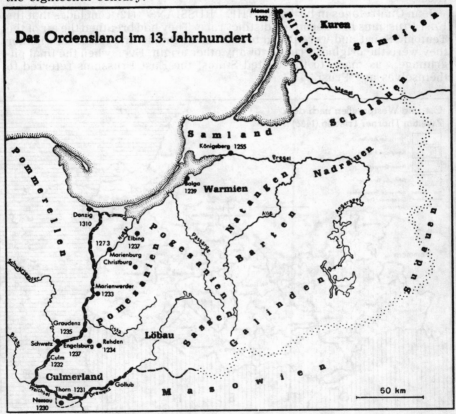

LAND UNDER TEUTONIC ORDER OF KNIGHTHOOD
THIRTEENTH CENTURY
(Courtesy Holzner Verlag Wuerzburg, Publishers
GESCHICHTE OST und WESTPREUSSENS by Bruno Schumacher)

5

The process of continual colonization and resettlement was necessary because of the substantial extermination of the Prusi and the constant drainage of manpower for military purposes by the rulers of the land.

Re-population was necessary not only because of war but because of the depletion of the population by famines and plagues combined with the almost constant requirement of military service. Few men returned from military service in good health. The Bubonic Plague, Cholera, Typhus as well as other diseases ravaged the population and as many as nine out of ten people died. Such loss of manpower made it difficult to develop an agricultural economy or engage in other economic enterprises or labors. (1), (2), (31 p 34.

The Thirty Years War, 1618-1648, while basically a religious war and not always continuous, did a great deal of physical damage to the countryside, devastating farms, workshops, villages, governmental structures and entire cities, leaving large areas in ruin for long periods of time. Fields grew up to weeds and brush. The people suffered for lack of food. Poverty was an even greater enemy than war in such years.

But the re-population process in East Prussia gradually altered the composition of the population and it became a land of mixed races, Germanic, Prusi, Slavic, French, Lithuanian, Bohemian and a miscellany of other races.

Jean Quatrefages in his book "THE PRUSSIANS" (12) concludes that the East Prussians had become a distinct race. They had breathed the air of the Teutonic Spirit and were proud to be called "Prusi" or Prussians, whether they were the original Prusi or of any other origin. Even when the final pilgrimage was made to the United States, the East Prussians referred to themselves as "Prusi".

**EAST AND WEST PRUSSIA AFTER THE
SECOND PEACE TREATY OF THORN 1466**
(Courtesy Holzner Verlag Wuerzburg, Publishers
GESCHICHTE OST und WESTPREUSSENS by Bruno Schumacher)

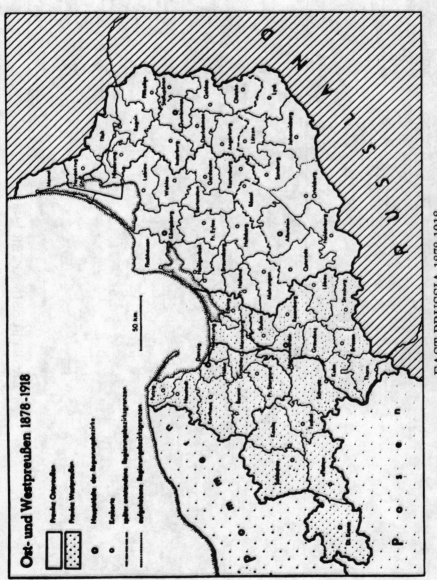

EAST PRUSSIA 1878-1918

(Courtesy Holzner Verlag Wuerzburg, Publishers
GESCHICHTE OST und WESTPREUSSENS by Bruno Schumacher)

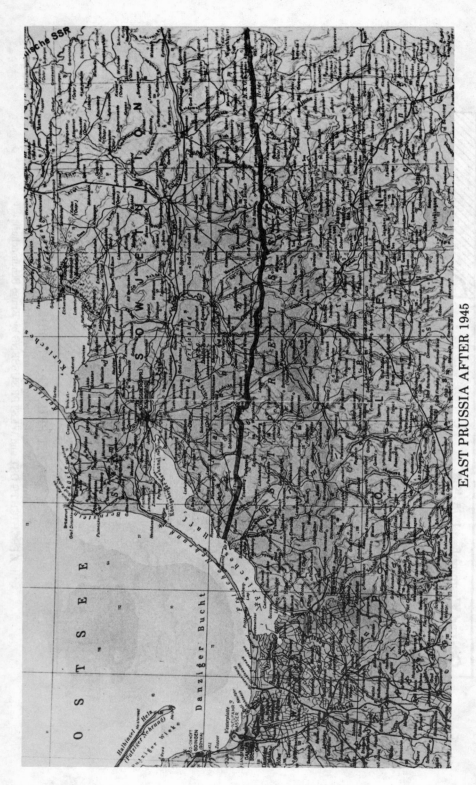

EAST PRUSSIA AFTER 1945

Chapter 2

A Refuge for the Persecuted

The Prusi, the original inhabitants of the East Prussian land are the first component of the new racial group which began the change of its people. Whether conquered or unconquered there were Prusi before and after the coming of Teutonic Knighthood.

A second component of this new people was the offspring of the occupation forces. Given a force of twenty or thirty thousand virile Knights, the flower of European manhood, and, a time factor of several centuries, and one must reckon with another product which is the mixture of the Knight and the Prusi, that is of the Old Prussian race. Examples are numerous where the presence of military occupation forces over a long period of time caused a new ingredient to be reckoned with within the native population.

The third element or segment of the new composition of the people was the settlement of vacated lands by settlers invited by the Knights from Germany. (The German Empire did not come into being until 1871 and the term "Prussia" was used to identify the previous commonwealth of principalities which later did become Germany.)

The fourth unit of our new population was the influx of farmers and nobility from Masovia to the south of East Prussia. It was a Slavic land but for five hundred years it was independent of Poland. These settlers came into the southern portion or "Masuren" land of East Prussia. However, the term "Masuren" (in German) was not used until the nineteenth century (1) p 140.

The fifth segment of this composition was the settlement of many settlers from all of Germany during the reigns of the Prussian rulers and from the small principalities where the ruling prince of one subdued and took over another and the people were required to accept the religion of the current ruler.

The sixth group were the Protestant refugees of the Reformation from France and Flanders.

The seventh ingredient of the new racial composition would be the Bohemian Brethren and Hussites fleeing persecution in Bohemia. Additionally there was a scattering of Scotsmen, English and Russians.

But, it was an invention, that of movable type and the printing press and the introduction of paper from the East more than any other development which stirred up the Reformation and transformation of all of Europe. Ultimately it spread to England and then to the English colonies in America. It is difficult to assign the honor of priority in the simple expedient of printing and multiplying books. It may belong to Holland for in Haarlem, one Coster was printing from movable type before 1446.

Far more important is the question of the manufacture of paper. Paper made the revival of Europe possible. Paper originated in China. Its use goes back to the second century B.C. In 751 the Chinese made an attack on Samarkand; they were repulsed. Among the prisoners were some skilled papermakers from whom the art was learned. Arabic paper manuscripts, from the ninth century onward still exist. The manufacture of paper entered Christendom either through Greece or by the capture of Moorish paper-mills during the Christian reconquest of Spain. Good paper was not made in Europe until near the end of the thirteenth century, and then it was Italy which led the world. Only by the fourteenth century did paper-making reach Germany. With lower cost and better quality, printing followed naturally and the intellectual life of the world entered upon a new and far more vigorous phase.

Jan Huss, in chains, bidding farwell to his associates
as he is being taken to be burned at the stake
(Courtesy WELTSGESCHICHTE F. Seckler Verlag von Carl Hirsch Konstanz)

MARTIN LUTHER
(Courtesy WELTSGESCHICHTE F.
Seckler Verlag von Carl Hirsch Konstanz)

JOHANNES GUTENBERG
(Courtesy WELTSGESCHICHTE F.
Seckler Verlag von Carl Hirsch Konstanz)

Johann Gutenberg (1398-1468) printed the Mazarin Latin Bible, so-called, because it was among the books found in the library and possessions of Cardinal Mazarin. The printing of this Bible is said to have taken place before August 1456

Jan Huss, a Professor of Philosophy at the University of Prague, and in charge of the University Chapel, began to lecture and later to preach about his convictions from reading the Bible. He was also, at that time, in correspondence with the English reformer John Wycliff. The Roman Catholic Church did not allow Huss to continue his preaching very long. He was duly charged with heresy and burned alive at the stake in 1415. (5) (41)

Wycliff's influence over Jan Huss and Huss's martrydom was followed by an insurrection by the Hussites in Bohemia in 1419. In 1420 the Pope, Martin proclaimed a crusade for the destruction of the Wycliffites, Hussites and all other heretics found in Bohemia. Under the generalship of Ziska, the soldiers of fortune found little to plunder in Bohemia. But the whole country was aflame with Hussite enthusiasm. The crusaders beleagured Prague but failed and the attack ended in retreat. A second crusade in 1421 achieved less. Two more also achieved little. In 1431 a fifth crusade of 90,000 infantry and 40,000 horsemen attacked Bohemia from the west under Frederick, Margrave of Brandenburg. By slow marches they advanced to Domazlice (Tauss) and Horsuv Tyn. At three o'clock on August 14, 1431 they encamped on the Tyn. The Hussites under the leadership of Prokop the Great were reported advancing, singing, 'All ye warriors of God'. When the chanting was heard the enthusiasm of the crusaders evaporated and the Margrave of Brandenburg advised flight. So ended the Bohemian crusade.

Later persecutions of the Hussites made many flee across the Carpathian mountains into Russian occupied Poland and to Russia itself.

Jan Huss then, was a part of the Reformation, then in its beginnings, more than a hundred years before the time of Zwingli, Luther, Calvin and other famous reformers. (5).

THE HUGUENOTS

The teachings of the reformers caught on much more rapidly than anyone had anticipated and the people began flocking to the reformed and evangelical faiths, leaving the Roman Catholic Church in large numbers. With their adherents diminishing along with their revenues, appeals were soon made by the heads of the church, in the countries where the reformation was taking place, for urgent Catholic action. The action came. The Inquisition with new and more frightening powers was revived. (5), (9), (13), (14), (19).

During this period, Holland and Flanders were under Spanish rule. Phillip II ordered a branch of the Inquisition into the low countries where the people had early responded and sought the comfort of the new faith.

Sir Thomas Gresham, writing to Cecil from Antwerp in 1566, said, "There are above 40,000 Protestants in this town, which will die rather than the word of God should be put to silence.". (9), (13), (14).

The Duchess of Parma, writing to Phillip in 1567, said, "In a few days 100,000 men had already left the country with their money and goods, and that many more were following every day". There was indeed a large emigration from Flanders. (9), (13), (14), (19).

The Inquisition burned Bibles, books, copies of Gospels (some of which had been printed at the request of a Roman Catholic Bishop and distributed by him for some time); it burned churches and it burned people as heretics because of their beliefs. The Protestants responded with similar acts of cruelty. Every method of cruelty that man could conceive was employed in the persecution of the non-conforming people as "heretics".

The French Protestants became known as "Huguenots". The origin of the term is obscure. It was first applied as a nickname. Some suppose the term was derived from Huguon, a word in Touraine to signify persons who walk at night in the streets—the early Protestants, like the early Christians, having chosen that time for their religious assemblies. Other origins are suggested but it is sufficient to know that the term was widely used to designate people who left the French Roman Catholic Church for one of the new Evangelical teachings. (4,p 29).

France, a Roman Catholic Kingdom and Nation, most vigorously persecuted the Protestants. People were deprived of their professions and livelihoods, they were tried or imprisoned without charge or trial. They were dispossessed. They were hanged, decapitated and bodies quartered, drawn and dragged through the streets. On August 24th 1572, the great massacre known as St. Bartholomews was carried out at the direct orders of the Queen-mother. Hundreds of Huguenots attending church were slain. The retinue of Henry of Navarre was murdered along with many guests present at the celebration of the marriage of the sister of the King of France. Admiral Coligny, one of the great leaders of the Huguenots (along with Henry of Navarre), was followed to his quarters and murdered and his body thrown out of the window to the courtyard below. Similar massacres took place at Vassy, at Lyon, at Nismes, in Dauphiny and in Bordeaux and throughout France. It made little difference whether the person was a man, woman, child or one of the nobility. Children of Huguenots were authorized converted in the absence of their parents. The clergy were authorized to take the children from Huguenot families by force, if necessary, and put them into Roman Convents. (9), (11), (13), (14), (19).

Additionaly, Huguenots were not only forbidden to hold public office but the children of Huguenots were denied an education. Huguenot young people could not attend schools or universities. These conditions laid the groundwork for home and church study and home and church education which became part and parcel of most evangelical religions. Likewise, these prohibitions against the exercise of their beliefs led to the holding of secret meetings and services. Meetings were held at night. Sometimes in woods or in the middle of large fields. (9), (11), (13(, (19).

When all else failed to return the people to the Roman Church, the dragonnades were resorted to. A determination would be made of the number of people in a particular household, farm or castle. Then a detachment of Dragoons would be ordered quartered in such household until the entire family signed their abjuration. Cuirassiers under the command of Marquis de Beaupre' Choiseul entered Rouen, sword in hand and the quartering of the troops on the inhabitants produced "conversions" wholesale. (14, p 194). When the quartering of troops took place, there was no room in the household for the family to sleep. Boarding the men soon consumed the food within the home. No imagination is required to know what happened to the women and girls. The family treasures—anything which the soldiers could carry away was appropriated. The men were chosen for their rapacity.

Small wonder that the Huguenots fled in the dark of night with nothing but the clothing on their backs and whatever they could carry in their hands. They fled to the nearest border or port, traveling at night, through fields and woods and avoiding places where church leaders, soldiers and police might be looking for them. They dared not seek help from friends or relatives for fear of exposing them or being themselves betrayed. It was certain death to be caught. Many changed their names and even destroyed such identifications as they might have with them. (9), (13), (14), (19). Some took ship to other countries such as England or the ports of Germany. Escape to Spain, Italy and other parts of the Mediterranean was avoided. Many did cross over the border into Switzerland and Germany.

HENRY OF NAVARRE

The Huguenot struggle had been going on for many decades before finally Henry of Navarre, a Protestant of royal blood, came into power in France as King Henry IV, in 1594. However, he had to yield to the Catholic Faith by attending at least one mass before he could be crowned. Henry IV brought peace to most of the strife within France, but only for a short time. Behind the scenes however the Protestants were still being persecuted and denied their full rights as citizens of France even after the promulgation of the Edict of Nantes in 1598. True, Huguenots were again admitted to public employments and their children were again allowed to go to schools and universities. But only limited church serices could be conducted and then in specified cities and places.

This restive peace under King Henry IV was completely shattered when the King was assassinated May 14th 1610 only sixteen years after he became ruler of France and only twelve years after the promulgation of the Edict of Nantes. (10) The Edict of Nantes remained the law of the land, but it was so disregarded and flouted that Louis XIV, revoked it on October 22nd 1685, stating that he considered it no longer of any use to France. Persecutions resumed in greater vigor and it has been the view of some historians and writers that this was one of the major causes which led to the French Revolution in 1789. The Huguenots continued to leave France for many years and into the eighteenth century, both before and after the French Revolution.

On October 18th 1663 Frederick Wilhelm the Great Elector
of Brandenburg (1640-1688) welcomes the distinguished
French Huguenots to Brandenburg and Presussen as their new
homeland in the reception hall of the Koenigsberg Castle.
(Courtesy DAS OSTPRESUSSENBLATT)

HENRY IV KING OF FRANCE
(Courtesy WELTSGESCHICHTE F. Seckler Verlag von Carl Hirsch Konstanz)

JOHN CALVIN
(Courtesy WELTGESCHICHTE F. Seckler Verlag von Carl Hirsch Konstanz)

FRIEDRICH I, KING OF PRUSSIA
1688-1740

14

EVENTS IN POLAND

Events affecting the nations to the south of East Prussia were not without their effect on the future of East Prussia. After the Polish partitional period 1138-1305 and toward the middle of the thirteenth century, the Tartars under Prince Batu invaded Poland, burned Sandomir and Cracow, defeated the Silesian princes at Leignitz, and finally entered Hungary, where they routed King Bela IV on the banks of the Sajo. The devastation of the land and cities was such that re-population was necessary. What was needed was a skilled class of people who were not only given to peaceful pursuits but capable of building and defending cities. Such immigrants could only come from the West, and on their own terms. Thus it came about that a new Germanic class element entered into Polish society. They were dependent upon the prince from whom they obtained their privileges, the most important of which was self government and freedom from taxation. In 1259 a second Tartar raid was made which was less dangerous to the nation but much more ruinous even though it lasted only three months.

Lithuania revived under Duke Jagiello and after much negotiating, Hedwig (Jadwiga) Queen of Poland, reluctantly consented to marry the Duke. He was crowned King of Poland and Lithuania. This union of separate states under one King was brought about by fear of the Teutonic Order. This combined nation extended its power and its borders from the Baltic to the Black Seas. It included all of the land between the Bug and the Dnieper Rivers. Jagiello became a Catholic and this conversion from paganism was an event of major importance in the history of Eastern Europe. What the Teutonic Order had endeavored to bring about with fire and sword for two centuries was peacefully accomplished by Jagiello and Hedwig by their marriage and in a single generation.

The new combined nation now threatened the existence of the Teutonic Knights and their rule of that part of East Prussia which they had conquered. Events mounted into incidents and Jagiello, leading the combined Lithuanian-Polish Armies with the help of the remaining unconquered Prusi in East Prussia and some Tartars and Russians inflicted a crushing defeat upon the Teutonic Order on the fields of Tannenberg-Grunewald.

The reign of Wladislaus II followed for some 49 years and was succeeded by Casimir IV, 1447-92. By the treaty of Thorn, October 14th 1466, Poland recovered much territory and the Teutonic Order was further reduced to East Prussia proper, roughly covering the area between the Vistula and the Niemen Rivers along the Baltic coast, with Koenigsberg as its capital. East Prussia was so overshadowed by the Polish-Lithuanian nation that it was for a time, really a Polish province.

The death of Casimir resulted in a temporary separation of Lithuania and Poland. John, Albert and Alexander, sons of Casimir, ruled for a time followed by brother Sigismund. In 1525, Sigismund was compelled to grant autonomy to East Prussia. In the reign of Sigismund the duchy of Masovia on the Southern border of East Prussia which had been independent for five hundred years, united with the Polish crown providing further unity and solidarity of this nation.

After 1555, Protestantism flourished exceedingly in Poland. In normally Catholic Poland, the Protestants were supreme in the Diet and invariably elected a Calvinist to be their marshal. Nearly half of Poland was Protestant. This condition reached its high-water mark in 1558-1559.

The then Polish King, perceiving the danger to the Catholic cause, supported the Catholic Bishops in a plan to regain the lost Catholic adherents. Protestants were then subjected to much the same persecution and denial of rights and freedoms as were the Protestants of France. In 1564 the more extreme heretics were banished. In 1565 the Jesuit Order mounted a strong counter-reformation. The persecuted Protestants fled the country. East Prussia was near and settlers were welcomed. Both farmers and nobility who had accepted the Protestant faiths settled in East Prussia much of which was still under the rule of the Teutonic Order although the Order was now in a vassal state to Poland. The refugees settled in the "Wildnis" or Masurian Lake area of East Prussia and became assimilated into the Prussian people during the course of three or four centuries. Thus, these refugees, farmers and nobility, added another element to the population of the province. There was no more appropriate designation for the total composition of the East Prussian area for these people than the designation of "Prussian".

Chapter 3

Developments under Prussian Rulers

In Prussia, Friedrich Wilhelm I, one week after the revocation of the Edict of Nantes, issued his Edict of Potsdam, on Ocotber 29th 1685, welcoming the French Protestant refugees to Prussian Germany. (See Note) Holland, England and the American English colonies opened their doors to the mass migration of French Protestants. Many settled in East Prussia in addition to those who settled in Prussia proper. Berlin had at least nine French Protestant Churches where services were conducted in French. (9), (11), (12), (13), (14), (19).

Friedrich Wilhelm I, therefore added greatly to the settlement of East Prussia by not only sending additional German settlers from the Rhineland regions but thousands of French Protestant refugees to the areas of Koenisberg, Insterburg and Gumbinen. He gave the refugees every assistance including food, lodging, transportation and assignments of lands and buildings. The King declared he would, if necessary, "sell his plate and silver if it would accomplish this great purpose." He looked after the welfare of the Swiss-German Salzburgers, the Heidelburgers, and welcomed as well the Mennonites who came in the early 1600's to West Prussia and who later moved to the Ukraine under special arrangements made with Catherine II of Russia. Most came to the United States and Canada in the 1870's and 1880's.

> Note: The Friedrich Wilhelm who welcomed the Huguenots to Prussia in 1685 was not King Friedrich Wilhelm I of Prussia. That Friedrich Wilhelm, known in history as the Great Elector, was the grandfather of the later King of Prussia of the same name.

In the administration of his domains Friedrich Wilhelm I, made three innovations: the private estates of the King were turned into domains of the crown; the serfs on the royal domains were freed; and, the hereditary lease was converted into a short-term lease on the basis of producivity. This policy reached into East Prussia and greatly changed the ownership and use of land in that province.

One of the most important actions of the Prussian Sovereign Friedrich Wilhelm I, was the "reestablishment" policy toward East Prussia. This was a major action of the Sovereign and government to provide East Prussia with settlers and colonists. A great deal of money was budgeted and expended for this purpose. The short-term lease policy was continued on the basis of productivity in order to make more land available to more people who would be willing to work it in order to retain it. Friedrich also instituted a general land tax (1), (2). which was administered mostly by French officials since it was patterned after the French system of taxation. Thus more French were added to those already there as Huguenots.

On a visit to East Prussia by Friedrich Wilhelm I, his son, the then Crown Prince, later Frederick the Great, wrote to the great Voltaire in Paris on July 27th 1739, as reported on page 418 et seq. Book X of the History of Frederick the Great, 1897, by Thomas Carlyle: (Vol II Carlyle's Works)

> "Prussian Lithuania is a country a hundred and twenty miles long, by sixty to forty miles broad; it was ravaged by the Pestilence at the beginning of the century; and, they say three hundred thousand people died of disease and famine. (31, p35) Ravaged by Pestilence and neglect by King Frederick I; till my father, once his hands were free, made a personal survey of it, and took it up, in earnest

17

Since that time, say twenty years ago, there is no expense that the King has been afraid of, in order to succeed in his salutary views. He made, in the first place, regulations full of wisdom. He rebuilt whatever the Pestilence had desolated; thousands of families, from the ends of Europe including seventeen thousand Salzburgers for the last item, were conducted hither; the country peopled itself; trade began to flourish again; and now, in these fertile regions, abundance reigns more than it ever did.

There are about a half million inhabitants in Lithuania; there are more towns than there ever were, more flocks than formerly, more wealth and more productiveness than in any other part of Germany. And all this that I tell you is due to the King alone; who not only gave the orders, but superintended the execution of them; and spared neither care, nor pains, nor immense expenditures, nor promises, nor recompense, to secure the happiness and life of this half-million of thinking beings who owe to him alone that they have possessions and felicity in the world.

To my great astonishment, I passed through villages where you hear nothing spoken but French— I have found something so heroic in the generous and laborious way in which the King addressed himself in making this desert flourish with inhabitants and happy industries and fruits, that it seemed to me you would feel the same sentiment in learning of such re-establishment.''

PRUSSIAN RULERS

Since Prussian rulers significantly affected the history of the East Prussians, a brief history of these rulers will aid in understanding the development of East Prussian history.

(1) Frederick William, the Great Elector was the ruler of Brandenburg. He was the eleventh in the line of Electors of this principality which was the real core and the central and largest province of the later Kingdom of Prussia. He assumed his rule as Elector in 1640 at a time when its position was very low. His success as a ruler returned Brandenburg to leadership and greatness. His aid of the King of Sweden in a war with Poland followed by a series of maneuvers put this ruler in a position where the King of Poland renounced his rights to Ducal East Prussia. Frederick William assumed the title of Duke of Prussia. In regaining East Prussia he achieved what the Teutonic Order had strove for in vain. This is the sovereign who welcomed the French Huguenots to his dominions as is later described in this work.

(2) Frederick III, son of the Great Elector, ruler of Brandenburg-Prussia from 1688 to 1713, crowned himself as King of Prussia at Koenigsberg and called himself Frederick I.

(3) Frederick William I son of Frederick I King of Prussia reigned from 1713 to 1740.

(4) Frederick II, called Frederick the Great, son of Frederick William I, King of Prussia, ruled from 1740 to 1786.

(5) Frederick William II, nephew of Frederick the Great, ruled from 1786 to 1797.

18

(6) Frederick William III son of Frederick William II ruled from 1797 to 1840.

(7) Frederick William IV, son of Frederick William III ruled 1840 to 1861.

(8) William I, brother of Frederick William IV was King of Prussia 1861 to 1888 and Emperor of Germany 1871 to 1888.

FREDERICK THE GREAT
(Courtesy WELTSGESCHICHTE F. Seckler Verlag von Carl Hirsch Konstanz)

FREDERICK THE GREAT

Frederick the Great was born January 24th 1712 and tutored by Friedrich Wilhelm I. Frederick the Great ascended the throne May 31 1740. He maintained all forms of government established by his father but ruled in an even more enlightened spirit. He tolerated all religions, abolished torture for major crimes except wholesale murder, conspiracy and high treason. He tried to improve the quality of justice. Justice was to be even-handed and applied equally to the high and the low, the rich and the poor. He disbanded the all-six-foot Potsdam regiment of Guards which was the most famous of Europe (and the most dreaded) but he gave a good deal of study to the real needs of his military establishment. His tax policies were designed to finance preparedness for his military objectives. He believed that a high level of military presence made for greater diplomatic and economic influence among the neighboring nations.

The Seven Year's War, 1756-1763, took all his energies but, with the aid of Catherine II of Russia, the war terminated favorably for Frederick the Great. Although ending in Germany's favor, this war did heavy damage to East Prussia where the Russians had invaded as far as Koenigsberg devastating the countryside. The king not only aided in in re-settlement of East Prussian lands which had sustained heavy damage, but he provided the people, farmers and nobles alike with means of rebuilding their properties so that they could sustain their people and re-establish their economy. Pomerania and Neumark were freed from taxation for two years, Silesia for six months. Many farmers obtained seed through the King's program. War horses could found all over Prussia.

The general land tax was further refined to reflect the French system of taxation. Unfortunately to the dislike of the Prussians the tax continued to be administered by French collectors. However, the new tax system did bring in the money Frederick needed to rebuild the nation. Prussian Germany was now recognized as a great European power even though handicapped by the existence of too many small principalities. Frederick's strong leadership did much to induce in the leadership of many of these small principalities the need for union and cohesion in order that Prussia might become a stronger power. Frederick's reign laid the real foundations for the coming of a genuinely united German Empire, though it did take until the time of Bismarck to reach the empire status.

Frederick's policies toward East Prussia were basically those of Friedrich Wilhelm I. Aided by his land Administrators, the Blumenthal brothers, much was done in East Prussia to build and continue a strong agricultural economy.

The author's forebears the Hannutta and Labusch families, among others, received grants of interests in lands and privileges from Frederick the Great through the Blumenthals.

UNREST OF 1840

In February 1840 a group of East Prussian farmers and landholders holding land from the King, met and declared that they were willing to give up their interest in the land and to provide for themselves in another way.

Among those in the Jurisdiction of Mensguth were Samuel Matrisch, Jacob Matrish, Johann Ollech, Jacob Hanutta and a widow who had been a Labusch family member. These farmers, or their descendents, who first went to the Russian Ukraine, came to the United States in the period subsequent to 1887.

Translation of the documents which follow this page is impossible except for names and date, and, that they got together for the purpose of protestsing the taxes, imposts, levies and other burdens which were mostly imposed upon the land and would rather give up their landed interests rather than carry on the responsibilities which attached to the leaseholder or land holder under the Sovereign. Undoubtedly, these burdens accumlated and resulted in the larger group of the East Prussians in 1865 in leaving their centuries old homeland for the unknown Russian Ukraine.

Bismarck did not come into the Minister-Presidency of the Greater Prussia until the early eighteen sixties. But the economic uncertanties as well as political turmoil and constant possiblity of war had a great deal to do with this action by these landholders. The fact that the second cholera epidemic had hit East Prussia in 1837 also may have contributed to the desire of these people to unload a portion of their burden.

The documents on pages 22, 23 and 24 following this page were explained by the German Archivist as follows: "Saemtliche Bauern der Anteile A und B erklaeren sich damit einverstand dass sie statt des Weges zu ihren Aeckern ueber den Schulzen-Dienstgarten einen andern Weg benutzen wuerden"

"All the farmers of sections A and B agreed to use another road to their land instead of the one across the overseer's garden."

Copia vidimata.   N° 177.

287.

Verhandelt zu Kummey den 13. Februar 1840.

Zu der heutigen Separationssache steht Behufs Ermittelung der [illegible] wegen Schulunterhaltung und [illegible] der Schul-[illegible] auf heute Termin an, zu welchem folgende evangelische Altsitzbesitzer des Dorfs Antheil B. erschienen:

1. Johann Gadomski
2. Michael Chittka.
3. Daniel Dembeck.
4. Johann Kruschewski.
5. Johann Glomada.
6. Samuel Matrisch.
7. Christoph Kleidasch.
8. Jacob Kanutta.
9. Wittwe Elisabeth Kruschewski geb. Labusch.
10. Gottfried Denski jetzt Jacob Kleidasch.
11. Friedrich Kruschewski.
12. Johann Dembeck.
13. Andreas Kruschewski.
14. Johann Przywa.
15. Jacob Matrisch.
16. Johann Olloch.

Der Stellvertreter des landesherrlichen Antheils, Herr [illegible] Menée aus Ortelsburg ist ausgeblieben, und hat selbiger nach dem Schreiben vom 15. d. M. durch eine [illegible] entschuldigt.

Dagegen haben sich freiwillig die [illegible] [illegible] und Nachbarn desselben

1, der Schulz des Antheils A. Adam Domnen, wohnt Pienatz

2,

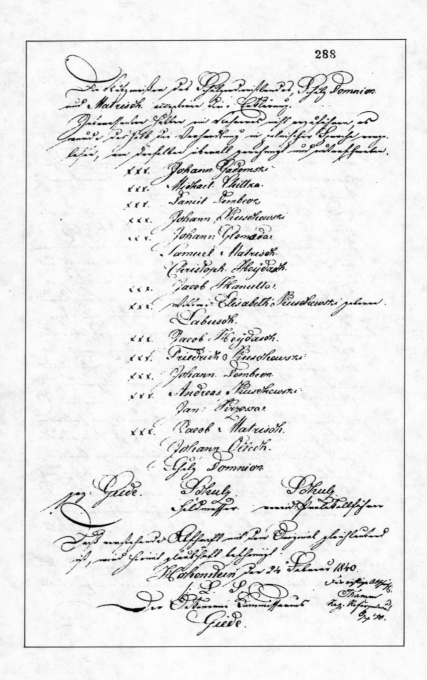

BISMARCK

The final period in the general background of the people of East Prussia and their emigration in the 1860's was the administration of Minister-President, Prince Otto von Bismarck (1815-1898). His leadership was one of the strongest old Prussia ever had. Strong leadership was needed because under the

MINISTER — PRESIDENT OF PRUSSIA
PRINCE OTTO VON BISMARCK
(Courtesy WELTSGESCHICHTE F. Seckler Verlag von Carl Hirsch Konstanz)

MARIENBURG GRAND MASTERS PALACE
(Courtesy "OSTPRESUSSEN" Unschau Verlag Frankfurt am Main)

Treaty signed at the end of the Thirty Year's War, each German principality was given its own leadership without having a national allegiance.

There were 265 secular principalities or powers and 65 principalities or powers which were ecclesiastically ruled. The remaining principalities numbering upwards of 1,200 and ranging in size from a few square miles to rather sizeable states, were all free to govern themselves. This was a chaotic and of course a very loose confederation held together mostly by common boundaries and language rather than any general federal form of government. It brought a time of great uncertainty in economics as well as in their relationships with each other. All of Prussia and northern Europe was affected.

Wars were frequent among these small principalities. Trivial claims were an excuse for battle. A bridge, a field, a wood, a lake, a stream, a river, a canal, a road along with tolls for the use of roads and bridges would provoke the ruling prince or the people to take up the sword to settle the matter.

Bismarck had an unquenchable desire to form a strong Germany through the leadership of Prussia. On becoming Minister-President under Frederick William IV, he took prompt steps to bring into the Prussian fold the territory of Schleswig-Holstein which was then claimed by Denmark. (1), (2), (5), (8).

In 1870 Germany and France were at war in the Franco-Prussian war. The Germans defeated France and this victory fused the German people and leadership into one of greater unity. Upon the restoration of peace after the Franco-Prussian war, Germany became an Empire in 1871, the unquestioned military giant of that time.

Birmarck, also believed in a high level of military strength, for, like Frederick the Great, he too felt that to maintain its supremacy, Germany had to lead and negotiate from strength. This meant military service for most of the male population. The calling up of large numbers of men deprived agriculture, industry and commerce of a rather high percentage of manpower. Family life suffered and women often had to do the work which ordinarily fell to the men of a farmstead.

A high level of military presence also required a high level of taxation of lands, personal property, produce and general productivity of the people. Poverty was a continuing depressive force and, as in most cases, fell most heavily on those least able to bear the burden. (1) (2).

With the possible exception of the Rhineland, it would be difficult to find an area in Europe which had so consistently, and for such long periods of time, been on a war footing as East Prussia. There were roughly three centuries of crusades in East Prussia when the Teutonic Knights and their allies battled the native Prusi. The Knights came in 1229-1230 and suffered a major defeat in 1410 but their rule continued over Teutonic Prussia through the 15th, 16th and into the 17th centuries. Other contending powers such as the Polish-Lithuanian combination, the Russians, the forces of Gustavus Adolphus of Sweden and others crossed and recrossed the East Prussian land mass in the course of their ventures. To the south, the lives of East Prussians were threatened and influenced by three events, the invasion of the Turks as far as Vienna, the battles between the Poles and Cossack-Tartars just before Casimir came to power in Poland (18), and, by the joining of Lithuania and Poland in a two nation union, as previously touched on by the marriage of Duke Jagiello with Queen Hedwig (Jadwiga) of the Polish royal family.

When Gustavus I Adolphus, King of Sweden invaded Europe through the Baltic countries, East Prussia was again in the middle of the battles which raged far into Poland until Poland was conquered and Adolphus was crowned King at Cracow. The remainder of the Thirty Year's war and, somewhat later, the Seven Year's War, were periods of great suffering as well as great physical damage. (31, p 36).

The invasion of Russia by Napoleon, after he had subjugated Prussia, again ravaged the East Prussian areas. Levies were made by Napoleon on the manpower, the food, grain, cattle, horses, wagons as well as great demands for money payments. There was some satisfaction, however, among the former French Huguenots who were living in both Prussia and East Prussia. They gave Napoleon's armies no little difficulty. Speaking perfect French, they frequently infiltrated the Napoleonic forces and obtained valuable information. They slipped into the French forces and in perfect French preached insurrection. The defeat of Napoleon and his return from Moscow was followed by peace. It gave East Prussia the first breathing spell in over five hundred years of warfare. East Prussia was relatively free of war from 1815 to 1914-15. (31 p37).

In addition to the burden of the military, nature contributed to the continuous suffering through famine, hunger, starvation and death. There were wet and dry seasons and crop failures. There was a potato disease in East Prussia which is said to have almost eliminated the potato as a crop to be depended upon from 1846 to 1864. (Kartoffelkrankheit) (1) p 276.

Even the great forests of East Prussia, the most extensive in Europe, were not spared by disease. A bark disease, caused by a beatle (Borkenkaffer) destroyed whole areas of fine trees. This was followed by the White Moth, which the inhabitants referred to as the "White Nun", which also killed vast stretches of the great timberlands, perhaps the same way as the Duth Elm disease killed off the Elm trees in the United States in the middle of the 20th century. Since it was possible to save some of the diseased trees for lumber and other uses, including firewood, many men were employed in the forests to salvage the affected trees. (1) p 276, (3). Other families were sustained by the employment of men on the building of roads and turnpikes, dikes, canals and military works. Thus, through a public works and employment program, needy people were enabled to sustain their families through these harsh years. (1), (3). But in the final analysis, it was the total Bismarck policy towards these East Prussians which decided them to seek a more peaceful land.

PROPOSED DRAINAGE OF MASURIAN LAKES

As land became scarce, proposals were made to drain the lowlands and the Masurian Lakes in order to provide lands for more settlers. Negotiations were entered into with engineers and contractors with a view of accomplishing this purpose when the military leadership heard of the proposed project. Military studies indicated that in summer the lakes and marshes, while not a major physical obstacle could be the equivalent of several army corps in defending Germany against an invasion by Russia. Von Hindenburg's view on supporting the retention of the Masurian Lakes and the lowlands was vindicated by his defeat of the Russian Armies in 1914-15 at Tannenberg. (45)

THE PLAGUES

The plagues which had swept many areas of Europe also cut a swath of horrible death through East Prussia. Cholera struck East Prussia in 1831, 1837, 1853, and 1867. (1) p 276.

In the visit previously mentioned (2) to East Prussia by Frederick the Great while he was still the Crown Prince of Prussia (the visit included that part of Lithuania which was then incorporated into East Prussia) he noted that the region had been swept by a pestilence at the beginning of the 18th century and that three hundred thousand people had perished of disease and famine in that region. Thus, even disease compelled people to flee from one land to another which offered a place of greater safety. (1), (2), (31) p 35. Every reason given by these poverty stricken, tax burdened, militarily oppressed people must be given weight and considered as a major compulsory reason, sufficient in and of itself, without the addition or cumulation of other reasons, for envisioning a land without such heavy burdens and sorrows.

One who has never experienced the necessity of giving up a home, a farmstead of estate size, a family, kinfolks, loved ones, as well as those asleep in

EAST PRUSSIA   MASURIAN LAKE REGION
(Courtesy DAS OSTPREUSSENBLATT)

the church yard, can not really appreciate the anguish and pain which these people experienced and the difficulties which goaded them into decisions they would rather not make. Generations of their families had put their labors and planning into the building of their estates and farmsteads, their equipment and the building up of their livestock herds. Surrendering them to the sovereign would mean great loss for they could not obtain adequate fair-market-value compensation. Last, was the trauma of parting with the place which was homeland (Heimatland), a nostalgic, emotional severence with the places of their birth, marriage, baptism and where they had lain their loved ones to rest. Once they left, there could be no return. There was no room. They did not expect to see their homeland or loved ones again.

"THE PRUSSIANS"

The East Prussians of this history were a part of the people of the province which had become a new stock or racial group. Historians do not agree upon the precise number or percentage of the Old Prussians or "Prusi" who were exterminated and how many remained. That the Prusi were not completely

29

EAST PRUSSIA   MASURIAN LAKE LOWLANDS
(Courtesy DAS OSTPRESUSSENBLATT)

exterminated as a race is clearly established from the conquests made by the Teutonic Knights. Others who were not conquered actually accepted the Teutonic way of life and submitted to the Teutonic Order's rule. Some of the Prusi became landowners and even nobility. Others were farmers and tenants, workers and artisans. But a large part of them were not conquered.

In the great battle of Tannenberg-Grunewald in 1410, (2) p 151; (3) p 6, it is indicated that the unconquered Prusi joined the Lithuanian, Polish, Russian and Tartar forces in defeating the Teutonic Knights.

The unconquered or revolutionary Prusi must have been considerable enough to mention in the history of this event and their participation in the battle. If the unconquered Prusi are added to those already conquered or submitted to the Teutonic Order, it would be fair to assume that upwards of one third of the population of East Prussia were the original Prusi or Old Prussians. If we now add to this number, the offspring of the occupation forces the percentage of Old Prussians or Prusi must have been considerable. The re-population of the province by the Knights, by Friedrich Wilhelm I, and eventually by Frederick the Great, with German settlers must have added at least another third. The remaining third were the French refugee Huguenots, Bohemians, Masovians, Polish protestants fleeing the counter-reformation in Poland and a sprinkling of other nationalities.

When the French system of taxation was begun by Friedrich Wilhelm I and continued by Frederick the Great, the administrators of the system were French and this strengthened the French element in the East Prussian

EAST PRUSSIA   MASURIAN LAKE SCENE
(Courtesy DAS OSTPREUSSENBLATT)

mixture. Thus the mixtures of these settlers with the Prusi in an area about
the size of the States of Vermont and Connecticut after the coming of the
Teutonic Knights had over a period of four to five centuries created a new
composition and a new population of East Prussia. A new race was actually
fused and created and a new culture evolved quite distinct from the pure
races from whence they came.

Jean Quatrefages (12) in his work "The Prussians" writes that one
Godron, given an account of the compositions put together in East Prussia
and considering the passage of time along with the new traits of character,
the crusading and questing spirit, said:

"The 'Prussians' are neither Germans nor Slavs ...
The Prussians are 'Prussians' ".

EAST PRUSSIA   MASURIAN LAKE SCENE
(Courtesy DAS OSTPREUSSENBLATT)

One need only to enter the borders of East Prussia from almost any direction and he was promptly met with evidence and witness of the spirit and times of the Teutonic Order in the monumental structures found throughout the province, especially at Marienburg and by the churches and castles that the order either built or inspired. (3)

That there has been a continuing and pervading spirit about East Prussians throughout this period of history cannot be denied. Everywhere in this province, one inevitably caught the feeling of an in-dwelling spirit of pride, of achievement, of quest for knowledge, of discipline, and of a high level of civic and national responsibility. This spirit was so well demonstrated by East Prussian's own Kant, Schopenhauer and Copernicus. (3). Copernicus was born in Thorn in West Prussia while it was under Polish rule but of parents of mainly Germans lineage, in 1473. He has been called a 'Polish' Astronomer. He received his university training in the University of Cracow, studied law at Bologna and lectured in Rome. However he was nominated to be cannon in the cathedral at Frauenburg in East Prussia and when he took up his duties there after 1512, it was in Frauenburg that he developed his heliocentric views of the universe. His thesis was published and presented to him on his deathbed in Frauenburg in 1543. (3), (Britannica 1968 Vol. 6 pp 466-7) His views were contrary to the theology of the Catholic Church. When Galileo accepted the Copernican views he found himself in serious difficulties with the Church. Galileo's studies and additional discoveries based on the Copernican thesis eventually turned this great science from a dogma to an understanding of the universe.

Johann Kepler, a German astronomer (1571-1630) found that the planes of all the planetary orbits pass through the center of the sun, coupled with his recognition of the sun as the moving power of the system entitles him to the rank as founder of physical astronomy and thereby confirmed the Copernican view of the sun being the center of our planetary system.

GRANDMASTER'S PALACE   MARIENBURG
1309-1457 Headquarters of Teutonic Order of Knighthood
(Courtesy OSTPRESUSSEN Unschau Verlag Frankfurt am Main)

EAST PRUSSIA   MASURIAN LAKE LANDSCAPE
(Courtesy OSTPREUSSEN Umschau Verlag Frankfurt am Main)

EAST PRUSSIAN "WILDNIS"
Southeastern part
(Courtesy DAS OSTPREUSSENBLATT)

Chapter 4

Our Forefathers in East Prussia

Several pictures of East Prussian landscapes and other views are included herein through the courtesy of the publishers of DIE DEUTSCHEN LAND, OSPREUSSEN, Band 16, Umschau Verlag, Frankfurt A.M. and from the newspaper "Das Ostpreussenblatt".

The variety of husbandry and life in this province was apparent as one views each geographical location. Along the Baltic Sea, amber was found and exported. There was fishing along the seacoast. Koenigsberg was pre-eminent in shipping, being an ocean port at the mouth of the Pregel River which brings canal traffic from deep within the east and southeastern parts of this land. The eastern and southeastern hinterland contained many large forest resources. Game was propagated. (3).

Everywhere, except along the coastal areas, there was farming. Villages and cities which have been built up in the agricultural regions had a bewitching charm peculiar to the East Prussian land.

Life in the middle area of East Prussia could be represented by the small village of Rummy in the jurisdiction of Mensguth, Kreis Ortelsburg. It was located in the area which was ruled by the Teutonic Order until the second Treaty of Thorn in 1466; then it was part of East Prussia under the Dukedom granted to the last Hochmeister of the Teutonic Knights under the Suzerainty of the King of Poland until 1525. In 1525 Duke Albrecht assumed the rule of the province until 1568. During his rule of the province he invited new settlers into southeast East Prussia, along with additional refugees fleeing from Masovia and other Polish sections because of the counter reformation. Rummy was nestled in the rolling hills not far from some of the many Masurian Lakes. This village was about 10 kilometers north of Ortelsburg.

According to the land registers in the Staats-Archives in Gottingen in 1977, the settlers in 1865 had been farming that area for upwards of two centuries. Some were Old Prussians whose land grants began before the middle of the sixteenth century. There are confirmatory documents dating from before 1581 and many granted by Frederick the Great from 1741 through 1785. The greatest number appear to have been given in 1753. Many holdings have been in families from the time of their settlement by the Teutonic Knights.

Some of the settlers held the type of limited leasehold instituted by Friedrich Wilhelm I and continued by Frederick the Great, which were based upon productivity. Others held hereditary patents. In any event, these folk whatever their origin in the distant past, were fully Prussianized and considered 'prusi', that is, "echte Deutsch" (true German citizens.).

The ice-age glaciers left many eskers and morains along with lakes, bogs and marshes. More than three thousand three hundred lakes dot the interior landscape of southern and southeastern East Prussia. In many instances they are situated in chains so that it was rather easy to create a waterway through them from the southern border of the province to the vicinity of one of the branches of the Pregel River. Canals were built where necessary and rail-type portages were constructed so that properly built canal boats could navigate between Koenigsberg and the southerly border of the province. The Pregel and Alle Rivers provided a convenient continuation of the waterway with which the canal connected the Masurian Lakes.

With more settlers coming in and more land required for crop and pastureland, the forests receded and the 'Wildnis' was such no longer. There are many great open fields with the soil running from sandy, to sandy loam and where the forest cover was heavy it has been called "garden rich". Much land was devoted to the raising of all varieties of grain. Cattle, sheep and horses were found in large numbers. In many respects this land was much like the land in central Wisconsin or Minnesota.

The crystal-clear waters of the Masurian Lakes have been a fishermen's paradise. It was a vacation type of country and often referred to as a 'schau-platz' or showplace of the nation. The countryside has a bewitching charm and splendor, expecially during the autumnal change of colors when the leaves of the hardwoods contrasted with those of the evergreens.

EAST PRUSSIAN "WILDNIS"
Southern Part
(Courtesy OSTPREUSSEN Umschau Verlag Frankfurt am Main)

In the wintertime, the woods and fields were covered with snow and the frozen lakes formed a great glistening ice chain.

The term "Masuren" is applied to the land area in the vicinity of the Masurian Lakes as well as to the people living there regardless of their prior origin. They are mostly protestant. A little further to the north in what was formerly Ermeland which for a time belonged to Poland, there are stately Catholic Churches and Catholic settlers.

EAST PRUSSIAN   MASURIAN LAKES
(Courtesy OSTPREUSSEN Umschau Verlag Frankfurt am Main)

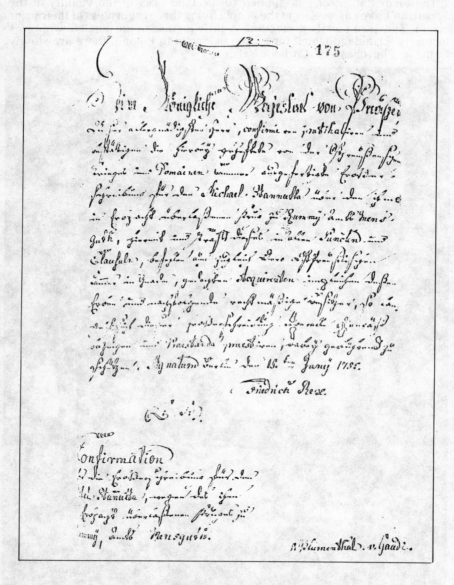

**Grant of Interest in Land
by Friedrich the Great to Michael Hannutta**
(Similar Grants were given to other East Prussians)

See English translation in Appendix, Page 200

1761

...

§. 4;

...

§. 5;

...

§. 2,

... Confirmation ... Contract ...

Trinitatis 1782 ...

... perpetuir ...

§. 3.

... 12 β. ...

zu concurriren, ... Kind ..., Gratis, Däm...... , Weg ...
.... Alleen ... den ..... sonst..... ... ...
.... zu ... ...
... ...
... , ... , ...
... ...
... . Was ferner

§. 11.

Die casus fortuidos ... ...
... ... Remissions statt, son
... der stipulirten Canon ... ...
... zu ... ... promt und richtig ... ...
... abgetragen ... ; ... soll ...
... große ... Calamitäten, ...
... , ...
... accidirt ... ...

§. 12.

... , ... Contract in allen seinen
Puncten und Clausuln ... ... , soll er
... ... maintenirt
... .
... ist dieser ... Contract in ...
... Exemplarien ... , ...

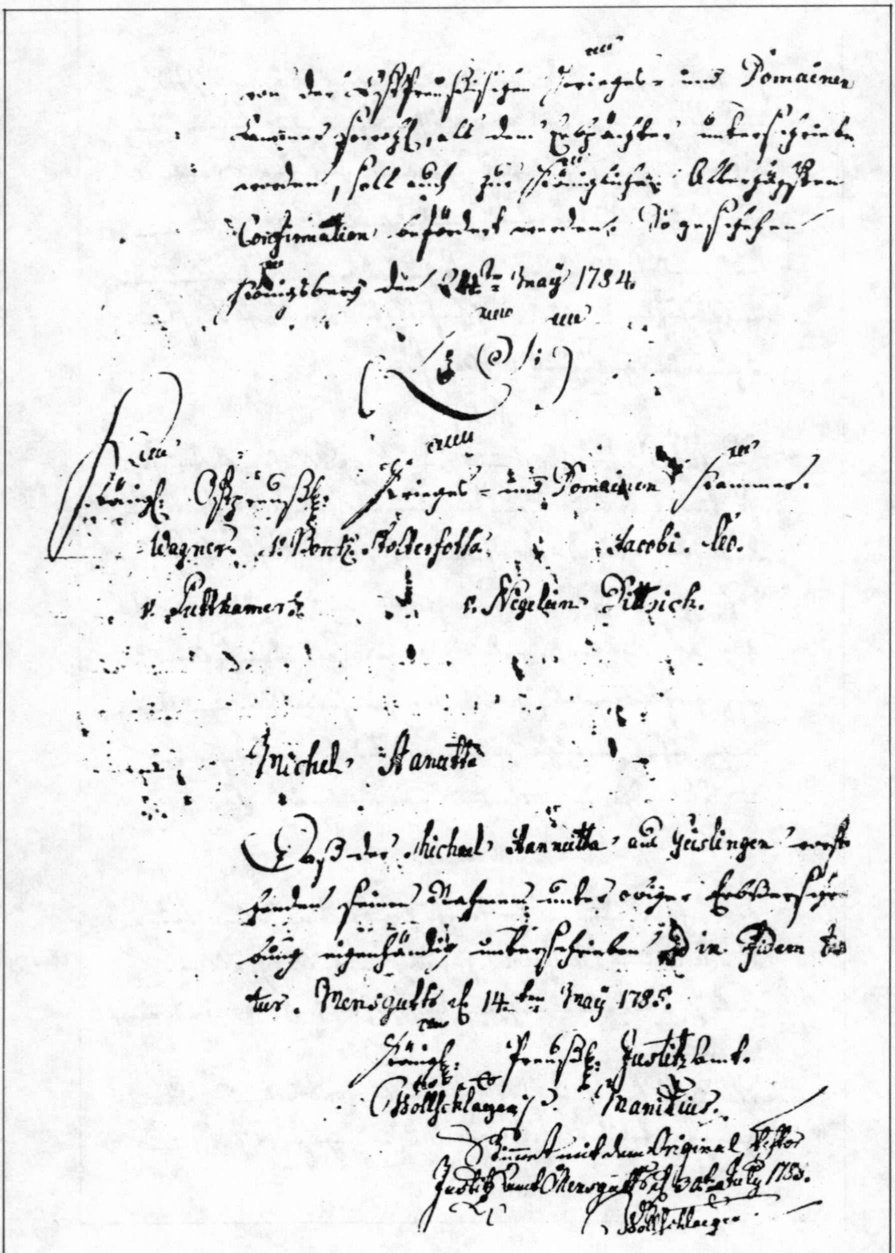

von der Ostpreußischen Krieges- und Domainen
Cammer sowohl als den Beklagten unterschrieben
werden, soll auch zur Königlichen Allerhöchsten
Confirmation befördert werden. So geschehen
Königsberg den 24ten May 1784.

(L. S.)

Königl. Ostpreußische Krieges- und Domainen Cammer.
Wagner. v. Bentz. [illegible] Jacobi. Leo.
v. Puttkamer. v. Negelein. Dittrich.

Michel Stanutta

Daß der Michael Stanutta aus Geislingen vorstehenden
seinen Nahmen unter der eigenen Erbverschrei-
bung eigenhändig unterschrieben, wird in Fidem at-
testirt. Mensguth d. 14ten May 1785.
Königl. Preußisches Justitzamt.
Vollschlaeger. Manitius.
Stimmt mit dem Original überein
Justitz Amt Mensguth d. 2ten July 1785.
Vollschlaeger.

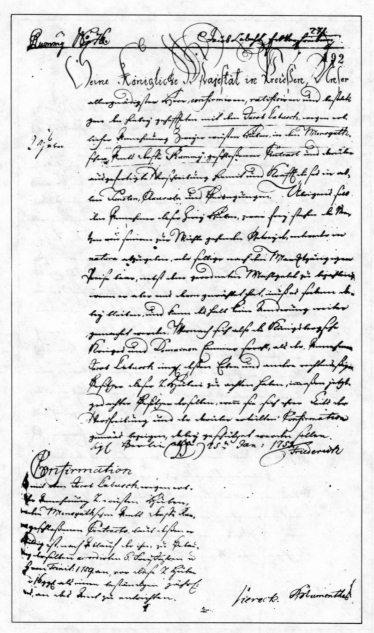

Fredrick (The Great) grants lands and privileges
to Jacob Labusch

192

277.

2 [illegible]

Nachdem sich laut Visitations Protocoll vom 16ten Mart: 17[illegible]
der Einsaß Jacob [illegible] aus dem Dorfe [illegible]
[illegible] von denen bis jetzo befindlichen wüsten [illegible] im Dorfe
[illegible] erblich anzunehmen und zu bebauen
so sind demselben folgende [illegible] zu Erbauung und Cultivirung
von allem Bauholz frey überlaßen und zu völliger Einrichtung der sämtlich daraus erforderlichen Gebäude 6 Freijahre [illegible]
freyen Haushaltung und Kriegs [illegible], von allen oneribus frey. [illegible]
[illegible] haben wie, als [illegible] worin [illegible]
[illegible] außer dem gewöhnlichen Metz und Mahlgeld
accordiret, mit der Versicherung, daß derselbe vor sich und seine
Descendenten von der Leibeigenschaft befreyet und allezeit
als [illegible] frey [illegible] tractiret, auch dessen [illegible]
[illegible] bey den Beamten als auch in Königl.
[illegible] zu verrichten, [illegible]
bey vorfallender Gelegenheit, auch in ein anderes Amt
auch an einem andern beliebigen Ort im Königreich [illegible]
[illegible], jedoch mit Königl. Kriegs und Domainen Cammer Con-
cession und [illegible] zu verziehen und diese [illegible]
[illegible] zu veralieniren befugt seyn
[illegible] bey [illegible]
mit ihm [illegible] nach Ablauf der ihm zugestandenen
von 6 Freyjahren, welche von Trinitatis 1753 den Anfang
nehmen von dieser [illegible] 30 [illegible] und

also

193

Königsberg den 27ᵗᵉⁿ Xbr 1752.

Vidit Oe

47

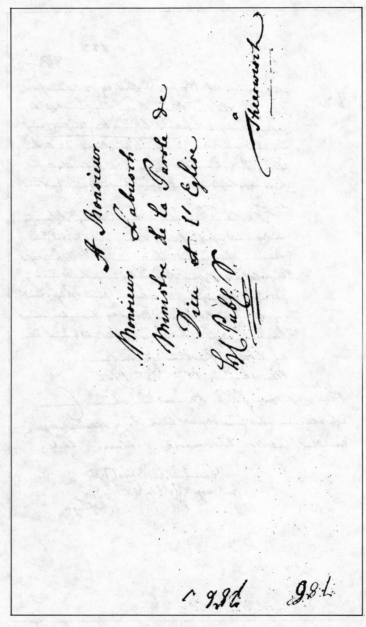

French
A document addressed to A Monsieur Labusch, Ministre
de la Parole de Dieu et l'Eglise
(Minister of the word of God and of the Church)

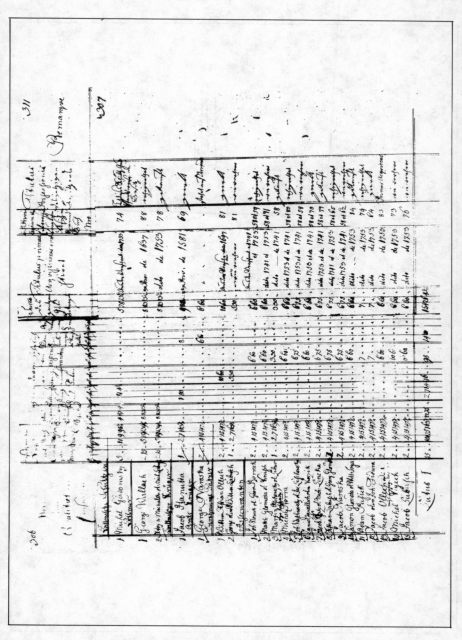

Census of 1775-81 Prastations Tabelle showing owners and dates
Jacob Hannuta   Amts Krueger
Michael Labusch   Zollmeister Krueger

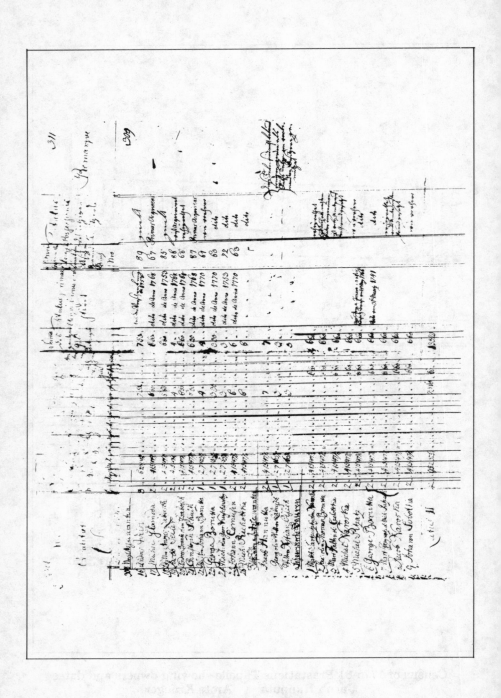

Land register showing family names of
Gottfried Hannutta, Michael Anutta
(Note first omission of use of "H" in "Anutta"

SUMMARY OF LAND HOLDINGS BY
LABUSCH AND HANNUTTA FAMILIES

Verschreibungen nach dem Grundbuch des Amtes Mensguth
Ostpr.Fol.15568
fur Labusch und Hannutta in Rummey

Nr.78	Michael Labusch	Berlin 4.August 1768	erebt
Nr.69	Jacob Hannutha	Konigsberg 2.Sept. 1581	eingeheirathet
Nr.69½	Michael Hannuta	Berlin 18.Juni 1785	gekauft
	Erbpachter vom Krug		
Nr.81	Witwe Labusch	Konigsberg 29.Juni 1697	ererbt
81½		Berlin 25.Januar 1753	
Nr.85	Adam Labusch	Berlin 25.Januar 1753	ererbt
Nr.83¾	Jacob Hannutta	Berlin 5.August 1751	ererbt
	Gottfried Hannutta		
Nr.68	Johann Hannuta	Berlin 25.Januar 1753	ererbt

Staatl.Archivlager Gootingen
Ostpr.Fol.15691a Bll. 93R 95V 96V 97V 100R
(Mitte 19.Jh. – keine genaue Datierung – evtl. etwas spater)

Besitzstand der Familien Hanuta und Labusch in Rummy A und B

Jacob Hanuta	140 Morgen	(= 2 Hufen)
Michael Labusch	67 Morgen 163 7/11 Ruten	
Georg Labusch zuzatzl.	3 Morgen 73 Ruten	
Jacob Labusch	135 Morgan 147 Ruten	
Georg Labusch		
Jetzt Michael Hanutta	11 Morgen 119 Ruten	
Jacob Hanutta	66 Morgen 45 7/11 Ruten	

In Rummy, there was a medium sized Baptist Church and the people here had been of this faith since about 1856, having been formerly Lutherans.

The typical farmstead would be from 80 to 250 morgen. (A German morgen is 2.47 American acres). The original grants and holdings were very large in terms of American ideas of the size of farm lands in the 1860's. The land census taken June 14th, 1788, Michael Hannutta had 5 Hufen (330 Morgen); Andreas Olech had 5 Hufen and 17 Morgen; Christian LaBusch 4 Hufen 15 Morgen; Adam LaBusch 4 Hufen, 15 Morgen; George LaBusch 5 Hufen, 19 Morgen.

In1775 Jacob Olech had 6 Hufen 60 Morgen along with the same amount for Jacob Labusch and Andreas Labusch. George Borutta had 4 Hufen. Krueger Jacob Hannutta had 8 Hufen in 1775. Thomas Borutta and George Borutta each had 6 Hufen 60 Morgen. William Ollech had 10 Hufen and 60 morgen. (In Schumacher's GESCHICHTE OST-und WESTPRESUSSENS page 73 he indicates that 1 Hufe is equal to 66 morgen and one morgen is equal to 16.5 hectare. One hectare is 2.471 acres.) However, as new generations came along and there was no additional land to be obtained, the family farms were subdivided until the farms were reduced to one family size.

By the 1860's with the land having been farmed for many generations, the buildings were well established. There were substantial well-built houses, large barns, stables, sheds for sheep and hogs, buildings for poultry and machine sheds, graineries and workshop buildings. Most frequently the buildings were constructed to form a square or "court". The courtyard or

Labusch Land
EAST PRUSSIAN HOMESTEAD
Courtesy Elisabeth Labusch Zander Malessa)
1945

German 'Hof' refers to the house, barns, yard, garden – namely the premises immediately forming the homestead. However, the term is often used in a broader sense to embrace the whole farmstead with all its appurtenances. 'Hof' is about the same as the English 'curtilage', but when speaking of one's "Haus und Hof" it means one's all.

Flower gardens were always included when vegetable gardens were planted. There was also an orchard or 'obstgarten'. Besides grain fields and pasture lands, there were wood lots, wetlands, rivers or streams and some land such as some of the glacial morains and eskers that were too rocky for anything except trees, shrubs and perhaps berry bushes.

Livestock on the farms of course included cattle, horses, sheep, hogs, geese and ducks, chickens and sometimes goats. Some land was better suited to sheep raising than other types of farming. East Prussia was a favorite recruiting area for all types of horses for military and governmental purposes.

Some homesteads remaining undamaged nor destroyed by fire or war had been built during the Wilderness pioneer days. They were a single structure and embraced in order the dwelling house, the granary, Machine or tool shed including the 'Werkstatt' or workshop, the hay storage area and last the stables for the animals. Usually the horses were separated from the cattle. These buildings were built for economy of materials but most of all for protection against thievery. They provided indoor access during the cold winter months to the feeding and care of the farm livestock

Some buildings of this type were built in the United States by the early settlers of these East Prussians and the author enjoyed the novelty of visiting the composite farmstead of his favorite aunt Wilhelmina's long structure strung out along the South branch of Beaver Creek. However, when fire or lightning came, (as it did), it was impossible to prevent the complete destruction of the farm structure thus built. It was an experience which meant great privation and suffering, cooking in an open field in the fire damaged cook stove, and, starting all over again.

EAST PRUSSIAN FARM SCENE
(Courtesy DAS OSTPREUSSENBLATT)

The agricultural areas of East Prussia were quite undisturbed by noise or factory smoke. Sugarbeet factories had not yet come. A quiet calm prevailed over the countryside broken only by the lowing of cattle and the call of birds.

The village church, the supply store, the blacksmith shop were the outer perimeter of the lifestyle of that day. It was seldom necessary to travel to the more important administrative center (Kreis) except on the most important business.

Religious and social life were closely associated because of necessity. Luther's teachings ("Luthers Lehre flog wie ein Glaubenstrum ueber die Ostgebiete") flew over the East region like a reformation storm.

In Rummy, the Baptist church was the center of life. In other villages there were Lutheran, Evangelical (Calvinist) churches. These provided the people with nurture and renewal of their faith and a closely-knit social life. In fact, the Baptists were so moved by the strength of their faith that they sent a young man from Rummy to the Rochester Theological Seminary in Rochester, New York, to study for the Baptist ministry during the years 1872 to 1875.

From 1815 to 1914 there was little to disturb the quiet pursuit of life in this province in a physical way. The principal disturbance was the continual enforcement of compulsory military service as men from age 18 and older were called into military service. Calls were also made upon the people for resources for military excursions elsewhere in Europe or for colonialism. In the far Pacific. The British, Spanish, Portugese and German explorers roamed far and wide making claims in the names of their Sovereigns.

In World War I the Masurian Lakes and Tannenberg again entered history and the people of East Prussia were once again subjected to the ravages of war.

But the end came in World War II when the Soviet Russian Troops and Soviet military might swept through this province, devastating everything rural and urban, and the civilization created with the coming of the Teutonic

Knights was wiped out. When one considers the geographic lines which caused East Prussia to be in an area where it was almost surrounded by its neighbors to the east and south and sometimes West for most of its history, the ultimate domination of this industrious land, resources and people was the realization of a long held Slavic dream.

Chapter 5

Invitation to Volhynia and Migration to the Promised Land

The emancipation of the serfs by Czar Alexander II in 1861 was not a decision made on the spur of the moment. It was the result of a process of social and economic thinking and development over a period of many years. The intellectuals of Russia, including Tolstoy, Dostoyevsky and others had been thinking of the freeing of the serfs long before 1861. (21) p 147-170, 190-91, 198, 214-15)

Serfs were considered as something between free men and slaves. They were not exactly the same as crops growing upon the land and sold with the land but in practice, it appeared that it did work out exactly that way. Yet, they were not slaves. They had certain rights beyond which the lord of the land could not go. Indeed, some of the serfs may have been landowners themselves who became indebteded to the lord, and, when they could not pay their debt, became serfs of the Lord or Noble.

If they could pay their debt and redeem themselves, in theory, they could be free. In practice, either because of the size of the debt and the Nobleman's system of keeping records, redemption by payment virtually was impossible.

Tolstoy ("TOLSTOY" by Henry Troyat 1967 Doubleday pp 114-147) indicates that Tolstoy had the Serfs on his mind in April 1856. He told his serfs on May 28th 1856, about his idea of freeing them. However, after listening to his plans, the serfs declined to accept their freedom. They saw Tolstoy's plan as a cunningly cruel hoax to cheat them of their status. The serfs interpreted the situation perhaps understandably, that they (the serfs) belonged to the lord of the land, but that the land belonged to the serfs. (21).

Tolstoy saw the coming of a great rebellion if the serfs were not freed quickly. (21) The change came finally, because the Czar and his court began to appreciate the possibility of great danger. The emancipation Act of February 19th 1861 did free the serfs. When they were free, they were entitled to an allotment of land in proportion to their fromer holdings. The government indemnified the owners but gave the serfs long-term loans with which to buy the land allotted to them. The loans were to be paid over a term of years.

Russia appears to have been the last large nation allied to western civilizations to deal with the question of serfdom. France extinguished serfdom by the French Revolution of 1789. Friedrich Wilhelm I freed the serfs on his royal estates (2) and thus contributed to the movement to do away with the system by a decree dated March 22nd 1719.

EAST PRUSSIANS AS UKRAINIAN SETTLERS

Some explanation about the Ukraine will further assist in understanding the conditions under which the East Prussians began their sojourn in this part of Russia.

When Poland and Lithuania became a united nation under Jagiello and Jadwiga (Hedwig), the territory of Poland and Lithuania extended from the country of Livonia in the North, along the Baltic Sea to and including West Prussia; thence southerly to the Hungarian border; thence southeasterly to the Black Sea on the Dniester; thence along the Black Sea to the Dnieper River; thence northeasterly to a point northerly of the Sea of Azov; thence generally northerly to a point southwest of Moscow; thence back to the

Map showing Russian Expansion into Poland
(Used by permission of Dr. Karl Stump and the
American Historical Society of Germans from Russia)

northwest and the Baltic Sea but excluding Teutonic held East Prussia. In 1667 with some concessions from the Russians, Poland ceded to Russia all of the Smolensk, Siendierz, Chernigov and all of the territory east of the Dnieper River subject to some division of territory with the Polish King later on. Kiev was to remain with Russia for two years. This part of the Peace Treaty with Poland has been the most durable of the centuries for Kiev never left Russian hands after this settlement. Volhynia was part of the Kingdom of Poland from 1569 to 1795. In 1795 most of Volhynia became a

Russia in 1865
(Used by permission of Dr. Karl Stump and the
American Historical Society of Germans from Russia)

Russian province as the result of the third partition of Poland. The native population of Vohlynia was Ukrainian. During the previous long reign of Poland over Volhynia the Polish Kings divided the land of the province among the Polish nobility. These subjected the native Ukrainian peasants to Serfdom from which they were not freed until the general emancipation of all Serfs by Tsar Alexander II in 1861. Russians as such, were not numerous in Volhynia except as appointed officials of the Tsarist government. Only in the immediate area of Kiev, Zhitomir and Chernigev were Russians more heavily settled although there was Polish influence in Kiev. (See maps in Dr. Adam Giesinger's CATHERINE TO KRUSCHEV, showing German colonies in Volhynia at pages 25 and 130)

With the freeing of the serfs in 1861 the noblemen owning land in Russia found themselves without workers to operate their farms and estates. The mere fact that one was of the nobility did not mean that such person or family was one of wealth unless their lands were productive. Many nobles lived beyond their means and many were burdened with debts and mortgages which would quickly lead them to ruin and insolvency unless the lands were put into production.

Since many of the landowners were Polish and the Ukrainian language was the one of every-day usage even though Russian was the official language, the land-owners frantically sent out representatives to seek farmers among the industrious Germans of East Prussia. East Prussians were especially sought because many of them knew German and Masuren which was a local native language made up of old Polish, some German and some Russian. Such settlers could be more easily worked into the economy of Volhynia in the Russian Ukraine.

The people who accepted the invitation of the nobles would go as farmers and workers but not as settlers in the sense of becoming Russian citizens. They went to Russia without the promises extended more than a hundred years ago by Catherine II. The Prussians preferred to retain their German citizenship.

The East Prussians were interested in a new life under more benign conditions than those which prevailed in East Prussia then under the leadership of Bismarck.

The representatives of the Volhynian landowners no doubt described the lands with their capacity to produce good crops. The descriptions probably indicated that there were fields and woodlands and considerable low land that needed to be drained to become workable farmland.

By this time, either the East Prussians knew or were informed by the landowner's representatives that the Russian government had instituted a new control of land under the laws and edicts of 1864 which established the Zemstvo, a first step toward Russification of land in the Russian controlled areas. The East Prussians were later to learn that this was to extend not only to the land and its control, but to the use of Russian language in schools and even in churches.

Apparently these changes did not give the East Prussians cause for alarm or concern. They were considerably more concerned about compulsory military service which they had lived with in East Prussia for a long time. As yet, in 1865, when the East Prussians began to move into the Ukraine, neither the landowners nor their newcomers knew that in 1871, universal compulsory military service would be decreed. The Prussians were doubtless given equivocal answers to their questions concerning military service. It was probably pointed out that they the East Prussians, would not be called into military service any more than the Germans who had preceded them under Czarina Catherine's invitation. It is reasonable to infer that such promises, either express or implied were made, for it is difficult to believe that the Prussians would be willing to leave all they had in East Prussia and make the great sacrifices they made in order to move to Volhynia where the military burdens would be as great or even greater than those at home in East Prussia. That their fears were allayed by the representations of the landowner's representatives must be an accepted fact.

The author's maternal grandfather, of minor nobility, was one of the three leaders of the forty wagon train which left East Prussia for the Ukraine with his family. He had however, a portion of his German military service to complete. He returned to East Prussia to fulfill his military obligation but because of travel problems, he arrived at his post several days after the required time for reporting. For his tardiness he was given a thirty day jail sentence but his sentence was suspended so he could serve his company as a cook. He did however, spend his nights in the guardhouse until his sentence was completed. Upon completion of his military duties, he returned to his family in the Ukraine.

In the operation of a large farm it was necessary to have considerable equipment. Much of it had to be hand made because this was before the mass production of the McCormick and similar reapers, mowers and thresh-ing machines.

The most valuable farm powertool besides that of horses or oxen was the windmill. It was necessary not only to grind the wheat and other grains for human use but also for the animals. Also resourceful farmers were able to invent home-made power tool uses for the windmills to minimize the use of hand tools.

PREPARATIONS TO LEAVE

After having met with the representatives of the noblemen from the Ukraine, it is reasonable to assume that representatives or committees went with the the representatives to explore the truth of the representations made by the Russians. The Mennonites and Roman Catholics of the Volga and other Germans sent such exploratory parties all the way to the United States and Canada and it would be almost impossible to assume that the East Prus-sians left all they had in East Prussia without first knowing what they were getting into in Russia.

The pilgrimage from East Prussia to the Ukraine was made in the Fall of 1865. The year's crops had been gathered. The traveling equipment over-hauled for a journey of perhaps 600 kilometers. The best horses were obtained. Wagons were built or prepared for heavy loads. They would have to carry seed, equipment, furniture, food, provisions for horses and people. Grain, hay, flour, dried peas and beans, smoked and salted meats, sausages, bread, herbs had to be taken along.

The wagon trains had to be organized under trained leaders. Usually a committee of three among whom the responsibilities for various phases were divided.

A sale of land or personal property under normal circumstances takes place between a willing seller and a willing buyer. However, when a rather large group of people in the same general area begin to offer their personal property, surplus animal food, equipment and other farm implements for sale, they create a buyer's market, that is, the buyer has the upper hand. The seller is under pressure to accept what he can get. They obtained for their property less than the fair market value for most of their property.

Thus the disposition of livestock, poultry, machinery, grain and all other items of personal property which could not be taken along because of lack of space, were sold under pressure and necessity.

They did take with them what their wagons could carry. Some of the items which had to be left were heirlooms that had come down through genera-tions. Extra animals were taken so that the teams pulling the wagons would not be worn out to such an extent that they had to be either destroyed or replaced enroute. While there already was a railroad in operation between Magdeburg and Leipzig in Germany in 1865. the great period of railroad building did not come along for another fifteen years or more. There was no other way to travel between East Prussia and the Ukraine except by wagon train. Since there were stage coaches between many European cities, there were roads of a kind so that the travelors did not face the primitive road bed of the American Western Pioneers. When a caravan stopped during the day to rest and feed the animals and the people, the men in charge of protecting the wagon train immediately set out guards around the camp to guard against highwaymen and groups of freed serfs. Night guard duty was most essential and not unlike that which was required by the American west bound wagon trains.

DEPARTURE

The East Prussians had come to East Prussia as refugees and pilgrims from some other part of Europe. They came fleeing from persecution and intolerable conditions whether from southern, western, central Europe or from the immediate vicinity of East Prussia as re-settled Old Prussians, settled by the Teutonic Knights or as refugees from Bohemia, Masovia or some of the many principalities of Greater Prussia where the ruling Sovereign was not of their religious faith and they would rather leave than be compelled to submit to the religion of the ruling prince. When they arrived in East Prussia they were either Lutherans or Evangelical. Some may have been influenced by the faith of the Mennonites from which came some of the Baptists. In any event, all of these folk were deeply religious and did not depart from East Prussia without holding a devotional service for themselves and the loved ones they were leaving behind. Assembled, the leaders read from the Bible and from Prayer Books:

"Lord, thou hast been our dwelling place
in all generations ..."
"O satisfy us early with thy mercy;
that we may rejoice and be glad all our days.

The lay leaders led in prayer and after prayer, all joined in a hymn. No instruments were used for all knew hymn tunes from childhood.

O God, Our Help (St. Anne C.M.)

Herr, unser Gott, du warst und bist,
Und bleibst in Ewigkeit;
Du bist's der uns're Hoffnung
In uns'rer Pilgerzeit.

O God, our help in ages past,
Our hope for years to come,
Our shelter from the stormy blast,
And our eternal home.

There was little cause for jubilation. Eyes were wet or reddened by tears. Departure and separation were ahead with no hope of return, no visitation, no place or room to come to for consolation except the comfort of their faith in God's eternal purpose and the nearness of His everlasting arms.

Assembled at a friendly relative's farm just north of Ortelsburg, the wagon train formed in a pre-arranged order which was to be followed throughout the journey. Forty wagons. Three wagonmasters.

One was a short dynamic young man but of towering intellect and personality to whom the two other wagonmasters looked for the final decisions. The word was given and the train moved out in its ordered column to the main road south through Ortelsburg, thence south to the southern boundary of East Prussia; thence southeasternly toward Brest on the Russian border. All of occupied Poland was within Russian control and had been for various periods from 1667 to 1915, by reason of the several partitions of Poland. The roads ran generally southeasterly through Kovel, Lutsk, Rovno and ended in Zhitomir. From Zhitomir the families were assigned to their respective lands. The distance was about equal to the distance from Hamburg to Koenigsberg, or Koenigsberg to Vienna. The wagon train probably made fifteen to twenty-five miles per day. Rest stops had to be made often as there were a number of pregnant women and quite a few small children. Wagon wheels had to be greased. Sometimes both harness and wagon repairs had to be made. Fortunately, the roads were clear of boulders and other obstacles which might cause a wheel to break or require a harness to be spliced. The demands of the journey were such that all able-bodied persons had to participate and each family had to provide for its own care of people and equipment. Night watch duty was rotated and the guard had to be sufficiently strong to repel raiding parties of freed serfs who would carry away everything except the millstone or a red hot iron. Every guard had to be prepared. Shot guns, knives and even swords were needed to deter attack or a feint on one side and perhaps a raid from the other side.

When the settlers came within range of their new homeland, riders would be sent ahead to notify the landowners of the prospective arrival time. Places were designated to which assigned families would report and be welcomed. Some families arrived to find no housing ready or only temporary quarters. In some cases, the "Izbas" formerly used by the serfs who had left the nobleman, were used for temporary quarters. The "Izbas" were miserable hovels for the most part and were hardly better than the stables provided for cattle, sheep, hogs or chickens in East Prussia. But when cleaned they did provide shelter from the weather until something better could be built. Other settlers, more fortunate, had housing provided on the noblemen's land in close proximity to the "Hof" or courtyard of the nobleman or landowner. But much of the building had to be done in order to provide the settlers with all of the housing necessary for the first winter with much more to be built the following year and in the years to come as the farmstead of each settler grew and developed. If the land had been previously cultivated the settlers found it had been neglected after the departure of the serfs since their release in 1861. Others of the settlers bought lowlands and paid exhorbitant prices for such lands. As in other cases, promised buildings and shelters were not ready or non-existent. The building of homes and quarters for the settlers had to be done when they came and did the work themselves.

Where settlers were sold and assigned wooded lands, such lands had to be cleared before any kind of crops or gardens could be planted. Likewise, sufficient housing had to be built that first Autumn to keep the settler and his family protected against severe winters.

Low lands had to be drained. The laying out of drainage ditches and the digging of them had to be done by hand with the help of their draft animals – horses or oxen. It was hard work but always the most difficult and stubborn to remove were the tree stumps.

The settlements of these East Prussians were not the close-knit colony type of community which the early Germans set up on the Volga and other colonies under the invitation of Catherine the Great.

These East Prussians were settled in an area of perhaps thirty miles from one direction to another, mostly in the Kries (county) of Zhitomir. The distance from Zhitomir to Kiev the capital of the Ukraine, was about 100 kilometers. Toporisc and Goroschke were about twenty versts from Zhitomir, the county-seat, in a northerly direction toward Korosten which became a railroad station between Kiev and Prostken on the East Prussian border. Thus, the settlers had to travel some distance to see each other. The most frequent place of visitation was at the Baptist Church at Toporisc or at Neudorf. Other places of visitation were the markets or fairs held by nearly every town where the people could bring their produce and trade with each other and with the merchants who brought their wares to the market. They referred to these fairs or markets as the "Jahrmarkt" because it supposedly was held only annually. However, with a number of villages having similar fairs, nearly every market became a "Jahrmarkt" whether annual or not. Everything from clothing to livestock, feed, grain, household wares and farm supplies were available. It was a gala occasion.

A COLONIST'S HOUSE

(Used by permission of Dr. Karl Stumpp and the
American Historical Society of Germans from Russia)

The climate in the Ukraine is continental. The average temperature in Kiev, latitude 50 degrees 30 minutes North, for January being 1° centigrade, which is colder than Hammerfest, latitude 70° 35' North. Since most of the Ukraine lies south of the 20° C. isotherm, high temperatures prevail in the southern portions in July and August. Rainfall diminishes from the Northwest to the Southeast. There are seasons of poor harvests. Travel during winter months, as indicated elsewhere, was mostly by sleighs. Heavy clothing was needed and women often wear boots and multiple garments to keep warm.

Heinz Heckel, Z. St. Beuthen (Oberschlesien) in his work DIE DEUTSCHEN IN WOLHYNIEN (32) p680. (Der Auslanddeutsche 1926) wrote:

> "Die aeltesten Siedlungen sind Zytomir, Heimthal,
> (beide in Ukrainisch-Wolhynien) und Rozyszcze.
> Die spaeter hinzugekommenen Deutschen siedelten
> sich in den Gegenden von Rowno, Luck, Kowel,
> Wladimir, Wol. Dubno und Chelm an"

> (The oldest settlements were in Zhitomir, Heimthal (both in Ukrainian Volhynia) (Russian) and Rozyszcze. The Germans who came later settled in the vicinity of Rovno, Luck, Kovel, Vladimir, Vol. Dubno and Chelm.)

The writer's grand-parent's land was located near the village of Goroschke. Their church was located in Toporisc. And this area was in Kreis Zhitomir.

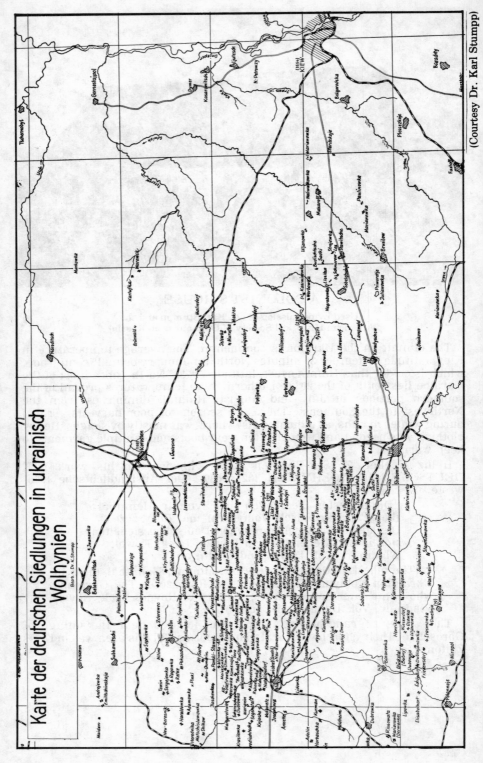

Karte der deutschen Siedlungen in ukrainisch Wolhynien

Bearb. v. Dr. K. Stumpp

(Courtesy Dr. Karl Stumpp)

Chapter 6

THE EAST PRUSSIAN SETTLERS IN VOLHYNIA

Social life in Russia was somewhat less church oriented than in East Prussia. Apart from regularly scheduled religious activities held in churches somewhat distant from the location of their lands, after an evening's work was done and especially during the shorter day-light hours of winter months, a lantern would be lit and taken along to light the way to and from a neighbors house.

Religion, current events of a local nature, farm problems and plans for coming events in their lives would be discussed and the family would all participate in the discussion.

At such social visits no one was expected to provide refreshments other than perhaps a cup of tea. No alcoholic beverages were served among the Baptists.

Neighborhood gatherings of young people would often include work bees or visits, such for example as a group of young women would take their spinning wheels with a quantity of combed wool to spin into yarn while they spun yarns about the village activities. If it was a gathering of older young men and little boys tried to get within hearing distance of their stories and jokes, the older boys only needed to reach slowly toward their back pocket where they carried a sharp pocket knife, which, when seen by the small boys, would send them headlong in flight. The dreaded mujhiks were said to mutilate little boys who got too inquisitive and the fear of being thus caught was deeply instilled in the boys at an early age.

But in a general visit when adults were present and there was safety because of the presence of parents, there was general story telling about wolves, witches, witchcraft, bewitched people, encounters with Russians on the roads when skilful handling of the wagon or sleigh could cause the vehicle of the unwary to be turned over and seriously damaged to say nothing of the danger to the driver and his load of produce or people. The Russians complained that the Germans were the aggressors; that they had heavier wagons with a longer wheel base, iron bound high wheels and steel axles that could absorb the collisions whereas the carts of the peasants were much more susceptible to damage. "The German" the Russians complained, "knew how to turn their wagon so quickly and so cunningly that the side and iron ends of the axles would hit the Russian peasant's cart and overturn it, and then leave immediately, without any damage to the German vehicle. (40) The colonists horses are well fed, very strong, and apparently, 'taught for such an attack'". When such practices became known, both vehicles would seek to avoid each other by the widest margins. These escapades told over and over, spread to all the Russians and the result was greater tension. Fights were frequent and it was not safe to travel or walk alone where one might run into difficulties. (40)

There were still some great forests in the Ukraine in 1865 and for many years thereafter. Wild animals could be hunted and wolves were seen. Wolves were a constant dread of travelers, especially in the winter months. Traveling even with a troika-sleigh, stories would be told how the horses would be attacked by large packs of wolves. They would concentrate on a single horse, hamstring him or attach to his throat to slow or bring him down with a consequent drag and imbalance on the rest of the team causing them to start rearing and screaming. This would bring the entire pack in for the kill of the horses and people. Stories were told how a supply of meat was sometimes taken along and the meat thrown out in chunks to delay the wolves while the sleigh would be driven at top speed to outrun the wolves.

Other stories were told of large pits being dug in the deep woods on wolf trails in order to trap the animals. One story related how a man traveling from a visit to a neighborhood musical gathering was carrying his violin with him when taking a trail through the woods. By accident, in the semi-darkness, he fell into a wolf pit. It was empty but it was also too deep for him to climb out of without assistance. he decided to await daylight when he might be missed or someone could hear his calls. Not long after falling into the pit a wolf came along and also fell into the pit. Having no weapon except the violin, the man started playing the violin and the wolf cowered in fear of the strange noise, and stayed on his side of the pit. However, when the man stopped playing the wolf prepared to attack. When the man did not return home, a search was started and his violin music led the rescuers to the pit where the wolf was dispatched and the man rescued.

But the story which topped them all for the children in our family was father's story of returning home from an errand to a neighbor. A great thunderstorm appeared on the horizon. Thinking to reach home quickly he took a trail through a patch of pine woods but he was caught by the storm while still in the woods. He sought some kind of shelter from a tremendous downpour. A large pine tree was near his path. Its base was about four feet in diameter and it had a large hole rotted out near its roots. The hole was large enough and deep enough for him to stand in protected from the worst of the storm. To his horror, in a few minutes a large wolf appeared. It was none other than old Grayfoot (Graufuss) a widely known and long hunted vicious killer. It was the biggest wolf he had ever seen.

The wolf did not seem to know he was there because of the thunder, flashes of lightning and the rush of wind and rain upon the leaves and trees. The wolf being familiar with this tree turned around and backed into the hole. The young man spread his legs apart to allow the wolf room to get in. What to do? The best defense, he decided, was an offense. He dropped down on the wolf grasping the wolf's ears with both hands and clamping his legs around the wolf.

The surprised wolf took off like the wind with the young man holding on for dear life. Now, he could not let the wolf go for he would turn and tear him up. He hung on and steered the wolf by his ears out of the woods and through a field toward one of the home sheds built for sheep. The shed had a sloping roof at the lower end of which was a pile of lumber. A hired hand saw the commotion and yelled "Uncle, grab hold of a bush". However there was no bush near and they were heading for the lumber pile and roof shed. The wolf as steered over the lumber pile, on to the shed roof and over the high side of the shed and into a duckpond on the other side. The wolf and rider plunged through the air in a furry whirling mass and into the water. Letting go of the wolf, the young man swam to shore while the wolf finding himself in the habitation of man, quickly disappeared. The young man had only a case of extreme fright, some, bramble scratches and an unbelievable story to tell his family by way of explanation.

TRAVEL

Travel for short distances was by foot and one did not say that the distance was "5 versts". Rather, one would say it was a walk of thirty minutes or two hours, etc. Travel for longer distances could be on horseback or by the one-horse unit called a Droshky or the larger unit used for heavier and larger loads, the Troika. This term applied to the wagon or the sleigh whichever was used. The Troika, of course, was for a three-horse team.

Railroads were slower in coming to Russia than to the rest of Europe or America. It was not until the early 1880's that any amount of railroad building was completed in Russia. European Russia – that is considering that part of Russia West of Moscow in that day as European Russia, had more railroad building than that part of Russia lying East. The region

UKRAINIAN TYPE WINDMILL
(Used by permission of Dr. Karl Stump and the
American Historical Society of Germans from Russia

between Moscow and Leningrad was earliest to receive good railroad service. The main Sea port for Russia had been Leningrad (St. Petersberg). Ocean service to and from that port was closed because of ice conditions from late November to Early April. The Black Sea ports, open all year were limited because of the lack of transportation to and from that body of water. Murmansk could be kept open all year but the distance from the area of production to the port was too great. Vladivostok could be kept open with icebreakers but the distances and burden of handling this commerce were expensive. For long years, long wagon trains would travel long distances over the Russian Steppes. The highway and road system was underdeveloped for a long time. However, there was much use of the many great rivers in all of Russia for many centuries and most of the larger centers of population grew up because of the water transportation which was available.

WINDMILLS

Many of the larger farms in the Ukraine, especially in the Zhitomir region, were equipped with windmills as soon as possible. Some made small hand turned grinding mills. But for the best production from a large acreage of land and thousands of bushels of grain, a good sized windmill was a necessity. It was the single most important source of power for there were no steam engines or internal combustion engines. Winds and breezes over the vast Ukrainian steppes were almost constant and the windmill could be put to use almost daily.

WIND

Cherney Vecher, Bely Sneg, Veter, Veter;
Na nogakh ne stoit chelovek,
Veter, Veter, Na vsem Boshem svete.
  - Alexander Block, "The Twelve"

(Black night, white snow, wind, wind!
A man can't stand up, wind, wind –
All over God's world)

 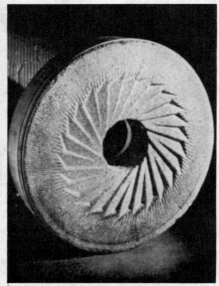

MILLSTONES: Left, Upper Stone. Right Nether Stone
(Courtesy of Orville Broderick)

The mill ground wheat and other grains into flour for human consumption. It also ground oats and other feeds for animals. Also, depending on the needs and ingenuity of the farmer, the windmill could power grindstones, corn'shellers, operate power tools, such as drills and saws and perform many useful operations that ordinarily were performed by hand.

If the farmer kept goats and they were allowed at large, it was necessary to secure the windmill doors so the goats could not enter and climb the stairs to the top of the mill. Goats loved to climb. But to retrieve them was a chore requiring much skill and patience in order to avoid having them jump into the machinery or to the ground from levels that might cause them injury.

GARDEN PRODUCE PRODUCTION

Fields for the raising of grain and other crops were of first importance. Pastures, both open as well as brush and woodland were needed for the sustenance of the livestock, cattle, horses, sheep, goats and swine. But the raising of a large part of the food for human consumption was in the garden. An orchard of fruit trees, apples, pears, cherries and plums were planted early and almost always adjacent to the garden. Most potatoes, pumpkins, squash, beets, beans, peas, carrots, herbs, rutabagas, turnips and cabbages were raised in fairly large fields for a rather large amount of each type was needed. Cucumbers, berries, lettuce, onions and many other types of vegetables were raised in large gardens which required much time of the women of the household. Additionally, during the fall season particularly, mushrooms would be picked and placed in clean bags and hung up to dry. Apples, pears, plums and other fruits were dried and used as needed. A root cellar, built as deeply as possible underground would be a very useful structure for the storage of root crops such as beets, carrots, potatoes, pumpkins and cabbages, although the latter two had to be consumed early as they did not keep very long. Barrels of sauerkraut would be prepared.

MEATS

Fresh meat was a luxury enjoyed mostly at butchering time. For winter use, much meat would be salt packed in a saturate solution of salt brine. Smokehouses also would be built and hams and other meats were smoked and cured for later use. Much of the food consumed on the farms was from flour and potatoes. Recipes by the hundreds were developed for the utilization of potatoes in many forms and the combination of flour with fruit, cheese and berries with only a small amount of meat required to supplement such a meal. Nothing has been indicated that meats were dried or made into "jerky"-type dried meats such as the American Indians used.

FUEL AND WOOD SUPPLIES

Fuel for heating purposes and for cooking was a concern wherever one lived. Fortunately, in the Ukraine, there was still much woodland and firewood could be obtained either on one's own land or could be obtained from mearby land owners. A. E. Vitovich, a Russian, wrote an article for the September 1915 Istoricheskii Vestnik IX pp 884-892 in which he described the relations which existed between the Germans and the Russians. He was strongly uncomplimentary to the Germans. His statements concerning the kind of land which the noblemen sold to the Germans was quite revealing for he said in part:

"When the foreigners received permission to acquire land or to lease it on a long term basis, a whole flock of Germans appeared in the Volhynia Province. ***two notaries, grew rich by hundreds of thousands thanks to a whole mass of completed merchant fortresses, which were sold by deeds and lease agreements. From morning till evening the offices of these notaries were filled by hundreds of Germans who came to complete the documents. The landlords willingly sold the land to the Germans for which the Germans paid advantageous prices, and besides this, did not lay claim to the best sections but agreed to take less productive land, which they soon turned into productive land. ***I saw sandy depressed, swampy places, which at first glance did not offer the correct conditions for agriculture. And after a short time, magnificent colonies appeared in these places thanks to the capital received by the colonists from the German government. ***At the markets only the Germans have the best livestock to sell. In this respect, the colonist Czechs posed the only competition.

(The author had the Russian article translated by William Lewus of the Department of Foreign Languages CSU Ft. Collins and a copy of this translation and the original article in Russian are in the Library of the American Historical Society of Germans from Russia, 631 D St., Lincoln, Nebr. The article is entitled "Nemetskiaii Kolonii Na Volyni" and was written when Russia and Germany were at war in 1915.

Vitovich indicates that much poor land was sold to the Germans at "advantageous prices", meaning that swampy, sandy, rocky, and other poor quality land was sold to the Germans. The clearing of these lands, draining them and preparing them for crops, gave the farmers and settlers, a great deal of firewood and wood for buildings and fences.

Fuel would be prepared in considerable quantities because of the difficulty of getting the timber out of the woods in winter. Stoves would be built into the dwelling houses in an arrangement where they could often be fueled from both within the house and from outside the house.

The stoves and ovens would be built of stone or home made clay brick. They were large enough so that the top of the stove could be used for sleeping during the coldest winter nights. Such a stove would retain heat long after the wood was consumed. But, as indicated, this was a never-ending chore for someone in the family and having participated in such chores, the author can attest to the hard, tedious labor involved.

SERVANTS

Because large families were the general rule, servants were seldom employed. During family illness or perhaps just after the beginning of a marriage, a settler having a large family might allow one of his children to work for a neighbor or relative for food and clothing. Such a person was considered a member of the household rather than a servant. When the farmers became more prosperous, they did hire farm help either from among themselves or from the Russians. The serfs were not generally considered satisfactory workers because they required close supervision and long years of poorest quality living accustomed them to have little regard for title to property. The writer had first hand experience with such a situation. For one whole summer he worked for John Doerk, a neighbor and relative, for One Dollar a month, room and board and a new pair of overalls at the end of the summer.

HARVESTING

Farming, perhaps excepting plowing and harrowing from the preparation of the soil to the harvesting, in those early days in the Ukraine, was largely hand labor. Agricultural machinery, except for home made items did not come along until the years just before the settlers decided to leave Russia. A settler was fortunate to have a plow and a home-made spike-toothed harrow or drag. There were no horsedrawn seeders (drills). Sowing was largely by hand. The sower would tie a sheet over his shoulder, fill the sheet with seed grain and reaching into the sheet and taking a handful of seed would scatter it with a wide practiced swing and taking two or three more paces would repeat the casting of the seed. A flag, usually a piece of cloth, would be tied on a long pole placed at the end of the field to give the sower a guide so the field would be evenly covered with seed.

"THE SOWER"
(Courtesy Orville Broderick)

The spike-toothed drag would then be dragged over the field with a team of horses or oxen in order to bury the seed.

When the grain was ripe, it would be cut with a scythe equipped with parallel wood tines – parallel to the blade of the sythe. This enabled the man wielding the "cradle", again with a wide practiced swing, to cut a considerable quantity of ripe grain and deposit it on the ground evenly. The bundlers, following after the man with the cradle, would gather an armful of

71

grain, then taking a handful of the stalks would pass them under the bundle. At the top of the bundle, the "tie" would be twisted, then bent into an elbow and the elbow tucked under the tie, thus tying the bundle as securely as if done by a McCormick binder. The writer has tied hundreds of bundles of grain in this manner and then placed them into shocks where they would dry to be later hauled into the barn for threshing. However, in the Ukraine, threshing Machines had not yet been invented and threshing was done by hand by the use of a flail for whipping the kernels of grain from the stalks or by the use of a four-bladed threshing stone, usually limestone, through which a hole was bored or chiseled for an axle. The threshing stone would be pulled and rolled over the grain scattered on the threshing floor, by a team of horses or oxen. The straw would be removed and the grain was then winnowed either by throwing it into the air so that the wind would carry away the chaff, or, primitive fanning or winnowing machines powered by hand or by the windmills helped to clean the great quantities of grain for bagging and shipment or for hauling to the granary where it would be stored in room-sized bins. Granaries had to have considerable capacity to take care of the large farms and to provide year-round storage so that there would be sufficient grain for food and seed for the spring planting. The great productions of grains by the Germans in all of the colonies and settlements proved a great safeguard against famines which now and then failed to provide sufficient food in all the Russian areas.

POTATOES

The planting and digging of potatoes was also usually done by hand. Cultivating, until cultivators were invented or potato-hillers were devised was also done by hand labor with a hoe-type tool. Insecticides were unknown so it was necessary to protect the plants against bugs by hand. When ripe enough to dig, they were also dug by either a potato-type fork-type hoe, or with a garden fork. In either case, it was hard, back-breaking work. The potatoes would be gathered into bags or into boxes built on stone-boats and hauled to the root cellers for storage. The potato was a dependable type of food that could be prepared in many pleasing ways. For potato and other German type and German-Russian type foods and recipies it is suggested that the KUECHE KOCHEN produced by the American Historical society of Germans from Russia be obtained, or the book on "Traditional Ukrainian Cookery" by Savella Stechishin, Trident Press Ltd. Winnipeg Canada 1967 be used.

SHEEP RAISING

Having wool for clothing and other uses in the days before availability of assorted textiles was a prime necessity. The sheep as an animal of domestic use was known before the dawn of known history. Pictographs and other evidences found by archeologists in excavations of lost civilizations indicate the presence and use of sheep. Wealth in Biblical times was reckoned in the number of sheep a man owned. They were an important economic unit for trading purposes. The sheep was a source of much needed wool, meat and fat. Thus, most farms had from a few to large numbers of sheep for one could not be self sufficient without a supply of wool. There was hardly a woman who did not know how to operate a spinning wheel to spin yarn for the knitting of stockings, caps, mittins or gloves, sweaters, blankets, filling for quilts and many other uses. Some yarn was loomed into cloth.

Some of the land areas not entirely suitable for other types of agriculture, were suitable for grazing of cattle, horses and sheep. On such farms horse and sheep raising might be the main product of the farm. Since much land was not fenced, shepherds would take charge of the large flocks of sheep and move them from one area or pasture to another and keep the sheep out of neighbor's fields or the farmer's own grain or other fields. Often a shepherd found it necessary to have a "lead sheep". Such an animal could save the shepherd much work as the other sheep would most always follow the "lead" sheep. The shepherd might select an injured lamb or another shepherd might even injure one and then deliver it to the shepherd who would bind its wounds and give it tender, loving care, carrying it about with him when he went out or in with the flocks. He would provide food for it, water it and build a special fold to keep it safe from further injuring itself or being injured by the other sheep. By the time the lamb recovered it would be well grown and so attached to the shepherd that it would follow him everywhere.

Sheep dogs were sometimes trained and used in herding of flocks of sheep to aid the shepherd. During the lambing season, a shepherd's presence was indispensable in the saving and protection of lambs from predators. It was also necessary to castrate the male lambs and, as soon as warmer weather arrived in the spring, the sheep would be brought into pens or buildings for shearing of the wool. After the shearing the wool might be cleaned and classified and bagged either for storage for later use or for sale at the "Jahrmarkts". If it could not be sold it might be bartered for other needed materials or supplies.

There is a large variety of sheep adapted to various climates and altitudes. They are found on all continents. They belong to the family of hollow-horned ruminants and in general are impossible of definition as they pass imperceptibly into the goat family. The pamir plateau on the confines of Turkestan, at elevations of 16,000 feet above sea level, is the home of the magnificent Ovis Poli named after the celebrated traveler Marco Polo who found it in the 13th century. There are sheep with long haired wool and some with short haired wool. There are characteristic British, Rocky Mountain, African, Asiatic and Australian breeds which fill needs for specific types of fibres. But sheep raising is much more than allowing them to breed and graze for they are also subject to diseases and ticks and many sheep raisers find it necessary to pass all the sheep through a sheep-dip to get rid of ticks or prevent other insect infestations. On a visit to Germany in 1974 the writer had the privilege of sleeping on a wool-filled mattress and under a down filled quilt from wool and down raised on the East Prussian ancestral agricultural lands granted the family by Frederick the Great.

Chapter 7

BAPTIST FAITH AND FEASTS

The East Prussians of this history were all Baptists when they came to the United States, starting in about 1885. Most of them were Baptists when they left East Prussia in 1865, although there were also some Lutherans and Evangelicals or Calvinists. The Baptist faith came largely through one man, Rev. Johann Gerhard Oncken, (1800-1884). Erick Amburger in his GESCHICHTE DES PROTESTANTISMUS (36) p 144, declares Oncken was Baptized in Hamburg by an American Baptist clergyman but had already been influenced by Methodist puritan teachings current in Scotland. His preaching was fervently evangelistic and he was eagerly heard by the spiritually hungry people of central Europe. By 1856 the Baptist faith had reached mostly Lutheran East Prussia and many were converted from Lutheranism to the Baptist faith. From East Prussia the Baptist faith moved into Poland and into the Ukraine. Oncken visited much of Russia and the Ukraine in 1869 and not only preached but helped form a conference or association type or organization through which Baptist churches could keep in touch with each other. Birth certificates of the writer's parents bore the seal "SIEGEL DER EVANGELISCHER GEMEINDE GETAUFTEN CHRISTEN ODER BAPTISTEN, Kreis Zitomir" or "Neudorf" as the case might be. Baptist literature was scarce. Song-prayer books which were brought from East Prussia were probably produced under Lutheran auspices. They were found in many Baptist homes of East Prussians Friedrich Wilhelm I had granted Johann Heinrich Hartung of Koenigsberg the privilege of printing the Bible, the new Testament and Prayer and Song books by royal decree executed May 17, 1738.This Prayer-Song book contained selected readings from the Psalms and other books of the Bible, prayers and songs.

Singing was without accompaniment of instruments. The song leader or "Dirigent", after obtaining the pitch from a tuning fork (Stimmgabeln) would read the first line of the Hymn and begin the Hymn. Just before the first line was ended, he would read the next line. This "lining out" would make possible the singing of the entire hymn without interruption. Printed or written copies of the hymn were not needed and the congregation soon knew the hymns by heart and they were sung without "lining out". Hymn singing either with or without "lining out" was a thrilling and soul stirring experience. In the early days of these Prussians in Marinette and Oconto Counties, in Wisconsin, some of the most beautiful reditions of music could be heard "a capella" whether sung by a choir or by the entire congregation. Whether in Russia or America, in cottage, home meetings or churches, choirs were soon organized and provided much inspiring music which greatly enriched the religious experience of the participants.

BIRTHS

Births were a happy occasion, especially where both the mother and child came through the ordeal in satisfactory condition. Medical services were scarce and most deliveries were handled by midwives. There was much made of births and the ceremony of baptism in the Catholic, Lutheran and Evangelical faiths which included the conferring of the honor to friends or relatives of being God-parents to the baby. Baptists, however, did not make a special festive occasion other than special thanksgiving that the mother and child were alive and doing well.

DEATHS

As it must to all men, death came to the pilgrims who came to East Prussia and to the Pilgrims who went to Russia and then came to the United States. Though man has dealt with this experience from the beginning of time, no single practice helped so much as a firm faith in one's God and the prospect of life after death. Conditions in East Prussia, at first a great wilderness, were primitive but improved somewhat more rapidly than in the Ukraine. Whether working in the woods clearing land or farming, this occupation is still one of the most hazardous. When added to this one deals with animals, with heat and extreme cold, getting up before dawn and working till after dark there is further exposure. Except for horse and ox power and the power of perhaps a windmill, there were no powertools, All work was hand work with primitive hand made equipment.

In those days if a husband and father lived to be fifty years of age, he was considered a man of extraordinary strength and endurance, for life expectancy was very low.

Children's diseases such as measles, smallpox, diptheria, scarlet fever, chickenpox and other diseases took their full toll. It was long before the discovery of vaccinations and antiseptic practices which advanced modern medicine. It was not uncommon to lose two, three and perhaps four children from a single contagious childhood disease in a single family.

Childbirth was always fraught with danger. many a wonderful marriage ended abruptly because of childbed fever or a breached birth. However, when one considers the pioneer conditions under which these people lived death in confinement cases appears to have been low. The womenfolk were hardy. They had to work hard physically at many tasks. With or without a good midwife, mother and child were usually brought through safely and without complications. The size of families was very large when compared to present day standards of maintaining zero population growth. Family size also indicated the excellence of the preparations and the skills of the midwives. Some families had sixteen or eighteen children. There was a high survival rate in such families, and, even with much intermarriage of the people of the group, there was an exceptionally high rate of physically and mentally healthy offspring. It has even been said that there were occasions when a wife working in a harvest field, haying or shocking grain, gave birth in the field and after taking care of the baby's needs and some rest for the mother, she returned to the work of the harvest.

A study of some early 1900 death records in Wisconsin disclosed that the cause of death entered for public record in the case of the death of a mother it was simply "Confinement". In the case of the baby, the cause of death was shown as "Weakness".

Farm accidents were more often the cause of death than disease. Being gored by a bull, kicked by a horse or seriously injured by primitive farm machinery or equipment which lacked safety features was quite commonplace. Thus, when death came in such form it was considered "before one's time" — that is, had safety precautions been taken or preventive medicine or a doctor or surgeon available, death might have been averted.

BURIAL

When death did come, preparation for burial in the scattered settlements of the Ukraine or the pioneer days in Wisconsin was taken care of by the immediate family and close neighbors and friends. The pastor, if there was one, or, the deacon of the church would be notified. No professional undertaking services were available for a long time. The body would be washed and clothed and placed in a cool place. A wooden box would be prepared. Wood shavings or sawdust would be placed in the bottom and the box lined with a material suitable to the age of the person. The funeral services would be held the following day. Friends and relatives usually came without their children. There generally was no preliminary "wake"— only the funeral service, when, at the conclusion of the service, all would file past the body uttering to their Maker their own personal prayer of thankfulness for the gift of that person's life and a prayer for their own salvation. If no clergyman was available, one of the deacons or other lay-leaders conducted the service with the use of the prayer book, scripture and an appropriate hymn. The coffin would be carried or conveyed to the cemetery and the people would follow for the committal service. Loving hands lowered the box containing the body to its final resting place.

A Hymn such as "God be with you till we meet again" (Gott mit euch bis wir uns wiedersehen") would be sung. Sometimes, a beloved childhood hymn would be sung:

"GOTT IST DIE LIEBE" (God is Love)

Gott ist die Liebe, laest mich erloesen
Gott ist die Liebe, Er liebt auch mich.
D'rum sag ich noch einmal
Gott ist die Liebe, Gott ist die Liebe
Er liebt auch mich.

The death would be reported to the local governmental unit and in the case of German citizens, it would also be reported to the German Consulate in Kiev.

Cemeteries in Russia were known as Kirkhof rather than Friedhof as in Germany. They were not usually adjacent to the church worship building. The first cemetary in Pound,Marinette County Wisconsin was about two miles from the church proper. In 1910 a new cemetery was located on the northern edge of the village about a half mile from the church building. The second or current cemetery in Pound is used by all of the Baptist Churches herein described, as well as by the Seventh Day Adventists and Assembly of God members.

Burial lots and plots were assigned to the pioneer family members of the church with additional lots set aside for others. Graves were mostly unmarked in the early days. A good example is the first Pound cemetery which has only a few grave markers or monuments as compared with the number of burials. The cemeteries are kept in good order by the cemetery board of the congregation. In the Ukraine, multiple church cemetaries for burials of more than one faith were generally unknown. Each church provided for the internment of its own faithful.

MARRIAGES

Marriages were celebrated with much festivity by most familes. Marriage and its estate was taken seriously and with much happiness by both families. When a family could afford more than a simple wedding. a messenger would be sent out to the persons to be invited. The messenger would be dressed in his best and the horse, or horse and buggy, including the whip, would be decorated with colored ribbons if not with flowers and streamers. Upon arriving at a farmstead, the messenger would assemble

EVANGELICAL CHURCH ZHITOMIR
(Used by permission of Dr. Karl Stump and the
American Historical Society of Germans from Russia)

the invitees and give his invitation in rhyme, with appropriate gestures.

Weddings might last two and sometimes three days with the people coming and going as their farm chores permitted. Most celebrations of marriage took only one day or a part of a day as there was always too much work to be done. When the wedding was of a member or members of a settler on a nobleman's land, prompt arrangements were made to obtain the assignment of additional land for the new couple upon which to found a new family unit.

BAPTISM

The ordinance of Baptism among the Baptists was performed by immersion. The person to be baptized and the clergyman would enter the water and the person to be baptized upon giving a brief testimony expressing the recognition of their sinful state and their acceptance of Christ as their Saviour, the person would respond in the affirmative to the clergyman's question, "Do you believe that Christ died for your sins and do you accept Him as your Saviour and intend to follow Him all the days of your life" Upon an affirmative declaration the clergyman would take hold of the folded arms of the person, place his left hand at the person's back and thereupon immerse the person completely in the water. It was a dramatic event and a highly emotional religious experience. It marked a significant change in the life of the person and most always profoundly affected their life thereafter. Baptists frequently referred to events in their lives as "before my Baptism" or, "after my Baptism". It was a definite line of demarcation of the before and after their "Christian birth."

Generally speaking, Baptist belief is that immersion or Baptism is like dying and being buried to one's sins and sinful life and being raised, resurrection-like to a new life in Christ and the becoming, in the words of the Apostle Paul, "a new creation".

Children of Baptist families were not baptized at birth or shortly thereafter. Their beliefs were that such an act was not necessary to the salvation of the child in the event of death.

Rather, Baptists believed that baptism could only be significant when a child reached the "age of discretion" or the "age of accountability" and could make the decision for itself whether by this act it wished to witness and receive baptism as an outward sign of the inward state of acceptance of this faith.

EVANGELICAL CHURCH DERMANKA
(Used by permission of Dr. Karl Stumpp and the
American Historical Society of Germans from Russia)

Only one who has lived the life of a Baptist and has experienced such a dying to sin and such a resurrection to a new life, can truly appreciate the significance of this religious experience. It is difficult if not impossible to describe in writing the major religious experiences and it is believed this is one such instance. It is considered the Baptist's deepest and most moving religious experience. There is some difference of views among the Christian churches concerning Baptism as a sacrament.

Baptism, most Baptists hold, is not of itself essential to salvation. Baptism is an outward sign of an inward state of grace (for we are saved by grace) evidencing one's repentence and conversion; the acceptance of the belief that Christ died for that person's personal sins and that person's redemption is only possible because of that death, such person can become a member of the family of God. Man cannot merit or earn salvation. It is a free gift paid for by the shed blood of Christ on the cross. However, Baptists do believe that a faith that does not manifest itself in a new life and in good works, is dead. If it were held that the act of Baptism was in and of itself an act of or essential to salvation, then, as the writer's father-in-law, a Baptist minister, after retirement, once declared, that the only way to really save a Baptist under that belief would be to immerse him in Baptism but not allow him to arise out of the water, for the moment he rose out of the water, he would again start sinning.

The foregoing is not intended to be a complete or even a partial exposition of Baptist doctrines. References to these beliefs and practices are intended to merely point the direction of this particular faith and not to set forth the fine details of which there can be many views. These East Prussians came to the Baptist faith first from the Catholic Church especially after the St Bartholomew Massacre of 1572; then the strong Lutheran teachings or the evangelical faith which was expounded by Calvin. Each change came with a pilgrimage from one country and one faith to another country and another faith.

LORD'S SUPPER OR COMMUNION

Another ordinace observed by Baptists is that of the Lord's Supper. In this act of communion, the believers again acknowledge within themselves their sinful state and commemorate the death of Christ for their sins. It is a memorial, for He said, "This do in remembrance of me".

Closely affiliated with this observance was the fellowship meal or "Liebesmahl" (Love feast). It was also referred to sometime as a"Abendmahl" or "Abendbrot" This was a church fellowship supper with devotions, prayers, hymns testimonies and a general atmosphere of deep commitment and strengthening of each others' faith and devotional life. Baptists believed that they were a fellowship of the redeemed and tried to so conduct their lives. Conduct unbecoming such a community of believers could and often did result in a visitation by a committee to counsel and admonish. If there was no sign of repentence and a return to the fellowhsip, there could be a dismissal. Baptists considered divorce unscriptural or at least the conduct leading to divorce was incompatible with their religious committment. Thus a divorced couple was often dismissed from the membership. This is somewhat different from the Calvinist view that the church is a society of sinners and one of the first qualifications for church membership is the acknowledgment of such a sinful condition and the acceptance of Gods grace and Christ's sacrifice which made it possible for one to become a member of the community of believers. It has been said that a church is not a group of saved people but a society of sinners who seek God's forgiveness.

Attendance at church services and participation in the corporate life of the church, the reading of the scriptures and the hearing of the preaching of the Word all being part of the climate of our christian nurture and growth. The Bible, the Word of God, is central in this church. Again, this is but a brief reference to these beliefs and is not intended to be a full exposition or interpretation. Baptist church services are marked with the fervency of their participation, witness and preaching of the Word.

MAHLZEIT

Pietism was a movement which arose in the Lutheran Church at the end of the 17th century. Part of it came as a result of the Reformed or Calvinist Church in spite of the doctrine of predestination. The Presbyterian or Reformed Church Constitution gave the people a share in the church life. One Philip Jacob Spencer who combined the Lutheran emphasis on Biblical doctrine with the Reformed tendancy to vigorous Christian life began pietism by preaching the Bible more than Luther's creeds; by holding religious meetings in homes; urged thorough private Bible study; believed that Christian priesthood was universal; giving prominence to devotional life and implanting in man a faith from which come the fruits of life. These views were accepted both by Christians and their pastors but of course not by all. "Pietism", was a derogatory term. Many of the East Prussians adopted significant parts of these teachings. For example, mealtime was not generally considered as a religious service or experience. True, grace was said at mealtimes by all faiths. However, among these pious folk, meal time was a blessed time and consequently there was a German expression which meant "Blessed Mealtime" (Gesegnete Mahlzeit). This was a combination of grace before the meal time with a devotional service consisting of the reading of a selection of scripture, a comment thereon, a prayer and the singing of a familiar hymn to a folk-tune known by all, at the conclusion of the meal. In the writer's experience for years as a young person, there would be grace before the meal and then after the meal, Scripture, devotional comment, prayer and Hymn. In the prayer the members of the household would be held up before God by name and condition. The "Mahlzeit" was then truly a Blessed Mealtime because it was not only a refreshment of the body's needs but also of the uplifting of the spirit to its Creator. But in those pietistic households, mealtime and private devotions were not the end of the day's religious life of the household. Before retiring there would be a further short period of prayer with many or all participating, one after another, and, in the commitment of their lives and those of their loved ones to the care and keeping of the Lord.

HOLIDAYS — CHRISTMAS

Christmas was observed and celebrated not only in the homes but in the churches. There was a Children's Church service where the children said their "pieces" (Spruch) Christmas carols, of course, were sung and "Stille Nacht" was never more meaningful or poignant thus far away from their original Heimatland. The Christmas story would be read and a Christmas message delivered by the minister. At the conclusion the small children would be given gifts or fruit or sweets. The sleigh ride to and from the church would be in the Troika sleigh with jingling bells on the harness trappings. Straw would have been placed in the bottom of the sleigh and the children nestled close to each other and covered with blankets and quilts. The snow glistened under a moonlight, reflecting millions of diamonds while the cold snow crunched beneath the sleigh runners and under the hooves of the horses. Since it was often a long ride before home was reached, the children would be sound asleep and were carried inside when home was reached.

EASTER

After a long winter of deep snows, when roads were obliterated at times because of several days of blizzards and high winds that wiped out the sky, covered the fences and other land marks; when the wind would howl for days,. at times sounding like a pack of wolves already at the door, with white sheets of snow turning this way and that shrouding the woods, the buildings and obliterating all of the horizon, Spring would be a most welcome time to which to look forward. It brought a resurrection of the earth as well as the celebration of the most holy Easter season with the observance of the resurrection of the Lord

Apart from the lenten period celebrated by most churches, there were small but happy customs that were observed in many households. The women prepared many colored eggs. Most were hardboiled with onion skins, a bit of cedar for green and saffron for yellow. Some eggs were made into artistic masterpieces. These were uncooked. An elaborate process was followed but the result was beautiful. Ukrainian women are world famous for their art work on Easter eggs. Each child was given a share of the hardboiled eggs some of which had drawings on them. Sometimes they were hidden about the household and an Easter egg hunt was part of the joys of the day. The children also enjoyed egg-pecking. If a challenger cracked the end of the egg of the child who was challenged the challenger was entitled to the cracked egg. If however, the challenger's egg was cracked, he or she lost it to the child who was challenged.

Another custom for the garnering of additional eggs was that of "sprinkling". Whoever awakened earliest on Easter morning and lightly "sprinkled" the other children in the household with drops of water from a cup, became entitled to an egg from each child who was thus awakened. The "Sprinkling" (Pobresgat) an adopted custom from the Ukrainian people, was done by dipping the fingers into a cup of water and allowing a couple of drops to lightly fall on the face of the sleeping brother or sister, or, by dipping a flower or piece of evergreen or cedar into the water for the "anointing." The physical resurrection was instant.

Fasting was also observed during the 40 days before Easter by some churches as a preparation for the celebration of the resurrection. In Christendom the resurrection is considered the central fact of the Christian faith. The name, Easter, like the days of the week is a survival of old Teutonic mythology but the origin of the celebration of Easter goes back to the Jewish Passover with the concept that Christ was the true Paschal lamb and the first fruits of the dead. In Baptist tradition this period was observed by special prayer services during the weeks before Easter. In the general Protestant tradition, the empty Latin cross was the preferred symbol of the Christian faith as it symbolized a risen Lord as Saviour of the World.

EDUCATION

The East Prussians came to the Russian Ukraine at the invitation of Russian and Polish nobility. Prior to the freeing of the serfs in 1861 only nobility could own or hold land. Thus the noblemen were the great landowners holding substantial areas of all types of land space. Because of the size of the estates the settlement of the settlers required separation of the Prussians at considerable distances from each other except for the concentrations of some settlers on the lands of a single nobleman. The East Prussians were not able to organize themselves for the education of their children as well as did the early German Colonists who came at the invitation of Catherine the Great.

The older, closely knit closed colony German communities not only had been given the privilege of organizing their own churches but their own schools and their own government. The East Prussians, on the other hand, distributed over the great estates at considerable distance from each other were subject to the Russian educational system under the Zemstvo law. Thus, such formal schooling as was obtained by the children brought to Russia or born to the East Prussians in Russia, was only in the Russian schools. If proper advantage had been taken of this system, the children could have been at least tri-lingual, that is, German, Russian and the Ukrainian provincial language. Working against the use of the German language was the use of the Polish language on the lands of the Polish noblemen. Russian was the official language for official records and the administration of governmental affairs.

From 1865 to 1887 and later, a period of 22 to 30 years was sufficient length of time within which the children born and reared in the Vohlynian Ukraine to have considerable contact with the provincial Vohlynian language while neglecting their German language. Some who took advantage of the Russian School system and with help from family tutors were educated in German, Russian and Ukrainian. It could be said that as a general rule, the East Prussian educated folk had better educational opportunities and training than did the Ukrainian children.

When these people arrived in the United States, only about one third of them preferred the use of German for their church services. Many knew the Masuren language spoken in East Prussia. These people were not Poles. They were not born nor raised under a Polish flag or government. Their citizenship was German but they could speak the "Masuren" language. A person speaking Russian was expected to belong to the Orthodox Russian Church. A Tartar, Turk or Moslem was expected to be a follower of Mohammed. Anyone capable of speaking the Polish language or even "Masuren" was expected to be a Roman Catholic.

This association and concept of unity of nationality and religion seemed to have been given more pronounced emphasis and effect in the United States in connection with the Polish language than almost any other. This was probably due to the general understanding that Poland was dominantly Roman Catholic. But this concept and association of Polish and Poland provided these Protestant German-Masuren speaking Baptists who had been Protestant in East Prussia from two to four centuries before they came to the United States through Russia, with difficulties. Roman Catholics regard former Catholics as "fallen Catholics" and as Godless people that are to be shunned and ignored even more than non-Catholics.

There were warm friendships between the French and other Catholic children and the Protestant children in Pound and Coleman as well as Klondike, where the French, Austrian, German, Bohemian and Polish folk belonged to the St. Wenceslaus Roman Catholic Church. In the field of public affairs both faiths served on school boards, Town Boards, on the Board of Supervisors of the County and in many volunteer, charitable and public-spirited organizations. Commercially, both faiths traded with each other. There were the Van Vonderen, Martin, Duquaine, Fortier, Neshek, Tachick, DeKeyser, Rice, Brooks, Boyd, Martens in Pound and Lauermans and others in Marinette.Blacksmith shops, garages, feedmills, and other enterprises were all patronized without discrimination. The spirit was greatly improved as well by the acts of the Ecumenical Council of Pope John and others in recent years. But there was and perhaps remains an underlying unity amoung the people of each faith and they are basically loyal to their own. The climate between the East Prussians and other folk in the Marinette-Oconto Counties area was friendly and more favorable than that which the East Prussians endured at the hands of the Russians in the last years of their stay in Russia.

Chapter 8

Change in the Russian Political Climate

The East Prussians arrived in the Ukraine in the late autumn of 1865. The serfs had been freed in 1861 and many of the lands were in a state of deterioration and a return to the wild.

The first years for the settlers were of hard work and extreme hardship because housing was limited and an even greater lack of equipment which had to be made by hand. Thus, the barest of necessities had to be provided for, shelter, food, warmth and the greatest care to preserve such stock and seed as they brought with them. Likewise, and also very important, was the preparation of gardens and fields for the seeding and raising of crops. Once prepared, especially the heavy sodded land, the land in the lowlands and woodlands, had to be kept worked up, fertilized and cleared of stones and roots so that the raising of crops would be unimpeded by obstacles in the fields.

Good crops became better and with good crops, other equipment and comforts added to the enjoyment of life. The amount of land worked by the settlers was largely equivalent to the amount of land the settlers owned in East Prussia which ran from 160 to 400 acres. The nature and tenure of their holdings can be gathered only from vague references absorbed during the lifetime of the writer, but according to Vitovich (40) much of the land was bought outright while other land was leased for a term of years with an option to purchase, or, upon the completion of the lease-term, the title would be delivered to the settler. Payments for lands purchased were made in cash but the leaseholds were paid for either in cash or produce of certain types on an annual basis. In general, after taxes on the leased lands, the total fees, charges or costs for the land and its use were much more favorable in the Ukraine than those paid in East Prussia. The arrangement between the settlers and the nobleman was a private one and from all that could be learned of the time prior to 1890, the landlord or landowner was responsible for the taxes due to the regional or central government.

ZEMSTVO LAND CONTROL

As has been indicated, only the nobility could own land prior to the freeing of the serfs. With the freeing of the serfs in 1861 and the allotment of land to the serfs, it soon became apparent that land would be a much sought item. Catherine the Great was opposed to the freeing of the serfs. She had not forseen the freeing of the slave-type labor and the prospect of land becoming available to other than the invited German colonists and the nobility. With much land assigned to the Catherine II invited Germans and developed by them to a high level of prosperity and productivity, the Russians could see that they had underestimated the value of their land. Their envy was aroused. It was easy to misinterpret the presence of the Germans who kept to themselves, had their own schools, churches and own government and did not wish to be assimilated. Jealousy led to rancor and malice and such attitudes led to open incidents and actual animosity.

Soon, Russians advocated that Russia be kept for the Russians and that no more land be sold to foreigners. In early 1895, a law as passed which made it illegal to sell to anyone but a Russian.

In 1864 the Zemstvo legislation set up a local government system, such as the county system in the United States. A Zemstvo was a council. A local administrative body. This legislation provided for land supervision by the local and provincial governments. This legislation was not limited to land. It was extended to jurisdiction over education, public health, roads, veterinary service, administration of prisons, building and use of roads and bridges, famine relief and numerous other matters, along with the power to levy taxes for such purposes.

From the beginning, land became more and more difficult to obtain by the Germans, either from the noblemen or from the government because of the limitations and veto power of the Zemstvo laws.

The Prussian Germans who had come into Russia had known land control on a much broader scale in East Prussia. However, their children became concerned by the creeping change which clouded their future life in Russia. On the other hand, the Russian intelligencia and politicians who were now urging the retention of their lands for their own people saw a threat to the nation by the presence of so many citizens of a foreign government who still maintained their allegiance to Germany rather than to the Czar or Czarina. They urged the Russianization of schools and even churches and the imposition of economic or other pressures to have the Germans become Russian citizens.

This was especially true after the war between France and Germany upon the conclusion of which Germany (formerly greater Prussia) became an Empire in 1871, after the defeat of France. The Slavophiles saw that the presence of so many people from the German Empire within its borders, could induce a desire for German expansion and conquest. The Germans were thus regarded as infiltrators of an unfriendly power. (10) p 170-3 (6) p 225 et seq. Bismarck being in power as the Minister-President under the Kaiser during this period of early German Empire, charges were made that the Germans were buying Russian land with German gold. That the Germans retained their citizenship and were loyal to the Kaiser rather than to the Czar. There was a bit of truth backing the claims of the Russians as far as the East Prussians were concerned. True, they were invited to settle in the Russian Ukraine by the nobility and on private lands of the nobility and not on lands of the Czar. But, they brought with them German money or gold which they had obtained from a disposition of their own assets in East Prussia. Nevertheless, it was German money and the East Prussian settlers were even more suspect and vulnerable than the colony Germans who had come in response to Catherine's invitation and with her aid and money. (6), (10). Vitovich confirmed the mistaken attitude that it was the German government which provided the settlers with monies for the expansion of their properties. This was contrary to fact as the German government gave the settlers no money at any time.

In 1889 the zemsky nachalnik system was put into effect to lessen the democratic control or character of the zemstvos. Under the Zemstvo system the Captain at the local level (Zemsky Nachalnik) was usually one of the minor nobility of the district appointed by the central Government to be the Czar's representative in the village area. (6) (10). This Captain had been given broad powers. All elected local officials had to be confirmed by the Captain and he could depose, suspend or change as he saw fit. Thus, the superficial democratic appearance of the Zemstvo change was still subject to veto power of the Czar or his representative. All decisions of the Volost local unit had to be approved before they became effective. He also had summary judicial as well as administrative powers for he could impose fines, penalties and punishments and was a little czar for his domain. The Nachalnik saw the East Prussians as a non-conformist group and he felt that he had a special mission to bring them all under the power of the Russian government and point of view.

As has been mentioned the East Prussians had retained their German citizenship. Children born to these people had a dual citizenship. Many as in the case of the writer's grandparents and parents, registered with the German Consulate at Kiev.

"Ownership" of land by a nobleman was a qualified term. Nobility obviously held their lands subject to the will of the Czar for the Czar was the autocrat of all of Russia and it was assumed that all land belonged to the Czar except insofar as the Czar granted it to his noble subjects in absolute ownership, subject to the rendition of certain payments, personal services, civilian duties, military services and the like. The nobleman had to render to his Czar the obligations imposed by his station. Provision was made for the noblemen's heirs to inherit but always subject to the same conditions and obligations due the sovereign, whether military or civil and at the pleasure of the Czar or Czarina.

The nobility was depended upon, especialy prior to the freeing of the serfs, to supply the manpower for the military forces. These obligations were usually discharged by the nobleman by sending his serfs to the military establishments where they were required to serve something like 25 years and seldom were returned to their families again except when crippled or in ill health when they could no longer contribute to or be of use to the family's welfare.

1871 CONSCRIPTIVE MILITARY SERVICE

The most shocking event in the lives of the Germans in Russia was the Russian government decree of 1871 establishing univeral compulsory military service at all levels. For the Colonists under Catherine's invitation this was an abrogation of promised "everlasting" exemption from military service. However, the Russian explanation was that "forever" meant 99 years and that since more than that time had passed since Catherine had made the promise, it was no longer valid. Actually, the Czar had taken a lesson from the German government and its form of universal military service, and, finding the Russian military establishment inferior to the German forces, he undertook the improvement of his military stance by means of the Decree of 1871.

The East Prussians could understand the change because they had lived under something very similar to this system and many of the older East Prussians had already rendered their six year term of service in the Prussian military. However, the East Prussians did not expect this change as Germans had been accepted into Russian life for over one hundred years prior to 1865 and were not expected to go into military service. While the actual conscription did not start until 1874, it did cause all Germans including the East Prussians to reconsider their status and future.

Like the German colonists who came earlier, the Prussians felt that they had been mislead, duped, cheated, defrauded, betrayed and trapped. When the representatives of the Ukrainian nobility came to East Prussia to solicit the Prussians, they led them to believe that they would be treated as other Germans had been treated in the past hundred years. Now, after they had built substantial properties, developed the lands from poor, non-productive, swampy-lowlands into prosperous and productive farms, they would have to surrender, sell, or forfeit (as in the case of leased lands) all their investments and structures. They could not possibly recapture their original investments. Consequently when the Prussians heard of the availability of land in America, whether by word of mouth, circulars or by direct solicitation by respresentatives of land owners and railroads, they gave immediate and serious consideration to giving up all they had built in Russia and to a departure at the earliest possible moment to avoid the loss of sons and husbands by induction into compulsory military service decreed in 1871 and began to be put into effect in 1874. Their whole world was pretty much turned upside down.

The East Prussians began to leave in about 1885. This is eleven years after 1874 when conscription began. It is possible the Russian draft system was not yet fully organized or the Russians were reluctant to provoke Germany by drafting German citizens or it is even possible that the Germans applied to their Consulate in Kiev for exemptions and extensions. It was said that an extension of ten years was obtained (19) p 179. However, there is no record historically that Bismarck intervened on behalf of the Germans who wanted to leave. True Bismarck had been the German or Greater Prussian Ambassador at the Russian court at St. Petersberg and was well acquainted and well received during his service in that capacity.

However nothing has been found which confirmed any intervention on behalf of the settlers, except the actual fact that the Prussians did not leave, as indicated, until 1885 and later.

Unlike the Catherine Colonists, the Prussians were not required nor did they take an oath to the Russian Government. Paragraph 5 of Catherine's manifesto of July 22nd 1763 provided:

"Upon arrival in Our Empire, each foreigner who intends to become a settler and has reported to the Guardianship Chancellery or other border-towns of Our Empire and as already prescribed in Section 4, has declared his decision, must take the oath of allegiance in accordance with his religious rite." (44) p. 16.

They, the 1865 Prussians, claimed and retained their German citizenship, registered with the German Consulate in Kiev and made no pretense of holding allegiance to the Czar. The main difficulty was the dual Russian citizenship of their children as well as that the law appeared to be applicable to citizens as well as aliens.

Some of the East Prussian and other Germans, particularly the older folk, were not willing to again risk the rigors of long journeys and the beginning of a new life under new pioneer conditions. Especially as the journey would take them about halfway around the world. They knew they would be sacrificing much economically and otherwise. They remembered how much they lost in East Prussia. They fatefully decided to remain in Russia and submit to Russianization. They were willing to accept full responsibility of citizenship, including military service. No one saw what lay over the horizon in the form of revolution, confiscation, dispossession, tearing apart of famililies, land marches to Siberia and death for more than half of them. But even those who did decide to stay, could not erase the stigma of being German. They seemed to be tainted and the discrimination continued right to World War I and World War II.

As has been mentioned, the Prussians were late comers to Russia. They came at a time when the climate had already begun to change. They were less welcome than the Colonist Germans of a century earlier.

The hostility of the Russians was such that coupled with the limitations on the acquisition of land and the prospect of conscription for military service of unknown length, convinced the Prussians that there would be no peaceful growth of their holdings either for themselves or their children. Beginning about 1885, they began to leave their hard won lands and properties. They went to America, Canada and South America. The Prussians who went to Wisconsin were only part of those from Volhynia to reach the Western world.

Chapter 9

PREPARATION FOR A NEW MIGRATION

In the summer of 1888 the writer's grandfather and father journeyed to Kiev from Goroschky through Zhitomir to register with the German consulate in preparation for leaving Russia. The story of this visit has been related to me by my grandparents and by my father. The visit was on July 11th and 12th of the Julian Calendar, or June 30th Gregorian Calendar, 1888. Copies of the registration documents included in this story confirm the dates of this visit. The passport was obtained at Zhitomir in 1890 but that was not nearly as interesting as the story of the mother city of Russia. It was founded in 864 and became an important port because the Dnieper River is navigable between Kiev and the Black Sea and through that Sea with the oceans.

Kiev is a cross-roads. It became famous for trade. As a city in which there was much trade, it became an attractive city to take by conquest and for plundering. It had been taken time and again as invasions swept back and forth by the Mongols, Tartars, Huns, Cossacks, Turks, the Swedish Nation under the leadership of its fighting king, the Germans, the Franks and by the Lithuanian-Polish nation.

One could not visit it without learning that it was a city of some 400 churches and that the most noteworthy decision of Vladimir was to reject Islam and Western Chrisianity for the Orthodox faith. This decision caused a deep cleavage between the Poles and the Russians even though Kiev was dominated by Slavs.

The multitude of national types seen by my forebears indicated how influential this city had become.

This was indeed, part of the main gateway of that corridor between the East and the West; between the ancient peoples east of the urals and those of Europe. The ancient Scythians had occupied the land north of the Danube and the Carpathian Mountains eastward along the north side of the Black Sea and the Sea of Azov to the Don River and then north toward the great steppes, the Pripet Marshes and the great wooded lands of the northern half of the Ukraine for 2000 years. The area between the Don River and Poland proper and roughly Kiev and north toward Lithuania had been fought over by the Kings of Poland and by the Hetmen of the Cossacks and Tartars. Sienkiewicz in his book (18) WITH FIRE AND SWORD wrote a fiery war novel based on this history where the disregard for human life was frightful beyond description. The land was drenched with blood.

The Cathedral of St. Sophia was the oldest church in Russia. Built in the eleventh century as a copy of St. Sophia in Constantinople it had been damaged by many battles and conquests and had been rebuilt so many times that its original form was hardly recognizable. But it still was a spectacular structure of inspiring imensity. At one time it had nineteen domes dating back to medieval times. The golden cupola and four storied dome was visible to the visitors for miles across the steppe.

A statue of St. Vladimir with his cross stood on the high west bank near the site where St. Andrew was said to have stood, looking eastward across the winding Dnieper. Walking about the city in the visit of 1888, seeing the statute of St. Vladimir, the domes of St. Sophia glistening in the sun or moonlight, seeing the great monastary of St. Michael with fifteen gilded cupolas, was an unforgetable experience for the young man. (The pictures of Kiev, including St. Sophia are courtesy of Mr. Dean Conger of National Geographic and JOURNEY ACROSS RUSSIA, by Bart McDowell and photographed by Mr. Dean Conger (16)) Archeology confirms that this territory was inhabited in Paleolithic times. There is a strong tradition about the ministry of the Apostle Andrew. He has been the patron Saint of Russia and the claim is made that St. Andrew first brought the Gospel to

Russia. In the MARTRYDOM OF ST. ANDREW By Budge (39) it is declared that he preached in the area around the Black Sea in what is now Russia but was then part of Scythia. Budge believes that St. Andrew was stoned and crucified in Scythia but some writers differ with his conclusions, understandably. Scythia is mentioned in Colossians 3:11 where Paul in his letter to the Colossians wrote:

"Where there is neither Greek nor Jew, circumcision nor uncircumcision, Barbarian, Scythian, bond nor free; but Christ is all in all."

The visit to the German Consulate in 1888 was not without some concern. No previous registration had been made when the family arrived in the Russian Ukraine in 1865, nor after the birth of the male children. However, the proofs were conclusive and the registration took place. The original documents are still in existence.

REGISTRATION AT GERMAN CONSULATE AT KIEV
1888

CERTIFICATE OF GERMAN (PRUSSIAN) CITIZENSHIP

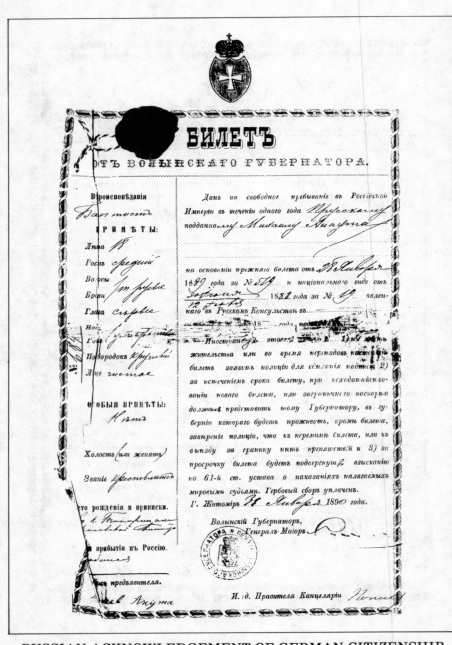

RUSSIAN ACKNOWLEDGEMENT OF GERMAN CITIZENSHIP

24 страницы. № 712

ЗАГРАНИЧНЫЙ
ПАСПОРТЪ

Подпись владѣльца ....

Михаил Анута

Unterschrift des Inhabers ....

....

Signature du porteur ....

....

PASSPORT OF MICHAEL ANUTA,
Page 1

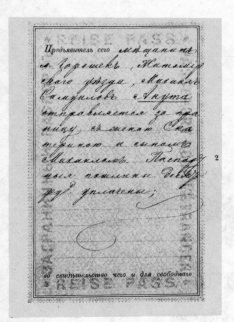

PASSPORT MICHAEL ANUTA,
Page 2

PASSPORT MICHAEL ANUTA,
Page 3

MICHAEL ANUTA PASSPORT
German and French side

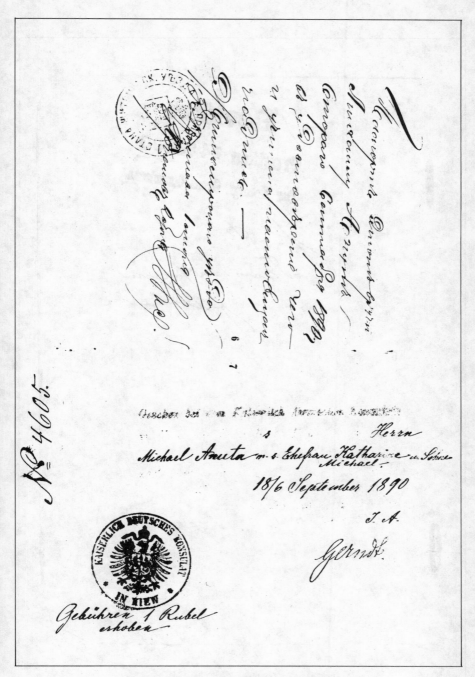

№ 4605.

Michael Aneuta m. s. Ehefrau Katharine u. Söhne Michael.

18/6 September 1890

i. A.

Gerndt.

Gebühren 1 Rubel erhoben

PASSPORT CONFIRMATION BY RUSSIAN AND GERMAN OFFICIALS

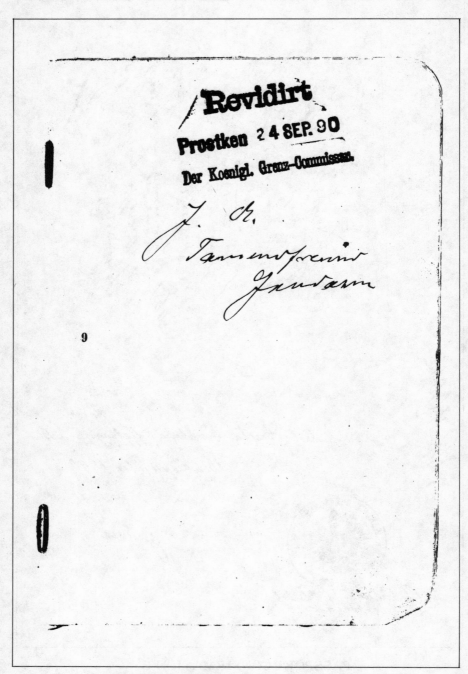

Revidirt

Prostken 24 SEP. 90

Der Koenigl. Grenz-Commissar.

EXIT AT PROSTKEN, SEPT. 24, 1890

ST. SOPHIA
RUSSIAN ORTHODOX CATHOLIC CHURCH
KIEV
Mother Church of Russia
Copy of St. Sophia in Constantinople
(Used by special permission of Mr. Dean Conger, National Geographic,
and used in JOURNEY ACROSS RUSSIA by Bart McDowell)

INTERIOR OF ST. SOPHIA
RUSSIAN ORTHODOX CATHOLIC CHURCH
KIEV
(Used by special permission by Mr. Dean Conger, National Geographic,
shown in JOURNEY ACROSS RUSSIA, The Soviet Union Today, by Bart McDowell)

The return journey to Goroschky was made in about two days but this time with sober thoughts of the necessity for termination of their sojourn in Russia. Now it was a certainty that the family must leave Russia as soon as possible and from that time until their departure in the summer of 1890, it was necessary to sell everything that could not be carried in order to have sufficient money for the long journey to the other side of the world; to a new continent, and, to make a new start in a new country with a new people and a new language. Personal property, livestock, stores of grain, farm equipment, tools, feed, furniture and everything of a tangible nature which could not be taken along had to be disposed of. Since others had similar personal and real property for sale the buyers again had the upper hand. Furthernmore, the land could not be sold to other Germans. Conditions were such that the Russians were the principal prospects. Thus, property was sold again, under pressure and for less that its fair market or invested value.

**ST. VLADIMIR LOOKING ACROSS DNIEPER
KIEV**
(Used by special permission of Mr. Dean Conger, National Geographic,
shown in JOURNEY ACROSS RUSSIA, The Soviet Union Today, by Bart McDowell

MOON OVER DNIEPER
KIEV
(Used by special permission from Mr. Dean Conger, National Geographic,
shown in JOURNEY THROUGH RUSSIA, The Soviet Union Today, by Bart McDowell)

**VIEW OF KIEV
WITH ICE CREAM VENDOR**

(Used by special permission of Mr. Dean Conger, National Geographic,
shown in JOURNEY THROUGH RUSSIA, The Soviet Union Today, by Bart McDowell)

PASSPORTS

The passport was applied for at Zhitomir (see photocopy) It was issued August 21st 1890. It was confirmed by the German Consulate at Kiev in September 1890 and also by the Russian Emigration Commissioner on the same date.

As the departure day approached, with all the property disposed of, it was necessary to stay with relatives awaiting the day of departure. A small group of their closest friends and relatives who remained in the Ukraine either permanently or to come in later years, assembled. Prayers and blessings were given, the farewell address (Abschiedsrede'') was given urging those who remained and those who were about to depart with the admonition to "Be strong in the Lord and in the power of his might"; that "Nothing can separte us from the love of God which is in Christ Jesus our Lord". They were further admonished to look toward the day when they would all see each other before the throne of the Lord.

Prayer-song book in hand they sang a hymn:

BREAD OF THE WORLD

(Loyd Bourgeois 1558)
(Harm. d'apres Goudimel-1565)

Bread of the world in mercy broken
Wine of the soul in mercy shed
By whom the words of life were spoken,
And in whose death our sins are dead:
Look on the heart by sorrow broken
Look on the tears by sinners shed,
And by Thy feast to us the token
That by Thy grace our souls are fed.

Brot fuer die Welt aus Gnad gegeben
Vergossen Blut im Kelch gereicht
Duheilig Wort, von dem wir leben,
O Tod, vor dem der unsre weicht
Wir bitten: vollest uns vergeben
Dass unser Herz in Reue schweight
Und wir noch vor dem Dunklen beben
Obgleich dein Licht uns laengst erreicht!

Chapter 10

JOURNEY TO THE NEW WORLD

By late summer of 1890 Russian railroads had been built between Kiev and Prostken, the East Prussian border and customs station. While British and American as well as other European railroads were build on what was called a uniform or standard gauge, that is, the rails were uniformly four feet eight and one half inches apart the Russian gauge was much wider, being as much as eight feet. Part of the explanation for the difference in the gauge was that any invading European power could not then use the Russian railroads without completely rebuilding them.

The railroad from Kiev ran in a northwesterly direction through Korosten. Korosten was about due north of Goroschky and about fifteen miles by wagon road. Upon boarding, the train proceeded northwesterly from Korosten through a number of villages and junctions to Prostken where the passengers had to change trains and pass through customs. The passport was duly stamped at Prostken by the Grenz-Commissar on September 24th 1890.

Once in East Prussia and still being German citizens they could not pass through without stopping a few hours at Rummy, in the jurisdiction of Mensguth, Kreis Ortelsurg to greet relatives and bid them goodbye. They found their East Prussian former homestead in good condition, looking prosperous. The taxes and other burdens were still the same, however, as they were in 1865. After final heart-rending farewells, they continued this, their third pilgrimage, hoping that it would be the last.

The journey from Rummy through East Prussia and Germany to the port of embarkation was also memorable. Some of these people were retracing journeys taken by their ancestors who were fleeing persecutions to the refuge of East Prussia. German industry and urban as well as rural life was a marvel of order and beauty such as did not exist in most of the pioneer Russian settlements. It reflected, of course, the centuries of living in a much closer knit country than the wide steppes of Russia. The hope was kindled that their new homeland could be made to reflect the prosperity of the older Germany.

EMBARKATION AND SEA VOYAGE

The arrival of the pilgrims at the port of embarkation was one of bewilderment and utter confusion. Hamburg, Bremen in Germany and Antwerp in Belgium, were ports through which the emigrants left the European continent. The traffic at the docks and wharves was almost as confusing as the middle of a battle. Horsedrawn vehicles, passenger and freight fought their way to and from the ships. Some of the travelers had to wait for their ships to arrive and dock. Others could board immediately. The greatest vigilance was required by each family to prevent their baggage and trunks from being separated from them and loaded on other ships. This was done with the purpose of depriving the travelers of sustaining themselves on food which they brought with them in their baggage. If they were separated from their belongings, they had to purchase food from the ship's captain at excessive prices. Captains would sometimes keep their ships at sea until they had disposed of their stores of food. Only then would they go to the port of entry and debarkation. Many passengers had prepared foods such as bread, sausages, butter, jam and items which would not deteriorate and would still provide sustenance on the ship's journey.

There were other hardships aboard most ships of that day. Sanitation facilities were minimal. Every inch was sold even to the marking off or roping off of space on decks or in holds which passengers could claim as their own area without having sleeping quarters. Doctors and medical services were limited. Some passengers arrived sick and needed immediate attention. Others took sick and died while at sea. The loss of a loved one and then burial at sea after all of the prior trials and hardships was almost beyond endurance. Burial at sea with the body of the loved one committed to the vast ocean, never being able to know where the body might repose, as distinguised from burial on land, was a most difficult experience. In 1861 William Whiting wrote a Hymn to encourage those facing the perils of an ocean voyage:

> "Eternal Father, strong to save,
> Whose arm hath bound the restless wave,
> Who bidd'st the mighty ocean deep,
> Its own appointed limits keep:
> O hear us when we cry to Thee
> For those in peril on the Sea.

A most touching story is reported in Work Book 13 December 1973 by Mela Meisner Lindsay in an article entitled SEVENTY CENTS FOR A LIFETIME OF FREEDOM, published by the American Historical Society of Germans from Russia, (30) where a young Polish mother refused to give up her dead child for burial at sea. In 1888, nineteen families left Zhitomir for Pound. Among these families were eleven infants in arms. Only three of these eleven infants arrived alive in Pound.

Contagious diseases were passed on to other passengers on board the ship, sometimes in epidemic stages. This might mean denial of entry. Also, Fall and Winter crossings contributed other dangers besides the misery of seasickness and disease because of almost constant storms tossing about ships that would not pass inspection for seaworthyness.

ARRIVAL

Those who came through the port of New York had an opportunity to see the new Statue of Liberty erected on October 28th 1886 on Bedloe's Island in New York harbor. The passengers learned the story of the statue and something of its symbolism along with the inscription:

"Give me your tired, your poor, Your huddled masses yearning to breath free, The wreched refuse of your teeming shore, Send these, the homeless, the tempest-tost to me, I lift my lamp beside the golden door."

Translations were made but it was a long time before the immigrants more fully appreciated this welcome. They were tired. They were sick. They were huddled masses, yearning to breath free. They were homeless and tempest-tost. They were too anxious to reach their new homeland to take note of their welcome by the statue of the lady holding the light of liberty at the golden door of Freedom as they entered New York.

ELLIS ISLAND

All of the immigrants at New York had to go to Ellis Island for customs and health inspections. Other ports of entry had similar inspections. Most were passed through, but occasionally, entry to the land of their dreams was denied because of health. These had to be returned to Europe and to their people. The separation was of unimaginable heartbreak and sorrow because this was unanticipated. They had assumed that mere passage on the ship was sufficient to pass them through to their destination.

There again was bewilderment, confusion and concern for baggage and the assembling of their family or group for the transfer to the railroad stations. In many cases, land agent or railroad representatives herded the people into horsedrawn buses to be taken to the railroad stations. Not being able to converse in the language of the country they had entered, they had to rely on the representatives of the land or railroad companies to get them safely aboard the proper trains.

The journey from New York, Baltimore, Philadelphia or Boston was quite different from the ride through East Prussia and Germany. In 1890, Americans lived mostly in rural areas for this was a rural economy for the most part. As the newcomers journeyed they saw that canals had been built in some areas notably between Baltimore and west thereof, and the Erie Canal connecting the Hudson River and Lake Erie. Many prior immigrants had traveled the Erie Canal after it was opened in 1825. But now the railroads were faster. On these trains, the travelers noted no separation into classes—all appeared to travel in the same class. The Pullman sleeper and the Pullman Chair car had not yet been put into general service for extra fare-paying passengers. Here everything appeared to be equal.

At night the coaches were lighted with kerosene lamps. The cars were heated by a coal stove set up in one end of the car. Traveling behind a smoke belching locomotive, now fired by coal instead of wood, the ride was a grimy, sticky, sooty, sulphur and coal-smoke smelling dusty experience. The passengers slept in their seats. They transferred from one railroad to another at rail ends as perhaps was the case at Albany, at the Buffalo-Niagara Frontier, at Toledo and of course, Chicago. In Chicago, they saw the same kind of congested confusion as was experienced at New York. But they were finally transferred to the Chicago, Milwaukee and St. Paul Railroad Depot. This train with its connections only recently made and its rails extended, took them to Coleman and to Pound. For a time Ellis Junction, (the railroad station to the North of Pound, serving the village of Crivitz, named by its founder for a German City) was the end of the line in 1882. The Milwaukee and Northern later built from Ellis Junction to Marinette and Menominee in 1884 and the northern line was extended through Wausaukee, Pembine, Iron Mountain and to the shore of Lake Superior at Ontonagon with a branch running to Crystal Falls and Iron River. Connecting with the Copper Range Railroad at McKeever Junction, there was through railroad service between Chicago and the Copper Country, Keweenaw Peninsula. A map of Wisconsin shows a shaded area in Marinette County and a small portion of Oconto County as the site of the East Prussian settlers.

Chapter 11

EAST PRUSSIANS IN WISCONSIN

The railroad station or depot at Pound in 1890 was a rather small one, of frame construction with a waiting room on the northern end, a freight warehouse at the south end, and the station agent's office and ticket window in between. The original station platform was made of planks, mostly two by tens and the platform was high enough so that it was level with the floor of the passenger train coaches. The passengers could thus alight from the train without using the coach steps. Apparently because of upkeep and some hazards, these platforms were removed in about 1910 with almost rail height concrete platforms. This required the passengers to use a step-stool to reach the first step of the coach in either getting on or off the coach.

The dark hashed area represents the general location of the settlement of the immigrants.

Relatives or friends who had previously arrived were on hand to greet the new immigrants. Temporary lodgings were arranged for and within almost hours, the men were at work either at a sawmill or at the site of their farmstead. The first impression of the village must have been one of dismay and depression. There were perhaps two stores, a saloon or two, a half dozen houses and a blacksmith shop. There were no schools or churches. Looking in any direction there was cut-over land as the local mills cut the trees nearest the sawmills.

A ride toward the west where the first land was acquired about a half mile west of the village, did little to encourage the newcomers. But no time was wasted in wringing one's hands. Hands were made with which to do things and with winter only weeks away, immediate steps had to be taken to provide housing.

VILLAGE NAMED FOR CONGRESSMAN

The name of Pound, was given the location when the railroad was extended northerly from Stiles, which was about twenty miles north of

104

Green Bay. In about 1882 the railroad was extended north to Braultville, a sawmill location of the Little Peshtigo River located about a mile and a half east of the present village of Coleman, in the southwest corner of Section 18 of Town 30 North of Range 21 East. At this point the Little Peshtigo crosses to the south side of County Road B for a short distance.

Joseph Brault attracted to his operation many people who had come from Canada and a large settlement of these hardy woods workers and farmers settled in and around Coleman. The author's mother worked for a short time in one of the Boarding houses at this mill site. Another sawmill was built just north of Coleman where the Little Peshtigo crosses US 141 by Waldron Dickinson. In the year 1882 the railroad was then extended to Pound, Beaver and Ellis Junction, the railroad station name for Crivitz.

The Dickinson sawmill was destroyed by fire and another mill was built at the same location in 1890 by Marshall Holmes. This too was lost by fire and a new mill was built by Fred and Harry Bolles. Meantime the railroad had been extended east to Marinette and Menominee in 1884 and also north to Wausaukee and later to Iron Mountain, Republic and on to the south shore of Lake Superior at Ontonagon. Near Ontonagon, at McKeever Junction, the Copper Range Railroad owned by a large copper company mining copper in

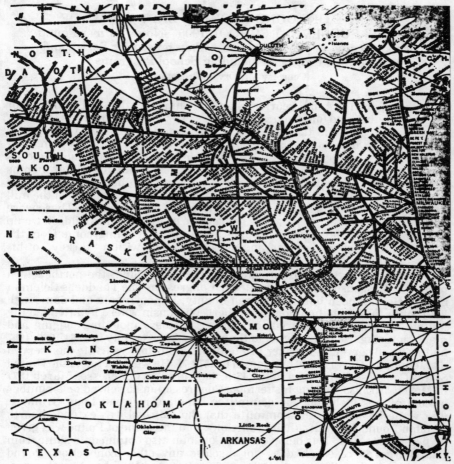

PART OF THE ROUTE OF THE
CHICAGO, MILWAUKEE, ST. PAUL & PACIFIC RAILROAD

the Keweenaw Peninsula built a railroad which gave the Copper Country access by rail to the rest of the country. The Bolles mill had a large mill pond extending upwards of a mile up river, a store, blacksmith shop, large boarding houses, a carriage barn and a horse barn. It operated successfully until about 1912 when most of the timber in the vicinity was harvested and it was not economical to operate the mill. It stood idle for a while and was then dismantled and sold. It provided the writer with a thorough knowledge of all the operations as the writer's father and mother lived on "Sawdust" street for a time and then while the mill was idle, all of the sawmill, shops, barns and other structures were fully explored.

VILLAGE OF POUND LOOKING EAST FROM TOP OF NEW ROOSEVELT SCHOOL 1905 Note: Former Pound School located in rear of St. Leo's Church used for Parish and Public Programs including School Programs
(Courtesy Mr. Orville Broderick)

The mill pond for many years was a fine fishing location and in the winter skating parties and old-time automobiles were driven over its surface. "Running the logs" in the mill pond in the summer was a very dangerous sport, but the barefoot youngsters, lighter than the rivermen with their caulked boots, rarely got wet. The mill, when in operation usually did its sawing during the summer months but was closed during the winter months when most of the men went to the logging camps to harvest logs for the summer's cut. The writer's father worked at an "edger" machine at the mill in the summer and spent a couple winters at the logging camp. These were lonely months and as spring drew nearer one or more of the children would be looking out of the windows hoping to see father coming home from the camp with a bushy mustache and whiskers, along with a "turkey" of his clothes on his back.

At the time of the railroad extension through Pound, the northeastern portion of Wisconsin was represented in Congress by one Thaddeus Coleman Pound. He had been born in Warren County, Pennsylvania and came with his family to Milton Junction in southern Wisconsin where he attended the Milton Academy. He entered the lumber business including logging and manufacturing. He was elected to the Wisconsin Assembly in 1864,1866, 1867 and 1869 and served as speaker pro-tempore in his last year. He then served as Lieutenant Governor of Wisconsin in 1870-71. He was elected to the United States Congress and served in the 45th, 46th and 47th Congresses March 1877 to March 3rd 1883. During his term as Congressman he served on a number of committees including the committee handling railroad Land Grants.It was while he was on this committe that the railroad was extended north through Pound to Crivitz (Ellis Junction), and the name of Pound was given its present location. It is believed that Coleman also obtained its name from this source as research does not disclose any other connection. Pound married Angeline Weston on October 29th 1866 and they had two children, Florence and Homer. Homer Pound was the father of Ezra Pound a famous but somewhat controversial man of letters. They were all related to the Henry Wadsworth Longfellow family in New England.

Homer Pound became the Assistant Assayer of the United States Mint. Roscoe Pound from another Pound eastern family was one of the greatest professors of Law serving at the Harvard Law School as well as others.

CLEARING: For Homesite, farm crops or for sale of logs
(Courtesy Mrs. Henry Johnson)

The earliest settlers in Pound were the L. D McMillan family and the Mathis family who came in 1874 and lived for a while in the Hamilton Lumber Camp buildings which were built on the north side of the present village of Pound. The evidence of these mills was there while the author attended the Pound Roosevelt School from about 1906 to 1914. J. A. Wagg, C. L. Adams, Peter Taftezon, Andrew Gissenaas, Hiram Moore, George Brooks, A. G. Brooks, William Squires, Charles Cunningham, Mathew Maloney, John A. Johnson, John Driscoll, L. G. Walker, William Jacobsen, H. W. Weed, Phillip Dwyer, R. K. Kelsey, Lars Jorgenson, W. Murdock, Henry Warrning, Nicholas Gillen, Adam Erickson, Ole Jensen, Henry Johnson and Charles Johnson, his brother and many others followed in such quick succession that it is difficult to assign the exact year of their arrival but it was all right after 1875. The Brooks Jacobson store and one operated by W. A. Wagg were the first stores. Mr. Mozdine operated the first lime kiln from about 1887. Later, Wagg also operated lime kilns and sold his product both locally and to the Green Bay and Depere Fuel Company. John W. Driscoll, C. C. Rice, P. J. Love, J. W. Dekeyser and B. Gissenaas built and operated stores. William Nasgovitz and Gust Tuttas operated Blacksmith shops. There were fires and the Rice-DeKeyser store was destroyed. A new DeKeyser store was built. DeKeyser operated it. Later it was Gibb's store. The Boyd hardware store was located on the site of the Rice-DeKeyser stores along with the Pound Bank. The first postmaster was J. A. Wagg, followed by A. G. Brooks, B. Gissenaas, Mrs. Julia Knapmiller and Mrs. Laura Culver up to about 1934. The Nasgovitz Blacksmith shop was located across from the four room Roosevelt School and nothing could convince the children attending this school that the "Village Blacksmith" was none other than Wm. Nasgovitz, for the description was perfect. But the area was pretty much cleared of pine except isolated small stands. There remained considerable hemlock and nearly all hardwoods.

VILLAGE OF POUND, MAIN STREET LOOKING EAST
(Circa 1904)
(Courtesy Mrs. Henry Johnson)

There were good stands of hard and soft maple, beech, oak, ash and elm. There were swamps filled with tamarack and white cedar for poles and fence posts. The poles were used for telephone and telegraph poles as well as for building and for the manufacture of shingles. Most sawmills operated shingle mills with their lumber operations. Both lath and shingles were in great demand for building of homes.

As in East Prussia, this area had been repeatedly visited by the ice ages. Glacial scars running northeasterly and southwesterly marked the entire northeastern part of Wisconsin and the Upper Peninsula of Michigan as the

POUND CMSTP&P RAILROAD DEPOT LOCATION
This is where most of the settlers landed and got their first views of their new homeland. Ed. Squires was Depot Agent for perhaps 50 years.

last glacier known as the Valders glacier extended some 100 miles south of Pound. (28) p 289 and (17) p 430. A large Esker (a serpentine hill of sand and gravel deposited by a river running under the glacier) extended for miles north of the village of Pound. For upwards of a hundred years, this esker sometimes referred to locally as "Hogsback" has furnished the sand, gravel and crushed rock for construction in a wide area of Wisconsin, including filling the railroad right of way during railroad construction days.

POUND FEED MILL BUILT 1900
(Courtesy Jerry Maloney)

C.E. MALONEY STORE & POST OFFICE POUND, WISCONSIN
(Courtesy Jerry Maloney)

POUND STREET LOOKING SOUTH FROM OLD HIRTON'S
HOTEL AFTER SNOW STORM (Circa 1904)
(Courtesy Mrs. Dorothy Brooks Fuelle)

POUND MAIN STREET LOOKING WEST About 1904
Note: Old two-room school sold St. Leo's Church 1905 still on School lot.
(Courtesy Mrs. Dorothy Brooks Fuelle)

JOSEPH BROOKS & WM JACOBSON STORE
(Courtesy Mrs. Dorothy Brooks Fuelle)

POUND LOOKING WEST FROM BROOKS & JACOBSON'S STORE
(Circa 1908)
(Courtesy Lloyd Gissenaas)

Because of the presence of sawmills in the vicinity, lumber was in plentiful supply and frame houses were promptly built by the East Prussians. Some of them found the cedar logs in such good supply that some fine log cabins or barns were built which endured for over a generation.

In the early pioneer days if the man of the family did not work in the sawmill or lumber camp between planting and harvesting seasons, and especially during the winter months, he would cut beech, hard maple, oak and other hardwood for cordwood, either for fueling the large wood burning heating furnaces or for the making of charcoal.

JOSEPH BROOKS & SONS GENERAL STORE (Circa 1910)
(Courtesy Jerry Maloney)

INTERIOR OF JOSEPH BROOKS STORE
(Courtesy Jerry Maloney)

C.C. RICE AND DE KEYSER STORES BEFORE FIRE (Circa 1905)
(Courtesy Mrs. R. Stadelman)

In the building up of the farms of the area, it was like Russia all over again with the clearing and draining of land and working up the soil. Many fields had stones in them and clearing the fields of stone was almost as difficult as clearing the hardy pine roots from the ground. Stone boats, a form of Indian Travois, were used to haul the stones off the fields to stone piles.

A considerable part of the area had been thoroughly burned in the great Peshtigo fire of October 8th 1871 which killed some 1200 people in the village of Peshtigo, located some 18 miles east of Coleman. So many were burned beyond recognition that hundreds were buried in a mass grave. Coleman, Pound, Beaver were ravaged in part by the fire which then turned Northeasterly into Menominee County Michigan and burned Birch Creek North of Menominee killing twenty-two people, burning the east part of Marinette (then known as Menekaune) as well as part of the city of Menominee, Michigan. People boarded boats and barges and went out into the Bay to escape the mighty blaze. (20) The fire happened on same day as the Chicago fire but with all communications down, it did not receive much publicity. The Giant pine stumps left either from logging or after the Peshtigo fire and measuring four or five feet across proved to be the most stubborn obstacles to the clearing of land for crop purposes. Digging these stumps out by hand was just about impossible. Other means were tried to remove the obstacle, including a giant tripod with a great iron screw to drive into the stump for the purpose of lifting the stump from the ground. This device was almost as dangerous as a medieval war-engine, for, when attempting to drive the screw into the stump either by hand or by horsepower, the long pole used as a giant wrench, when loosened, by accident or otherwise, became a deadly instrument, swinging around and demolishing everything in its path. A cousin of the writer, lost her husband, Samuel Krause in this manner. Dynamite appeared to be best suited for breaking up the pine and other stumps so that the remaining portions and roots could be chopped out or pulled by logging chain by a team of horses or oxen.

These pioneer settlers, with the most arduous and trying labors, with hand hoes, grubhoes, axes, hand saws, canthooks and other hand tools literally whittled away the wilderness so that crops could be planted and a livelihood provided. There were no luxuries in these homes. The people were poor but they did not know it because they enjoyed the richness of a freedom of conscience and faith which made nothing else matter.

Village of Pound looking East.
Depot hides St. Leo's Church but spire is visible above Depot.
(Courtesy Mrs. Henry Johnson)

INTERIOR GISSENAAS STORE & POST OFFICE
Mr. Gissenaas on left.
Bearded man at left rear Pound's first settler Mr. L.D. McMillen

(Courtesy Mr. Lloyd Gissenaas)

**VILLAGE OF POUND LOOKING WEST ON MAIN STREET
POUND HOTEL IN RIGHT FOREGROUND (Circa 1910)**
(Courtesy Jerry Maloney)

JOSEPH DE KEYSER STORE 1912
Rebuilt after fire. Main Building still used for Hardware Store
(Courtesy Jerry Maloney)

Crops included much the same grains and vegetables as were raised in Europe, whether in East Prussia or in Russia for Pound was in the same general temperate zone and latitude. Cash crops at first were mostly the cordwood or sawlogs cut by the land owner. The housewife would exchange eggs for sugar or other staples of food. But then a cucumber processing plant was established in Pound and many farmers raised cucumbers as a cash crop for the pickle factory. A sugar beet factory was built in Menominee, Michigan twenty miles away (across the Menominee River from Marinette, the county seat) in 1901. For many years, this was another cash crop raised by many farms. One of the most tedious chores in the writer's memory as a boy, was the blocking and thinning of sugar beets on the farm of Albert Graetz. The wage was ten cents a row but the row seemed a mile long. During harvest time in late September or October beets were taken out of the ground either by machinery or by hand garden forks. After cleaning off the clay or dirt, they were thrown on a pile where another worker "topped" the leaves from the beets with a heavy machette type topping knife. All of it was hard uncomfortable, cold work.

The beets were then loaded in wagons and hauled to the railroad station siding for weighing and loading them with a heavy beet fork, into a railroad gondola car for shipment by rail to the sugar beet factory at Menominee, Michigan.

GIBBS STORE
Mr. Tousignant, James Calwell and Dorothy Brooks
(Courtesy Mrs. Dorothy Brooks Fuelle)

FORMER DE KEYSER STORE, LEO BOYD STORE,
NOW ACE HARDWARE STORE
(Courtesy Cy Maloney)

SEILS BROTHERS GARAGE IN POUND (Circa 1910)
(Courtesy Mrs. Lorraine Woller)

SEILS SNOWMOBILE SHOWING IT
CAN STAY ON TOP OF A DRIFT

SEILS BROTHERS INVENTED SNOWMOBILE (Est. Circa 1912)

(Photoes courtesy Mrs. Lorraine Woller)

POUND ROOSEVELT SCHOOL 1905

(Courtesy Mrs. Dorothy Brooks Fuelle)

FIRST POUND VILLAGE SCHOOL ROOM (Circa 1902)

(Courtesy J. Maloney)

The potato harvest was also one to remember as it too usually was done after frosts had killed the vines. Where a potato digger was not available, digging with potato hand tools was necessary. The potatoes were then bagged and brought to the root cellar for storage or loaded on a wagon to be taken to town to be sold. One year the potato crop was so great that potatoes were selling for 10c a 100-pound bag with the bag included.

Most farmers had dairy cows and milk was sold either whole to the cheese factory or separated and the cream was sold to creameries. The skim milk or whey was fed to the hogs.

Threshing time was an exciting time especially for the young boys. Each member of the threshing crew was a hero but most especially the engineer of the steam threshing machine engine. They admired his familiarity with the monster and the skill of repairing the thresher by crawling into its inward parts. The smell of pine-pitch roots which were used to fuel the steam engine was an aroma never to be forgotten.

The feeding of the threshing crew was a modern miracle. How the poor hosewife could marshall the food and supplies to satisfy the amazing appetites of the threshing crew was a great wonder.

But there was fun too. Swimming in the Little Peshtigo River or one of the lakes, was enjoyed by all children. In the winter there was sleighing and skating. In summer there was raspberry, blackberry and blueberry picking near White Potato Lake with a milk can full of fruit brought home for canning.

Fishing too, was enjoyed now and then. A special trip would be made to Montana, Rost, Bass, Little Squaw, Big Squaw, Muskrat, Kelly, Crooked and White Potato Lakes as well as others for blue gills, perch, bass, northerns and crappies. There was hunting for partridge, rabbits, deer and bear.There was also some trapping as furs in good condition brought a good price.

As a young man, before taking up the study of Law, the author worked as a telegraph operator, first for the Western Union in Milwaukee and then on the railroad running through Pound and Coleman. He was the relief operator and agent at Coleman at both the day and night shifts. He also worked at Ellis Junction, just north of Beaver, at Wausaukee, Pembine, Sagola and other stations on this division. Edward Squires, son of William Squires, one of Pound's pioneers was the Depot Agent at Pound for an estimated fifty years or more. Louis Bergeron was agent at Coleman. Charles Lubin was night agent there.

EDUCATION

Prior to 1889 there were only a few schools in the general area. The elementary school in Pound was built in 1891. In 1905 it was sold to St. Leo's Church for a parish hall and a new four room school was built. This was the Roosevelt School of 1905. No transportation system such as a bus system was provided for school children. They walked to school both ways, in all kinds of weather. Walking distances for little children were considerable. A Normal School was built in Marinette for the training of teachers for these country schools. Coleman had a high school before one was established in Pound. After graduation from high school, there were many fine private colleges and public universitites for higher education. The first to take advantage of the University of Wisconsin was Albert E. Schwittay who graduated from the Law School and was admitted to the bar in 1901. He was later elected District Attorney, Sheriff and Assemblyman. He took office January 7th 1913 as Assemblyman but died of pneumonia at Madison, on January 19th 1913. The writer attended his funeral. Most of the East Prussians from Russia worked on farms. There were some who engaged in sawmill operations and forest products cutting and distribution. The Mattrisch family operated a sawmill for many years. Others worked in industry or woods or mill operations.

First Wilson School Building ½ Mile West and ½ Mile
North torn down in 1918 for Second Wilson Building.
(Courtesy Cy Maloney)

1918 Class of Old Wilson School Building
(Courtesy Cy Maloney)

1918 WILSON SCHOOL
Located ½ Mile West and ½ Mile North of Pound
(Courtesy Jerry Maloney)

The author's father, Michael S. Anuta, came from Russia at the age of 17, married at 21 by the Rev. Ludwig Hein, whose example and influence led him to a lifelong dedication to christian service, worked within and without the church to reach and serve many who could not come to church services. His work as a young man in the backwoods settlements did much toward the establishment of the Section Eight Church before 1902. He participated as a carpenter in the actual construction of that church. He continued his calling, holding prayer meetings, young people's meetings until he took employment with the American Baptist Publication Society as a Colporteur for the area. His missionary report for the year 1909-10, shows that for that year he held thirty-one meetings. In 1911, he held 79 meetings, visited 368 families and traveled over 3,000 miles.

In 1914 the Society urged him to go to the Milwaukee field and work there. He also worked in Grand Rapids, Wisconsin (now Wisconsin Rapids) and established a small church group there. In 1921 he moved to Hammond, Indiana where he became a director of a settlement House known as "Brooks House" and another settlement house in Gary, Indiana known as "Catherine House". He was ordained to the Baptist Ministry in the large First Baptist Church of Hammond, Indiana in March 1923 and was named an Associate Minister. He also served for several years for the Chicago Tract Society. He retired to his small farm in Pound in 1937 and died August 23rd 1940, fifty years after he left Russia.

The young children who came with their parents from the Ukraine as well as the American born children attended both the village and the one-room country schools. They were good students and many made outstanding scholastic records. The first generation Americans worked hard at their education, regardless of the field. Most studied agriculture, others worked in the forest products industry. They became lumber dealers, blacksmiths, hardware dealers, farm equipment and automobile salesmen, garage operators, storekeepers, business executivies, teachers, principals, ministers and attorneys and other callings. The children of the first generation American did much better. They became graduates of schools of higher learning and became professors, engineers, teachers, doctors, dentists, geologists, curators of museums, orthodontists, physicists, lawyers, judges, librarians, nurses, school administrators, dairymen, industrial and commercial executives, historians, writers of textbooks, and too many other fields of science and knowledge to here enumerate.

WILSON SCHOOL CLASS 1919 (?)

(Courtesy Mrs. Dorothy Brooks Fuelle)

Two reasons why this photo is included in that it shows the Parsonage
of the First Baptist Church and a Baby-Sleigh with Goose-necked
faces on the tips of the front runners. This baby is
believed to be Charlotte Gross and her brother.
(Photo courtesy of Mrs. Charlotte Gross)

Dr. Lloyd G. Walker

Dr. Walker treated nearly all of the East Prussians from Russia during some 50 years of medical practice in Pound and vicinity. He served three years in the Civil War and was the son of Capt. Jonathan Walker, "the man with the branded hand", made famous by a poem by Whittier in the days before the civil war. In 1844, after the birth of his son, Lloyd G. Walker, his father was branded with a red hot iron at the order of a Federal Court, after conviction of aiding slaves to escape to the Island of Nassau. He also served a year in solitary confinement and was fined $500.00, a great sum of money at that time.

(Courtesy Mrs. Dorothy Brooks Fuelle)

1978 View of Village of Pound Main Street looking West

ROOSEVELT SCHOOL
This four school-room building replaced old two-story
(plus basement) building which burned.

VILLAGE OF POUND: Looking south on US 141 from cemetary

POUND: Looking west across US 141 to north side of street

POUND: This is 1978 but is first view which met the settlers 85 to 88 years ago looking west along main street with vine covered bank building on left. (Dark building with vines is Pound Bank)

BARN & STABLE: Built of lumber and Cedar logs by William Perrault who came from Canada in about 1890. Neighbor of author's family. Children went to Pound School and built up enduring warm friendships
(Courtesy Mrs. Ann Perrault)

POUND EQUITY COOPERATIVE FEEDMILL

PATZ PALLET SERVICE COMPANY POUND

This marker of US 141 marks the half way point between the equator and the North Pole. It is located a short distance North of Pound

THRESHING MACHINE OUTFIT
Joe and Glen Perrault on Thresher
Other threshing outfits were operated by a number of Threshers among whom were the Seils brothers, Matt Stankevitz and sons Otto, Willie and Adolph

(Photo courtesy Mrs. Ann Perrault)

PESHTIGO FIRE MUSEUM
Formerly Congregational and later St. Mary's Church

Mass Grave and Peshtigo Fire Cemetary

COLEMAN DEPOT: CMSTP&P RAILROAD before 1900
(Courtesy Family of Louis Bergeron, Agent for many years)

PATZ COMPANY Pound Wisconsin
Founded by Mr. Paul Patz, First Generation American who has
didicated his talents and abilities to the support of his faith
throughout northeastern Wisconsin

INDUSTRY AND COMMERCE

Since this work concerns itself primarily with the EAST PRUSSIANS FROM RUSSIA and the conditions which they faced here and how they overcame them, this portion will deal with their industry and commerce. An example of a highly developed dairy farm is shown in the photograph of the Patz Farm. Paul Patz, one of the first generation Americans was raised on this farm. From his work and experience on this farm, he felt that there could be much human labor saved by mechanizing certain farm operations. His inventive mind developed the barn cleaning machinery and system as well as other agricultural equipment and aids. From this man's genious came the large Patz Company industry located on US 141 between Pound and Coleman on what was part of the John Dirk Jr. farm. Patz, a dynamic, dedicated christian man has a philosophy which calls for action in all his interests. He is a most generous supporter of religious causes. He was probably the main reason for the educational building erected by the First Church. He has given funds to missionary enterprises and to the building of churches at Wausaukee and other locations.

Another view of a dairy farm is included largely because the property belonged to the author's Aunt Wilhelmina. The buildings are now located on the top of the high hill, but, when the land was first settled, the home, workshop, granary, machine shed, hay and grain barn and finally the stalls were built old-country-style, in one structure along the north bank of the South Branch of Beaver Creek. It is now the Kapla farm.

The Gust Krause family established a large lumber, building materials and hardware establishment, just south of Coleman on US 141.

Gust Charnetsky established and operated the Chevrolet garage sales and service business for a number of decades.

THE PATZ FARM
Mr. Paul Patz was born and raised here and has made this farm a showplace in northeastern Wisconsin

The Graetz Manufacturing Company operates a very substantial manufacturing plant together with a sawmill and woodworking plant on Highway 64 just west of the east Oconto County line. Albert Neshek and the Fred Tachicks, operated grocery stores. Donald Gusick now operates the Ace Hardware store at the location formerly occupied by the Boyd Hardware store for many years. Truly, these men and women, whether on farm or in industry, were men to match the tall timber as well as the monumental tasks they faced to subdue and develop the land. They grew tall and straight morally under the climate of their faith. Their moral and spiritual fibres were as straight and as tough as the hardwoods they harvested.

KAPLA DAIRY FARM Beaver Township

Just before this house was built in about 1908, the Old Country Type of farm single structure consisting of house, granary, workshop, machine shed, hay and grain barn and finally stable — all one long building stood on the North bank of the South branch of the Beaver Creek, was struck by lightning and completely destroyed

GRAETZ MANUFACTURING COMPANY, INC.

GLACIERS

The northern portion of the United States, especially in the Great Lakes area was greatly affected by the ice ages. Authors Robert H. Dott Jr., and Roger L. Batten in a college textbook on the EVOLUTION OF THE EARTH, second edition, McGraw Hill 1976 page 442 et seq. discuss the visitations and revisitations of the glaciers to the North American continent and particularly the Wisconsin and Michigan area where the glaciers made their deepest penetrations. The scarring of the glaciers has marked the land area settled in Pound by the Prussians and others even as it scarred the northern European area of East Prussia. In the Pound area there are numerous evidences of these glacial visitations. There are a number of lakes, rivers, swamps, marshes, bogs, old lake beds, blueberry marshes together with hills and valleys, morains and sizeable eskers. An esker is interesting because it is the residue from an under-glacier river of considerable size, which, over hundreds and thousands of years, deposited sand, gravel and stone in a serpentine "hog's-back" or hill winding through otherwise flat or rolling country. (See also Geology of the Great Lakes, Jack L. Hough, Univ. of Ill. Press 1958) Since the last glacier visited the area between ten and twelve thousand years ago and there was little or no cultivation of land for agricultural purposes by the Hopewell or the Woodland Indians, these East Prussians, Germans, French Canadians, Bohemians, Irish Scandinavian and others were the first people of our civilization to cultivate the land for sustaining themselves and producing food for others.

The Pound Esker has been furnishing sand, gravel and stone for various construction and building projects for the white man for over 100 years. A large part of the Pound esker still remains in a virgin state. It runs mostly easterly and westerly about a mile north of the village of Pound. The materials from this esker were used for building of the railroads, the highways and both private and public buildings. The pictures herein show that this source material is still being used and constitutes a substantial industry.

GLACIAL ESKER still provides construction materials after over 100 years of use. Many parts of the Esker are untouched. They provide a resource for future needs.

POUND GRAVEL PIT — a glacial deposit in use over 100 years

GLACIAL ESKER used for sand and gravel for 100 years
(This section remains in its original state)

All immigrants took their citizenship in the United States seriously. Shortly after arrival, most declared their intention to become citizens and when the five year waiting period expired were naturalized in the Marinette or Oconto County Circuit Court. The author's paternal grandfather arrived October 15th 1890 and filed his Declaration of Intention December 30th 1890. Learning about their new government along with the learning of the English language was not easy for English language is one of the more difficult languages in our western culture. Further, they used their old country languages within their households and in their churches but insisted on their children becoming proficient in the language of their adopted land. Unfortunately they did not insist on the children becoming proficient in the two or three languages known to the immigrants. They thus inadvertently deprived their children of knowledge of not only more of their own older culture but their need to take courses of foreign languages later in schools and colleges.

For the older people who had been raised in Europe, religion in their native tongue was somewhat more personal and meaningful than in English. There was a closeness and intimacy in their ability to communicate their inmost feelings to their Creator in the old tongue rather than the new. While English has been in use in all Protestant Churches for upwards of fifty or more years, the older folk still love to hear "Stille Nacht" "O Tannenbaum" "Ihr Hirten Erwacht" "Ihr Kinderlein Kommet" "O du Froehleche" "Cicha Noc" "Wsrod Nocnej Cisy", "Gdy sie Chrystus rodzi" "Sainte Nuit" "Ecoutez le chant des anges" "Emerveillon'nous ensemble" "Je vien a vous du haut des cieux" or "O peuple fidele" "Les Anges Dans Nos Campagnes". While these are Christmas songs, there are others that are still loved by even the second and third generations.

SUCCESORS TO AMERICAN INDIANS

In actual fact, these East Prussians from Russia came to a land that had been vacated by the aboriginal American Indians, a renmant of the later Woodland Indians, but a few years before. Menominee Indians had entered into treaties with the Government of the United Sates in 1817, 1820, 1821, 1826, 1830, 1833, 1836, 1842, and 1848. The last treaty was supplemented in 1854 whereby the Menominee Indians ceded all of the remaining lands which they claimed as a tribe.The Menominees were a peaceful tribe and allowed some Winnebagos, Sauk and Foxes to occupy a part of their lands in central Wisconsin. Their original claims extended from Escanaba and west to the Mississippi River, thence south to Prairie du Chien; thence easterly to a little below Milwaukee; thence north along Lake Michigan to Green Bay and Escanaba and including the Door County Peninsula. The government moved into the area some of the New York Indians such as the Oneidas, Stockbridge and Brotherton Indians. But when the Menominee finally gave up their claims of sovereignty, they were moved to the Menominee Indian Reservation near Shawano, Neopit and Keshena. Some of the Menominee and some of part blood refused to move and remained in the areas of their original homes and became assimilated. A neighbor Indian widow lived near the author's home in the early days of this century. Remembered most is the fact that she smoked a corn-cob pipe and would deposit the smoking-hot pipe in the bosom of her dress without flinching. Indian men made excellent river-men and workers in the logging camps. But the East Prussians and their neighbors were the people who really took possession of the lands and made them productive for the first time in the history of any fully agricultural people.

Chapter 12

Church Life in Pound and Coleman

Following the establishment of the lumber industry, first at Braultville, then at Little River and other mills especially at Peshtigo, Marinette, Menominee, Goodman, Wausaukee and other settlements not too far from Coleman and Pound, the influx of population brought in many French Canadians, Irish, Bohemians, Poles, Germans, Scandinavians and the East Prussians. There were fine Roman Catholic Churches in Pound, Coleman, Crivitz and Klondike. St. Leo's of Pound was founded in 1902 by Phillip Dwyer, A. B. VanVonderen, Patrick Murphy, Joseph Brooks and Henry

POUND ST. LEO'S CATHOLIC CHURCH
Before Steeple remodeled
(Photo courtesy Jerry Maloney)

Warning. Land was acquired from E. Mariner and a beautiful church and rectory was built. Some of the extra land was first used as a garden, then for recreation, and, when the new Roosevelt school was built, the old school was moved to the rear of the lot for a Parish Hall. Many community and school exercises were held in this Parish Hall which was called Olympic Hall.

One of the largest French Catholic Churches in the area was located at Coleman. It was the St. John the Baptist Catholic Church. The French probably originally called it St. Jean the Baptiste Catholic Church. The Pound and Coleman churches now form one Parish under the name of St. Francis of Assissi and under one priest. Peshtigo also had a number of Canadian French Catholics as did Marinette and Menominee.

POUND'S ST. FRANCIS OF ASSISSI
ROMAN CATHOLIC CHURCH
Formerly St. Leo's

137

ST. FRANCIS OF ASSISSI PARISH
Former St. John's Coleman

ST. JOHN THE BAPTIST CATHOLIC CHURCH
Coleman
Before Steeple remodeled
(Courtesy Mrs. Ann Perrault and Geraldine Dupuis)

COLEMAN: St. John's Cemetary
now St. Francis of Assissi Parish Cemetary

ST. JOHN THE BAPTIST
CATHOLIC CEMETARY, COLEMAN

Before the reformation, all of these people were of one faith. Now, they were divided into Catholic and Protestant. But the bitterness of the reformation with its carnage was not evident. Lutherans, Baptists, Catholics and other faiths lived side by side. They traded at the same stores, sent their children to the same schools (there were no parochial schools until recent years), participated in community events and organized their municipal government and schools along non-partison lines. A congregationalist congregation built a church in Peshtigo. The building was sold to the St. Mary's Roman Catholic Church. When the latter built a new building, the former congregational church was sold to the City of Peshtigo for its Peshtigo Fire Museum.

During the Reformation, much of the resettlement of Protestants of France took place in other countries such as Germany, England and the United States. Northern Ireland also had a considerable settlement of French Huguenots. Several large groups were settled in East Prussia by Friedrich Wilhelm I and by Frederick the Great, particularly in Koenigsberg, Insterburg and Gumbinnen.

When Henry IV of Navarre, a former Protestant leader came to the throne of France, he heartily entered into plans with his minister to colonize Canada. The object was to establish a colony granting complete religious freedom. On November 8th 1603 Henry IV granted a commission to Pierre de Monts, a Huguenot gentlemen of Saint Onge, authorizing him to "possess and settle that part of North America embracing what is now Nova Scotia, New Brunswick and Canada." The King's commission granted him a monopoly of trade for ten years. The Royal grant stated in part:

> "With the help and assistance of God who is the
> author, distributor and protector of all kingdoms
> and states, to seek conversion, guidance and
> instruction of the races that inhabit that country
> from their barbarous and godless condition,
> without faith or religion, to Christinity and the
> belief and profession of our faith and religion,
> and to rescue them from the ignorance and
> unbelief in which they now lie".

Sieur de Mont was appointed the King's Lieutenant-General and took with him two friends, Samuel de Champlain and Baron de Pourtrincourt. Two ships sailed from Havre in March 1604 taking 120 persons of both high and low birth, Protestants and Catholics, with a Protestant minister and a Roman Catholic priest to look after their spiritual interest. (44) p 174 et seq.

Sieur de Monts settled on a small island at the mouth of the St. Croix. De Pourtrincourt settled on Port Royal. Selection of the island at the mouth of the St. Croix was bad, for many died during that winter. Among those who died were both the minister and the priest. The remainder of the groups consolidated at Port Royal. In the emergency Marc Lescarbot, a Protestant lawyer and writer became the teacher, minister and priest to all.

However, Commercial rivalries interfered with further settlement of Canada as a land of religious freedom. De Monts surrendered his commission to Huguenot Minister Admiral Conde. By the change of times and events, the rights and titles to the continent which belonged to De Monts, through one of the romances of history stranger than fiction, passed from Protestant to Roman Catholic hands.

On May 23rd 1633, Champlain, now Governor, received the keys of Fort Quebec from the Huguenot de Caen and from that hour Canada was closed to the Protestant Huguenot as a colonist. But Port Royal became the first settlement in North America north of the Gulf of Mexico.

The neighbors next to the Pound Protestant Baptists were almost all French Canadian Catholics. Families with names such as Archambeau,

Bergeron, Brault, Brazeau, Beaupre, Chartier, Dupre, Durocher, Fortier, Gaudette, Lesperance, Gendron, Neveau, Perrault, Rivet, Rocheleau, Thibideau, Duquaine, Lantereur, Beaudry and upwards of 400 others became neighbors and friends of the Protestants. (35, THE FRENCH BLOOD IN AMERICA by Lucian J. Fosdick, Baker 1911. See also Chapter III The Huguenot Colony of Canda p 112 et seq. in the same work).

Baptist, Lutheran and other Protestant children attended schools with the French Canadian or other national origin children. Only once was there a bloody fight lasting most of the day between French Canadian Gaudette and East Prusssian Tuttas, to settle a personal feud not involving matters of faith.

ST. WENCESLAUS CATHOLIC CHURCH
KLONDIKE

In the earlier days, mixed marriages were frowned upon by both groups. As in other parts of the world, with Pope John's leadership many changes took place in both Catholic and Protestant Churches as they moved toward each other. A Catholic Priest and a Protestant riding together to a community ecumenical meeting agreed that there was a real danger for both church groups to fear "passing each other in the dark".

In the Town of Brazeau in Oconto County immediately West of the Marinette County line there is a cross-roads village community known as Klondike. Here the St. Wenceslaus Roman Catholic Church ministers to a large area of French, German, Belgian, Austrian, Bohemian and Polish people who came there at about the same time and experienced the same kind of living as the Prussians living near them and further away in the Pound and White Potato Lake area.

PROTESTANT CHURCHES

When these East Prussians came to Pound, they found that there was no organized Baptist Church. There were some Baptist families in the vicinity as early as 1876 or 1877. Mr. & Mrs. C. L. Adam who lived on the east side of the school house lot on the west side of the village had been baptized in the Little Peshtigo River in 1885 by the Rev. Mr. Frederick Mueller, who was a state traveling Baptist minister and missionary. As the East Prussians began to arrive in the community their first concern was for their physical welfare in the form of housing for their families.

Daylight hours were short enough and they spent their working hours building homes and barns as well as preparing some of their land for the raising of food for themselves and forage for their livestock. There was not sufficient time to build fences so the cattle were either hobbled or allowed to roam in the brush and woods with bells tied on them so they could be located at milking time. But the people were also hungry by this time for spiritual sustenance and meetings began to be held in homes for prayer, scripture reading, exposition, discussions, devotions and the singing of hymns. The C. L. Adam home was used most often for such devotional meetings.

The fellowship of these meetings helped to relieve the loneliness of life in the wilderness where one could not see a neighbor's house or even the evening lights that might send forth a friendly glow because of trees and brush. Finally, enough of the people felt that a congregation should be organized. The Baptists organized a single or union church in 1889. A church building was built in 1890 at the intersection of what is now US 141 and a side street.

The American Baptist Home Mission Society contributed the sum of $200.00 toward the building fund. A parsonage was built about 1905.

The Rev. Ludwig Hein who was born, educated and ordained in Germany was called from Nebraska to be the first Pastor of this Baptist congregation. Rev. Hein was trilingual and was able to minister to the entire congregation. One part of the congregation met in the morning and the other in the afternoon. One of the first marriages performed by the Rev. Mr. Hein was on May 5th 1894 when he united the writer's parents in marriage. Martha Heisel and Gustave Gross were the witnesses. As more and more immigrants arrived, it became apparent that the original church building was too small to accommodate all the people. At a congregational meeting called to consider the matter after the Sunday morning service July 16th 1899 it was unanimously resolved to meet the following day, July 17th 1899 to adopt the resolution of dissolution of the union church.

GERMAN BAPTIST CHURCH

Immediately after the dissolution of the union church on July 17th 1899 a group of the German members met and organized the GERMAN BAPTIST CHURCH. Charter members were Mr. & Mrs. C. L. Adam, Mr. & Mrs. Carl Dams, August Gross, Carl Gross, C. G. Gross, Mr. & Mrs. Fred Heisel, Mr. & Mrs. Ludwig Heisel, Mr. Reinhold Heisel, Mr. & Mrs. Heinrich Krause and Mr. & Mrs. Fred Ziegenhagen. Mr. C. L. Adam was Moderator, and C. G. Gross, Clerk. Trustees were Fred Heisel, one year; Fred Ziegenhagen, two years and C. L. Adam, three years. Mr. Fred Heisel was elected Treasurer.

"Articles of incorporation" were executed before Notary Public B. Gissenaas by C. L. Adam, Fred Ziegenhagen and John Coppicus, the provisional trustees January 16th 1901 and affirmed by L. Heisel and John Salewski on July 5th 1901. The separation agreement provided for the payment of the sum of $200.00 to the German church as representing one third of the value of the building. Both congregations continued the use of the building under an agreement until a new building could be constructed. In 1902 a new and somewhat larger church building was erected at the west end of the village by the German congregation

Pastors who have served the Pioneer Baptist Church, formerly the German Baptist Church are:

Rev. C. L. Dietz	1903
Rev. Adolf Schultz	1905-1907
Rev. F.W. Socolofsky	1908-1911
Rev. Julius Matz	1911-1912
Rev. L. B. Holzer	1913-1918
Rev. C. Fred Lehr	1918-1921
Rev. Wm. Zeckser	1922-1925
Rev. Robert Ziebart	1925-1926
Rev. John Meyer	1927-1937
Rev. Herman Bothner	1938-1943
Rev. Fred Mashner	1943-1947
Rev. John Grygo	1947-1950
Rev. James Conner	1950-1954
Rev. G. W. Blackburn	1955-1961
Rev. Curtis Haas	1961-1963
Rev. E. S. Fenske	1964-1966
Rev. Anthony Guenther	1966-1973
Rev. Wilfried Bruns	1973-1974
Rev. Nevin Beehler	1975-1978

They also acquired a parsonage on the north-south road which is now US 141 at the south village limits in 1907. The writer's earliest recollections of church memories were of attending The German Church Sunday School. The German church applied for affiliation with the Wisconsin Vereinigung (German Association) in 1899. On January 1st 1940 they changed the name of this church to PIONEER BAPTIST CHURCH. In 1929 they built a new brick-veneer church just south of the First Church on US 41. This congregation has been served by an excellent ministry and it has a dedicated and active congregation.

FIRST BAPTIST CHURCH

As in the case of the German Church, the present FIRST BAPTIST CHURCH is a continuation of the original church organized in 1889 with the exception of the division because of language and accommodations. There were members of each continuing group which were part of the first 1889 church in each of the separated groups. Ministers who came to this Pound field served all these people until separate pastors could be called. Beginning in the year 1899 the American Baptist Home Mission Society supporting a missionary church in Detroit asked the pastor of that church to go to the Pound field every two months to minister to the most important needs of the people. In 1905 he was called to the Pound field. The Rev. C. V. Strelec assumed his Pound pastorate in June 1905 and served this field in both the First Church and the Section Eight church until July 1912 when he was called to serve a Milwaukee Church.

During the Ministry of the Rev. Mr. Carl V. Strelec, the parsonage was built, the SECTION EIGHT CHURCH building was dedicated and a new large brick veneer church building was dedicated in 1908 in Pound. About a fourth of a mile further south on US 141 a parcel of land was acquired for picnic and recreation purposes. A brass band was organized and led parades and gave concerts. It became a very well known and respected musical organization. At the east end of the church lot a long shed was built for the housing of horses and wagons or carriages during church services because most people drove in considerable distances. With the general use of the automobile the sheds were no longer used and were removed.

When the German language group separated from the union church, the First church had articles of incorporation executed and filed in the court house in Marinette but not at Madison. The articles were executed on November 11th 1901 by Fred Dobrzewsky, Michael Schiwy, Michael Will, John Salewsky and William Murrach. After the dedication of the First Church the old union frame church built in 1890 was sold to the Modern Woodmen who moved it to another location for a meeting place. Later it was used for Municipal purposes. The original Town of Pound cemetery was located nearly two miles northwesterly from the church. A new church cemetery plot was acquired in about 1910 on US 141 at the north edge of the village. The writer's grandfather Anuta was one of the last persons buried in the old Town of Pound cemetery, March 5th, 1907.

PIONEER BAPTIST CHURCH
Formerly German Baptist Church

While this is a history primarily of the East Prussians from Russia rather than of individuals, it is felt that the history would not be complete without reference to several individuals and particularly the ministry of the Rev. Carl V. Strelec. Strelec's ministry strengthened the congregations of the First and Section Eight churches and undergirded the faith of all of the Baptists who came here from Europe.

Carl V. Strelec was born in Russian occupied Poland not far from the southern border and near the Carpathian mountians. His people had fled from Ruthenia which had been part of Austria, because of the persectuion of Protestants in that region.Of minor nobility, Strelec's forebears embraced the faith of the Bohemian Brethren, followers of the martyred Jan Huss, one of the earliest reformers. The Strelec family were in the leather business. When they came to Russian dominated Poland they entered into an arrangement to supply saddlery to the Czar's Cossack troops. They found that it would be more convenient to perform the service to the Czar's forces in a more central Russian location so they moved to Berdecev a little south of Zhitomor and west of Kiev. It was while the Strelec family was in the Ukraine that the Baptist movement which had been initiated by Johann Gerhard Oncken reached there and Mr. Strelec had a moving conversion to the Baptist faith. His entire family followed his example and were all baptized.

Mr. Strelec vividly recalled the time and the place of the baptism but no one in the family could recall the location. Strelec served an enlistment in the Cossack Cavalry attaining the rank of sergeant. He came to the United States and went to Montana to work on a ranch as a cowhand believing that his knowledge of horsemanship would be valuable. He realized that this would not be his life work in view of his faith and he returned east and enrolled in the German Department of the Rochester Theological Seminary in 1894 and graduated in 1899. He was ordained May 24th 1899 at the First church in Buffalo under the auspices of the Buffalo Baptist Association. He assumed his first pastorate in Detroit shortly thereafter. While in Detroit he met Mayme Honsa and they were married January 20th 1902. They had one daughter, Marianne Mildred who is the writer's wife. Mayme Strelec died of

ORIGINAL UNION BAPTIST CHURCH OF 1890
With Parsonage added about 1905

145

puerperal fever December 8th 1902. The American Baptist Home Mission Society asked Strelec to make bi-monthly visits to the Pound field which he did commencing in about 1899. He was called to the Pound field in June 1905 and served until July 1912 when the Society again asked him to further mission work in Milwaukee. He served in Milwaukee from 1912 to 1915 when he became head of the Slavic Baptist Training Seminary in Chicago. In 1920, the Baptists sent him to Poland to head up Baptist relief work.

FIRST BAPTIST CHURCH 1910
(Courtesy Mrs. Dorothy Brooks Fuelle)

1978 VIEW FIRST BAPTIST CHURCH
View from North

THE REV. C.V. STRELEC

1978 VIEW FIRST BAPTIST CHURCH AND EDUCATIONAL PLANT
View from South

147

He served in the Baptist relief administration until 1924. During this time he edited and published a weekly magazine called "New Ways". In July 1924 he accepted a call to serve the church in Cleveland, Ohio and he continued in that church until he retired because of ill health in 1938. While doing relief work, Mr. Strelec visited widely in Europe, Poland and Russia. He tried to locate his father and members of his family but the Russian revolution had apparently taken all of them as he could find no trace of them.

He was acquainted with many Baptist pastors in the Polish and Ukrainian areas but the devastation of the churches during the Russian revolution at first doubted by him, was fully confirmed. The churches were totally destroyed and the congregations dispersed. Cemeteries were plowed up. Mr. Strelec was a prolific writer and publisher. He edited and published not only "New Ways" but "HERALD OF TRUTH" "OUR LIFE" and "SPRINGS OF TRUTH". He contributed hundreds of articles to the secular press. During the course of his ministry he translated or composed some sixty one hymns into various Slavic languages. He preached in Bohemian, Polish, Ukrainian Russian, German and English. He was capable of handling some twelve languages, all of them, he said "with an accent". He was born October 1st 1869 and died September 15th 1962 at Cleveland. He is buried in part of the former Anuta family plot in the Pound Baptist Cemetery given to the church for Mr. Strelec's burial.

The list of ministers who served the Pound field in all its branches includes many distinguised pastors. Each served with great distinction and for long periods of time. Rev. Strelec's ministry was significant in that he came at the beginning of the major pioneer life of the East Prussians from Russia. He brought to them a corporate ministry which brought a unity of Baptist theological thought and practice. However, it did substantially replace the home-centered worship and devotion of the earlier pioneer period.

BAPTISM ON THE LITTLE PESHTIGO RIVER NEAR US 141
The presence of both the remains of the North and South Dams indicates that this scene occurred in about 1920, possibly during the Pastorate of the Rev. Mr. Henry Schilke
(Photo courtesy Mrs. Dorothy Brooks Fuelle)

One of the families prominent in the First Church was that of Adam Patz, who originated in Koenigsberg, in East Prussia. This family came through New York in 1888 and settled west of Coleman. The writer recalls the family driving their double-seated surrey with the fringe on the top to church Sunday mornings. On December 26th 1906, Rev. C. V. Strelec and Wilhelmina Patz, daughter of Mr. and Mrs. Adam Patz were married by the Rev. Mr. A. Schultz of the German church.

ORIGINAL SECTION EIGHT BAPTIST CHURCH
Built 1901-2

The couple had four children: Mrs. Angeline (Charles Spangenberg, Mrs. Ruth (Leslie Mugford (both now deceased), Mrs. Helen (Oliver) Robinson, and one son Eugene B. Strelec.

While in Europe, Mr. Strelec met with Mr. Rauschenbusch and other Baptist leaders. He also met some of the political figures of those days and personally knew Jan Masaryk of Czechoslovakia and other leaders in Poland and East Prussia.

While at Pound, a number of Baptist leadership conferences were held under his leadership and that of the Northern Baptist Convention. Pastors who have served the First church are:

Rev. C. V. Strelec 1905-1912
Rev. G. A. Alf 1914-1916
Rev. Henry Schilke 1918-1947
Rev. Bill Erickson 1947-1950
Rev. Michael Evan.............. 1950-1955
Rev. Ivan Bachtell 1955-1965
Rev. Don Vietz, (Assistant) 1965-1968
Rev. Robert Dow................. 1965-1968
Rev. James Morgan............. 1968-1971
Rev. Frank Thompson 1972-1975
Rev. Richard Reece............. 1975-

1970 NEW SECTION EIGHT BAPTIST CHURCH

Section Eight Baptist Church

The later pages to this history contains copies of a number of Town Maps of Marinette and Oconto County, Wisconsin showing thereon the names of farm owners. The Plat book is published by the Rockford Map Publishers of Rockford, Ill., and these maps are shown by their courtesy. The names shown on the land parcels are those of current owners. Of course, many changes in ownership have taken place since these people came in the late 1880's or 1900's. However, many farms have descended from father to son or to daughter and son-in-law but the maps show the distribution of the settlers over the area.

Many of the settlers were located so far back in the woods that with poor road conditions, pressure of work and plain poverty, attendance at the village church was difficult. It was to these people that Michael S. Anuta as a lay worker devoted himself, as he had dedicated himself to this purpose under the influence of the first pastor, the Rev. Mr. Ludwig Hein. He held home meetings, young people's meetings, choir rehearsals and either tramped through the woods, winter or summer or drove a sulky, buggy or small sleigh. On more than one day-long trip the author accompanied his father to a distant backwoods home for services and Sunday School home in late evening.

One day while a-foot to a choir meeting father took a trail through an extensive woods. About half way through he came upon a huge bear who felt that the man was invading his territory. The bear gave immediate chase. A large hard maple was nearest at hand and the man clambered up the tree with the bear breathing hard behind him. When they got to the top of the tree where the branches were too small to hold a four or five hundred pound black bear, he stopped. They stared at each other only four or five feet apart. The bear decided to descend and wait at the bottom of the tree. When the choir director did not show up a searching party went out and heard his calls. When the search party came near, the bear departed. There was no rehearsal that night but the treed man had his own season of prayer in the tree-top.

Other laymen became dedicated leaders in these bockwoods areas and eventually the people in the oulying areas on their own initiative formed the SECTION EIGHT church. On Tuesday, November 12th 1901 a meeting of the FIRST church was called with the request that the SECTION EIGHT BAPTIST CHURCH be recognized. This request apparently made a major issue of the separation of yet another group from the Pound First church. The Rev. T. V. Jackimovicz of Chicago apparently representing the American Baptist Publication Society and American Baptist Home Mission Society was present along with the Pastor of the Marinette church, the Rev. C. F. Vreeland with a layman, Mr. William Jacobson.

The German Church delegates were Mr. John Coppicus and Mr. Carl Dam. The Section Eight church was represented by M. Anuta, Mr. August Nasgovitz and Mr. Michael Charnetsky. Minutes of previous meetings were read which indicated that the Section Eight church was already organized on November 2nd 1901, officers were elected and at that meeting they voted to call for this council meeting.

More than fifty members were present at this recognition meeting from the Section Eight church. The members expressed themselves as wanting a church nearer to them so that they with their children might have more easy access to church services; that they might more speedily serve God and keep the Baptist Covenant. They wanted to construct their own building without any help from the mother church in the village. The recognition was granted by the council and the Section Eight Church commenced to erect its own building and conduct its own services and Sunday School classes. (See Volume 1 of Corporations in Marinette Court House page 396 for a complete copy of the minutes of this meeting). In 1976 a Seventy-fifth Anniversary of the founding of this church was observed. This author and his wife attended some of the anniversary meetings. Charter members shown in the Annniversary program were John Stank, Wilhelm Kobus, Michael Charnetsky, Fred Jashinsky, Jacob Gusick and John Shevy. Mr. Stank gave the land for the church lot and building. After the church was completed in about 1902, Rev. Mr. Strelec preached in this church about once every two months until he was called to the field when he would preach once every month. Laymen conducted services in his absence with most of the preaching done by Mr. John Shevy. The writer's father filled this pulpit on

REV. MICHAEL S. ANUTA
1871-1940 Born in Toporisc Dreis Zhitomir

many occasions. Emil Kobus became the Sunday School Superintendent and served as a most effective lay minister to these people. The Section Eight Church is one of the rare churches in which every member feels called to service whether there is a professional leader or not and thus has rendered a most effective ministry in this area. The 75th Anniversary program listed the following pastors:

Carl V. Strelec	1905-1912
Gustav A. Alf	1914-1922
Albert Alf	1922-1926
Leon Jesokow, student Pastor	1920
A. Soltys	1927-1929
Samuel Kostreva	1930-1939
Gerald B. Smith	1939-1941
Lowell L. Young	1941-1943
Warren J. Thompson	1943-1955
Walter Cecil	1955-1959
Floyd Sheppard	1960-1965
Ronald W. Hoffman	1966-1974
Gerald Longjohn	1974-1976
Gerald Van Prooyen	1976-

Samuel Kostreva was one of the Russian-born generation of East Prussians who became an ordained minister having been nurtured in his faith in this church. His father served as a lay minister in East Prussia.

Seventh Day Adventist Church

A series of tent meetings were conducted in 1895 by a Seventh Day Adventist minister by the name of Rev. Herman, assisted by a Rev. Dirkson from North Dakota. This resulted in the organization of the Seventh Day Adventist Church with the following charter members:

Mr. Coon	Mrs. G Pelot	Mr. G. Badora
Mr. F. Cole	Mrs. Furlitt	Mrs. G. Badora
Mrs. O. F. Cole	Mrs. Correy	Mrs. F. Wathing
Mr. M. Anuta Sr.	Mr. Mozdine	Mr. Gust Gross
Mrs. M. Anuta	Mr. C. Rosner	Mr. Ed. Gross
Mr. G. Pelot	Mrs. John Dirk Sr.	Mrs. Ed. Gross

All but six of the members were East Prussians from Russia.

There presently is a beautiful modern Church on US 141 just north of the First Baptist Church serving the Seventh Day Adventist membership.

SEVENTH DAY ADVENTIST CHURCH, POUND

ASSEMBLY OF GOD

The inspiration for the Pound Assembly of God Church appears to have come from a few of the Pound people who had assembled in the old Bethel Temple of Chicago in the 1920's. Their spiritual concern for their relatives led to an invitation from the Pound First church to Bethel Temple's pastor Raymond Fosteque.

Prayer meetings were held in homes and a young Bible School graduate Gust Schultz was secured as pastor. After a time E. B. Block of Marinette conducted services in Pound. Then Mike Wascos came but with it tragedy struck when a fire destroyed the former German Church building. Under the leadership of Julius Hein, Louis Olson and Joseph Staniszewski a new building was undertaken using materials from a Lutheran Church building located east of Coleman. The first members listed included Joseph Staniszewski and wife, Julius Hein and wife, Louis Olson and wife, John Leisner and wife, Mrs. Charles Bieber, Fred Salewsky and wife, Mrs. Fred Jashinsky, Frank Gengler and wife, Mrs. Fred Pusich, Mrs. Louis Shevy, Otto Nichols and wife, Mrs. Emil Rakouaki, Mrs. Gottlieb Lentz, Mike Nichols and wife. Adolf Freiwalt and wife and Fred Badora and wife. The year of the formal organization was 1935 with R. L. Sharnich of the District presiding. Miss Lillian Johnson, Rev. George Price, John Haags, John Timms, Elmer Hoff, Gilman Hanson, Wilbur Mandigos, Revivalist C. M. Ward, Roy Reed, Ed. Lutze, Dwight Sheltrowns and Herbert D. Kolenda have since that time ministered to this congregation and erected a beautiful Lannon stone church edifice. Missionary work has been done in Gillett, Armstrong Creek and other locations. This church has a strong leadership and congregation and is ministering to a substantial number of people of the community.

ASSEMBLY OF GOD CHURCH, POUND

(MJA)

TRINITY EV. LUTHERAN CHURCH

Beginning in about 1877, Pastor Adolph Toepel of Peshtigo began conducting divine services for the Lutheran Christians in Coleman. As in other cases, services were first conducted in homes. Other Pastors who served after Rev. Toepel were Hilleman; Hermstead; Eisenbach; Strommer; D. Oamman and M. Kionka. An organization was perfected May 25th 1902 with Pastor Kionka acting as chairman of the meeting. Fourteen members were present and signed the constitution. The first officers were Max Schwahn, Secretary and Frank Olsnefsy as Treasurer with Samuel Kaminski. Later Carl Semrau Sr. became Treasurer. Pastor Kionka served until 1903. In that year the congregation united with the parishes of Crivitz and Athelstane called Otto T. Hoyer. A renovated school house was made into a house of worship and was dedicated March 12, 1905. This building served until 1942. Pastor Hoyer was called to Winneconne. In 1906 Hugo Kock a young graduate came to serve the parish but left shortly for another field. Theodore Albrecht another graduate served the parish until 1910. He was succeeded by Pastor Weber who remained until 1914.

The congregation asked for synod's support to call its own pastor and Wm. Wojann was called. A home was purchased for the Pastor. In 1918, the congregation voted to unite with St. Matthews Ev. Lutheran Church of Beaver Township. This union continued until 1958 when again because of continued growth, the church wished to have its own pastor. Some land was purchased and a new parsonage was erected. It still serves as the minister's home.

Pastor Wojahn accepted a call to go to Eldorado, Wisconsin. In September 1930 Pastor Wm. Fuhlbrigge assumed the pastorate of the Coleman-Beaver parish. The congregation began to think of a new church or expansion of the old. On June 15th 1941 the congregation voted to build a new church building.

The beautiful new building was dedicated August 30th 1942. Pastor Fuhlbrigge in 1949 accepted a call from the Jacksonport, Wis. Church. In the spring of 1950 Pastor Louis Pingel of Phoenix, Arizona began to serve this church and stayed until January 1958. The Tower chimes purchased by the Ladies Aid Society were installed and dedicated May 19th 1957.

A Fiftieth Anniversary was observed on June 22, 1952 with special services. It was shown that after fifty years the congregation numbered 287 baptized members. 173 communicants, 74 voting members, 18 lady members and 87 families represented. Pastor Reinhard Schoenbeck from West Allis, Wis., followed Pastor Pingel, being installed in May 1958 but accepted a call to New Ulm, Minn., a year later. Pastor Donald Laude came from Lone Star, South Dakota and was installed in February 1960 and served until June 1964, going to Jenera, Ohio. Many improvements to the building were made during his service. On June 29th 1960 the Trinity Lutheran Cemetary Association was organized. Pastor Laude was succeeded by Pastor Waldemar Zink from Kewaunee and was installed Feb. 7th 1965 and is the current pastor in 1978.

Many physical improvements have been made to the parsonage and the church building. In 1975 an addition was voted to the church to replace the old entry and ground was broken for a new addition on August 3rd 1975. A corner stone was laid October 12th 1975 and the new addition was dedicated March 7th 1976. At the 75th Anniversary celebrated May 15th 1977 the congregation numbered 500 baptized members, 365 communicants, 150 voting members, 50 lady members and 179 families represented.

The Ladies Aid Society dating back to the early 1900's contributed a great deal to the work of the church including giving to charity and to church causes.

This church is an outstanding witness of its faith in this community.

TRINITY EVANGELICAL CHURCH, COLEMAN

ST.MATTHEW'S EV. LUTHERAN CHURCH

A group of the German Lutheran people in the Beaver Creek Settlement organized a Lutheran church in 1877. At first they met in homes and in the school house. From 1881 to 1918 they formed one parish with St. John's Ev. Lutheran Church of Grover. But St. Matthews was incorporated in 1885 and joined the Wisconsin Synod in 1886.

St. Matthew's Ev. Lutheran Church, Beaver Township
Congregation first church, built in 1899

On October 11 1891 it was decided to build a church. It was completed in 1899. On the night of Ascension Day in June 1916 it was damaged by lightning. When Rev. Wm. Wojahn came to Coleman, St. Matthews formed a joint parish with Trinity Ev. Lutheran Church of Coleman from 1918 until 1958. The present parish hall was built in 1952. With the installation of Pastor Ed. Stelter of Crivitz, on April 13 1958, St. Matthews became a joint parish with Grace Ev. Lutheran Church of Crivitz. Fire destroyed the 75 year old church Feb. 9th 1975. The present church was dedicated April 25th 1976. Pastsors who have served this church are 1877-1881 Rev. Adolf Toepel, Rev. Hilliman; 1881-1888 Rev. Anton Pieper; 1889-1898 Rev. Christ Gevers; 1898-1907 Rev. Martin Kionka; 1907-1918 Rev. C. C. Kleinlein; 1918-1930 Rev. Wm. Wojahn; 1930-1949 Rev. Wm. Fuhlbrigge; 1950-1958 Rev. Louis Pingel; 1958-1960 Rev. Ed. Stelter; 1960-1969 Rev. E. Kitzerow, 1960-The Rev. William

Besler. At the Centennial of the Church the congregation had 150 baptized souls and 115 communicants.

The Kirchenbuch der St. Matthew's Gemeinde shows that the first Baptism was Oct. 13 1878; Bernhard Carl Ludwig Baumann, son of August Baumann and Albertine nee Rothe. The first confirmation was April 14th 1878. Confirmands were Hermann Maerz, Friedrich Carl Maerz and Elisabeth Kunz. The first wedding on April 23rd 1880 united in marriage Carl August Kunz and Wilhelmine Caroline Freidrike Rust. The first funeral was Nov. 22 1878, for Ludwig Krueger. The list of members clearly shows the German origin of families such as Albright, Bauer, Bauman, Bayer, Behrend, Besler, Braun, DeWolfe, Ellie, Frank, Gove, Guenther, Hanneman, Heil, Hoffman, Johnson, Kienitz, Klein, Krueger, Kuntz, List, Mansfield, Martz, Meyers, Nowak, Pelot, Peot, Polzin, Prestine, Prue, Rhode, Rickling, Risner, Seefeldt, Seils, Steer, Winkler, Woller, Woulf, Zechel, Zeitler, Zempel and Ziech. This church gives a strong and faithful witness to their faith in Beaver Township and vicinity.

ST. MATTHEW'S EV. LUTHERAN CHURCH

Baptist Church Picnic and Recreation Park
on US 141 one half mile south of Pound

Orlando Dam of Little Peshtigo River where it flows under US 141

Coleman, Wisconsin Post Office with Mr. & Mrs. Al Van Vondern and their son Earl Van Vondern. Rigs of two mail carriers shown but carriers not identified. (Circa 1905)

(Courtesy Mrs. J. Van Vonderen)

View from Coleman looking north toward Little River and Pound with highway now US 141 and CMSTP&P Railroad. In distance can be seen smoke, steam and dust of E.E. Bolles Lumber Company sawmill at Little River. Only known photograph of the mill location scene.
(Circa 1911)
(Courtesy Rene Durocher)

HOTEL COLEMAN, Coleman, Wis., about 1920
The author lived here while working as telegrapher at the Coleman Railroad Station for Louis Bergeron, Agent and Charles Lubin, Night Agent.

Courtesy Mrs. J.E. VanVonderen)

A spectacular railroad wreck at Coleman
with some twenty cars derailed. 1918
(Courtesy Rene Durocher)

VILLAGE OF COLEMAN IN 1912
The presence of so many buggies indicates a shopping day
(Photo courtesy Mrs. Henry Johnson)

EARLY COLEMAN LOOKING EAST
(Photo courtesy Mrs. Ann Perrault)

EARLY COLEMAN LOOKING WEST
(Photo courtesy Mrs. Ann Perrault)

COLEMAN MUNICIPAL BUILDING & FIRE DEPARTMENT 1978
(MJA)

COLEMAN: Elevator and north side of street looking west, 1978
(MJA)

COLEMAN: North side of street, looking east, 1978
(MJA)

COLEMAN: South side of street looking east, 1978
(MJA)

COLEMAN HIGH SCHOOL 1978
(MJA)

KRAUSE LUMBER & HARDWARE, 1978
(MJA)

COLEMAN: Looking Westerly, 1978

COLEMAN: Main Street, Looking East, 1978

E.E. BOLLES COMPANY (1909)

Sawmill located at Little River where now US 141 crosses the Little Peshtigo River.

Picture taken from boom out in mill pond looking southerly. The engine room and flywheel was housed in the lean-to on west side of Mill. The Shingle Mill was the part jutting out to the east, a portion of which is visible in picture. (See other picture of Shingle mill crew)

Mill was closed in about 1912 and remained intact until about 1914 when it was dismanteled. A large Boarding house was located behind mill along with company store located on East side of road (now US 141). Horse barns were located on hillside northerly of present Orlando Dam.

This mill provided employment for many of the East Prussians from Russia along with its predecessors whose mills were destroyed by fire.

This mill settlement was complete with sawdust streets and electric lights for mill and street lighting provided by the mill generator. Housing was provided in company houses for a number of families.

The outlets from the mill pond were two dams the remains of which are seen in the picture showing a Baptism taking place just below southerly dam.

(Courtesy of Patricia Rudolph)

The only known picture of a part of the E.E. Bolles Shingle Mill shipping dock located on southeast side of building. Mill in back.

(Left) *Chippewa* train 21 arches through the intersection of 5th and Clybourn in Milwaukee in its original form: gaily painted F-3 Pacific, standard M&E, two 4400 coaches, and standard diner and parlor. The veteran 4-6-2 spread its cinders across the first subdivision of the Superior division at 65 or 70 mph, then assumed a more relaxed pace for the remainder of its run.
(Below) A year or two later — in 1938 — CMStP&P had completed its last steam resumbering and had added the Beaver Tail as 21 eased alongside a classic lineup of waiting automobiles at Coleman, Wis. Note the Ford bus and the stately Packard. — *Left*, TRAINS *collection*; *below, Keweenaw Central Railway collection.*

Near last run of CHIIPPEWA, Milwaukee Road fast passenger train to Copper Country. (Circa 1940)

(Courtesy M.L. Hanson)

Chapter 13

EAST PRUSSIANS BECOME AMERICANS

Unlike their reluctance in Russia to accept citizenship and the duties and responsibilities of that status, the Prussians from Russia took prompt steps to become naturalized in the United States. Most of them were naturalized in the Circuit Court for Marinette County but some, from Brazeau and Lakewood Township in Oconto County took out their final papers in the Oconto circuit Court a part of the same circuit.

The list shown in the appendix endeavors to show both those who declared their intention to become citizens and those who were admitted. Some went to court individually. Others took a wagon with a hayrack and went together in a group making a festive occasion of the trip. Unfortunately, the records are not fully complete. Many blanks calling for information are not filled in. Others were filled in improperly. If John Smith was naturalized the wife was most often shown as Mrs. John Smith instead of giving her maiden name, date and place of birth and names of her parents. Children who were minors were often omitted when the order should have listed them. All who came, came to work as farmers or laborers. After becoming settled, some began studies for upward mobility into better oportunities for living. Two who came from Russia were ordained to the Gospel ministry in the Baptist Church, Michael S. Anuta and Samuel Kastreva Sr. John Kastreva served as a lay ministor.

Among the first generation of American young men to become thus ordained, Samuel Kostreva Jr., Asaf Jashinsky and Harry Kovnesky, Robert Shevy and Lloyd Graetz. Gottlieb Kostreva a lay preacher, father of Samuel Kostreva Sr., also a lay preacher was born in East Prussia August 30th 1862. He died in Pound October 30th 1936. Rev. Michael S. Anuta officiated at this service.

COURT HOUSE, MARINETTE, WIS.

OLD MARINETTE COUNTY COURT HOUSE BUILT ABOUT 1890
(Photo courtesy of Mrs. Henry Johnson)

In the legal profession, one young man who arrived here at 16 resented being paid a boy's wage for doing a man's work. He decided a better way could be found. He began studies at the University of Wisconsin and graduated from its Law School. He was admitted to practice law in 1901. This was Albert E. Schwittay, son of Mr. & Mrs. Frederick Schwittay, both born in East Prussia who came here in 1890. More of his career is referred to in the section on Education.

Those of the East Prussians who settled in the towns of Lakewood and Brazeau in Oconto County journeyed to Oconto either by train to Stiles Junction and the branch line to Oconto, on the CMSTP Railroad, or, to Marinette over the CMSTP Railroad and then the Chicago & Northwestern Railroad to Oconto.

Oconto was the county seat of that County and the Circuit Judge who usually resided in Marinette went to Oconto to hold court and take the proceedings to naturalize the East Prussians who settled in Oconto County. The airline distance was almost the same but to get there by railroad or highway was much further than from those Town areas to Marinette County. However, Oconto County had jurisdiction of its residents and they had to be naturalized there. The picture of the Oconto County Court House below shows the court house building before additions to the north and south. The original building was built in 1891.

IN DEFENSE OF LIBERTY

Wherever these people lived, they did not like war nor wish to participate in it. Yet, when called to duty, whether in East Prussia, Russia or the United States, they too gave their last full measure of devotion in World War I, World War II, Korea and Vietnam etc. Wherever duty called them, their response was prompt and complete. The people at home supported the war efforts. All executed their duties as citizens with honor and distinction.

NEW MARINETTE COUNTY COURT HOUSE BUILT 1942

OCONTO COUNTY COURTHOUSE

Casualties there were and the losses were borne by the families and loved ones with the same grief and sorrow as well as pride felt by any other American family.

This was true whether the young men were German, Prussian, French, Scandinavian or other national origin. Young men, the flower of the youth of these people perished in the service of their adopted country in the Atlantic, Pacific, Pacific Islands, in the southwest Pacific, Africa, Italy, France, Germany and the low countries. Some were taken prisoners and were imprisoned for months and years. Most have come home well but there are some whose physical condition was affected in one way or another and they have been handicapped for the rest of their lives. A price is paid for every victory and for every liberty.

CM&STP RR. DEPOT AT MARINETTE, WISCONSIN

The Immigrants who came to Marinette and Oconto County came to Oconto and Marinette mostly by railroad to make their Declarations of Intention to become citizens and later to appear at their Naturalization Proceedings before the Circuit Courts.

LEVEL OF CITIZENSHIP

From a background of nearly fifty years of general law practice which included ten years as Prosecuting Attorney, six years as Circuit Court Commissioner and ten years as Municipal Judge and by reason of being related by blood and marriage to many of the people of this group, the writer has been able to observe the ethical and moral level of conduct and citizenship of these pople even though located in an adjoining County and State but only within a distance of 20 to 30 miles. The daily newspapers published in Marinette County were a good reflection of the general pattern of life.

In comparison with the generally known and observed course of conduct of young people as well as adults in this central region of America, these folks rated an exceptionally high level in their relations with each other and in the observance of the laws of the state and nation.

Divorce and serious crime were remarkably low while the general morality of these people, Prussian, French, Bohemian, Polish, Scandinavian and others, reflected an above the standard level of ethical and moral living. They not ony reflected great courage and dedication to the ideals of their forebears, they were and are generous in their giving of self and substance to build up the moral capital of the area and thus stand tall and high among the citizens of their adopted land.

PILGRIMAGE'S END

A few days prior to the writing of this page and the next, the writer visited the villages of Pound, Coleman and Klondike. The site of the first sawmill east of Coleman, Braultville, the village of Little River at the point where the Little Peshtigo River intersects US 141, the French St. John the Baptist Church and Cemetary in Coleman, the St. Leo's Church and Cemetary in Pound, the Old Town of Pound Cemetary, the present Baptist Cemetary in Pound, the Lutheran church and cemeteries in Pound and Coleman, The First, Pioneer, Section Eight, Seventh Day Adventist, Assembly of God, Trinity Ev. Lutheran and St. Matthew's Ev. Lutheran Churches and the St. Wenceslaus Catholic Church at Klondike.

All of the pilgrims who came seeking a new life have now finished their course and are restsing from their labors in their final pilgrimage. To the best of this author's knowledge, all of those born in East Prussia have passed on to their reward. Just about all of those who were born in Russia or Canada have also ended their pilgrimages. Whole families lie serenely in their family plots. For them, this is their "holy ground", for them this is "the place". The ultimate pilgrimage is ended.

The turreted tower of the Pioneer Church reminds all of Luther's Hymn: "A Mighty Fortress is our God" (Ein Feste Berg ist unser Gott") ("C'est un rempart que notre Dieu") The double spire of the First church and the spires of all of the other churches with or without crosses stoutly point heavenward proclaiming to all whence came their foundations.

> "The Church's one Foundation is Jesus Christ her Lord"
> She is His new Creation by Water and the Word;
> From heaven he came and sought her
> To be His Holy Bride; With his own Blood He bought Her
> And for her life He died.

Der Kirche Grund hienieden, Der Fels, auf dem sie ruht,
Ihr leben, Heil und Frieden, ist Christus und sein Blut,
Durch Leiden und durch Sterben, Hat er sich ihr vermaehlt,
Ihr Leben zu erwerben, Den Kreuzestod erwaehlt"

L'Eglise universelle a pour roc Jesus Christ;
Elle est l'oeuvre nouvelle Que sa parole fit,
Habitant le ciel meme, Il vint se l'attacher,
Et, par un don supreme, Mourut pour la sauver!"

The basic faith of these people and their descendants still sustains them though a large number are now spread throughout the world. Some have become members of other churches but their work ethic drive has not lost its strength nor its cunning for they, even as laymen in such churches, have become elders, deacons, presbyters, officers and leaders of their faiths. The faith of their fathers is indeed living still. They are the leaven, they are "our Hope for years to come".

All of these pilgrimages have been a continuing labor to sink their roots of faith deep enough so that nothing can completely destroy the growth and upward thrust through the soil of life and to produce the fruits of that faith. The fruits are in part, a society which recognizes their creator and Saviour. But it also is a recognition that this faith comes from the greatest recorded source of moral and spiritual truths; truths which confront men with a Loving God and his grace. There is no comparable source and we instinctively ask, as did Thomas, "To Whom Shall we go Lord?" This deeply founded and continuing belief and faith, coupled with the appropriate works will sustain them to the end.

NUN DANKET

Now thank we all our God, With heart and hands and voices,
Who wondrous things hath done, In whom His world rejoices;
Who from our mother's arms, Hath blessed us on our way,
with countless gifts of love, and still is ours today.

Nun danket alle Gott, Mit Herzen, Mund and Haenden,
Der Grosse Dinge tut, An uns und allen Enden,
Der uns von Mutterleib, Und Kindesbeinen an,
Unzaehlig viel zu gut, Und noch jetzt und getan.

LIST OF IMMIGRANTS

The lists of names shown on the following pages have been taken from the Public records of Marinette and Oconto Counties.

This list is not perfect. The author has made diligent search for all who belong to this group and such as were found, were copied as accurately as possible. Many of the blanks in the court forms were not filled out. Names were not spelled correctly. The author personally knows of people who came here and died here and yet there is no public record to be found.

Naturalization forms changed. At first, they were much more complete. Later, about all that can be depended upon was the name of the man and his country of origin from whose allegiance he was severing himself and pledging new allegiance to his adopted land. Dates of arrival are guesses in most cases. Where a maiden name was called for for the man's wife it was given the same as the man's. Names of parents of both man and wife were omitted or unknown.

The author has undoubtedly made errors but the major error is that this history was not written by someone some fifty years ago when many of the original East Prussians were still living. The author confesses his guilt in not having done his part, for when his mother was living, even in her 90th year, her mind was sharp and clear and she could recite relationships now impossible to trace. Gone too are the intimate glimpses of those who lived in Prussia and came here at a time when they could remember conditions over there as well as here and the journey across the ocean.

It is hoped that this book will awaken interest in our ancestry and heritage and bring forth records and information that can result in a more accurate presentation.

IMMIGRANTS FROM EAST PRUSSIA AND RUSSIA

Abbreviations: An = Antwerp, B = Boston, Ba = Baltimore, Br = Bremen, C = Country, G = Germany (East Prussia), H = Hamburg, N = New York, P = Philadelphia S = Sweden, A = U.S.A., Q-S = Quebec-Soo.

Immigrant	Birth	C	Exit	Entry	Year	Death	Spouse	Birth	C	Death
Frederick Anutta	1851	G	Br	N	1890	6/27/1893	Louise Bednarz	3/ 4/1863	G	12/ 4/1917
Frederick Anutta Jr.	1888	R	Br	N	1890	1918	Clara Burgo	3/ /1893	A	9/25/1924
John Bedford Anutta	1886	R	BR	N	1890	11/ 9/1963	Olga Bolander/Lydia Stanton	1886	S	6/15/1955
Michael Anuta Sr.	1833	G	Br	N	1890	3/ 3/1907	Katherine LaBusch	9/ 1/1833	G	4/16/24
Michael Anuta Jr.	1871	R	Br	N	1890	8/23/1940	Charlotte Czudnochowski	12/22/1876	R	3/16/1967
William Anutta	1890	R	Br	N	1890	4/ 3/1960	Hattie Edleman	9/ 2/1893	G	7/13/1972
August Badura	1871	R	Br	N	1890	9/12/1897				
Charles Badura	1867	R	Ba		1887	1/ 9/1944	Louise Will	6/ 6/1888	R	7/ 2/1955
Frederick Badura	1882	R	Br	N	1890	7/12/1947	Caroline Schwittay	11/18/1884	R	5/26/1956
Gottfried Badura	1832	G		N	1890	3/29/1901	Regina Pelot/Maria Kupachky	1842	R	7/ 5/1936
Paul Badura	1879	R	Br	N	1890	3/11/1925	Augusta Czudnochowski	1883	R	3/20/1954
Michael Bedura	1876	R	Br	N	1890	8/15/1951	Minnie Shevy 1883/Martha Bieber	1889	R	1908/1974
Wm. Beaber	1869	R		N	1888	1931	Jennie Mosdzen	1872		1931
Frederick Bednarz	1876	R	Br	N	1890	1/ 5/1955	Mollie Swenty	1876	R	
John G. Bednarz	1879	R	Br	N	1890	11/12/1954	Maggie		R	7/21/1905
Martin Bednarz	1861	G		N	1890		Louise		R	
Michael Bednarz	1861	G		N	1887		Carolin Kutrib		R	

Immigrant	Birth	C	Exit	Entry Year	Death	Spouse	Birth	C	Death
William Bednarz	1862	G		N	1888		Jennie Tibusch		R	
William Bednarz	1863	G		N	1888	1940	Bertha Olshefski	1885	R	7/26/1962
Charles Beissel	1880	G		N			Augusta Patz			
Henry Beissel	1878	G		N		1952	Minnie Czudnochowski	1890		
Louis Beissel	1876	G		N		5/29/1967	Wilhelmina Wertelewski	1890		2/ 9/1972
Frederick Bertsch	1851	·G		N	1893					
Gottlieb Bertsch	1858	G		N	1892	8/ 9/1946	Amelia Mundt	5/ 5/1869	G	8/15/1946
Michael Bertsch	1860	G		N	1892					
Fred Bieber	1869	R		B	1889	7/17/1939				
Fred Bieber	1886	R		N	1889	9/25/1978	Emma Dams	5/14/1891	R	5/23/1974
Fred Bieber	1855	G		N	1888		Anna Tomcek	1860	R	4/ 8/1945
Adam Bieber	1853	G		N						
Frederick Borkowski	1879	R		Ba	1893	1942	Mollie Stankevitz	1885	R	10/28/1968
Gottlieb Borkowski							Minnie Czudnochowski			
John Borkowski	1887	R		Ba	1893	9/27/1949	Mollie Kobus	10/18/1885	R	2/18/1925
Ludwig Borkowski	1849	G		Ba	1893	1917	Frozyna Plewka	1850	R	1909
Gust Borkowski	1888			Ba		5/17/1970	Minnie Guseck	4/18/1892	R	4/22/1970
Gottlieb Borutta	1890	R	Br	Ba	1903					
William Borutta	1870	G	Br	N	1928	1940	Anne	11/30/1866		1942
John Broderick	1844	G		Ba	1891	9/15/1901	Lizzie Gusick			

Immigrant	Birth	C	Exit	Entry Year	Death	Spouse	Birth	C	Death
Gottlieb Broderick	1878	R	Ba	1897		Gustie			4/24/1902
John Buxa	1874	G	N	1900					19___
Gottlieb Buxa	1877	G	N		1955	Bertha	1899		
Ludwig Charnetski	1846	G							
Michael Charnetski	1850	G	N	1888	5/20/1941	Mary Buxa	11/15/1861		5/25/1942
Frederick Czudnochowski	1840	G	Ba	1891	10/16/1939	Louise Shevy			
Fred Czudnochowski	1852	G				Charlotte Shevy	4/25/1855		2/22/1925
Frederick Czudnochowski	1880	R	N	1891	10/17/1953	Minnie Czudnochowski			2/13/1954
Gust Czudnochowski	1881	R	Ba	1891	10/ 9/1967				
Heinrich Czudnochowski	1880	R			3/14/1943	Augusta	1850		1914
John Czudnochowski	1852	G	Ba	1891		Jennie Rakowsky	1867		
John Czudnochowski	1864	G	Ba	1891	1950				1944
John Czudnochowski	1880	R	N	1890		Augusta Jakowski			
Michael Czudnochowski	1842	G	Ba	1891	5/31/1931	Catherine Shevy			5/25/1899
Michael Czudnochowski	1872	R		1892	1955	Louise Salewsky	2/20/1874		
Michael Czudnochowski	1875	R	N	1892		Minnie Shevy			5/10/1953
Michael Czudnochowski						Caroline Shevy			
Wilhelm Czudnochowski	1844	G	N	1892	6/ 4/1937	Mosdzen/Louise Czak	1/10/1836		8/16/1924
John Dirk (Doerk)	1858	G	Ba	1892	1927	Anorta Suchalla	1846		1939
John Heinrich Dirk	1884	R	Ba	1892	1956	Mollie Stank Div			

Immigrant	Birth	C	Exit	Entry	Year	Death	Spouse	Birth	C	Death
John Denkhaus	1884	R		N	1890	1956	Martha Anutta	1884		1958
Fred Dobrzewsky	1867	G			1888					
John Dora	1896	R	Br	N	1903	11/ 2/1947	Gusta Tachick	4/30/1899		
Frederick Dudek	1851	G		N	1887					
Oscar Dudek	1877	R		N	1887	1955	Martha	1887		1937
John Ermis	1855	G	Br	Ba	1892		Wilhelmina Swenty			
Ludwig Ermis	1844	G		Ba	1891		Regina Gusick			
Louis Ermis	1868	G		Ba	1891	9/16/1942	Jeannette Bieber	1876		8/ 5/1960
William Ermis	1872	R		Ba	1891	1953	Mina Broderick	1879		1957
Frederick Freivalt	1851	G				1927	Louisa	1863		1927
Gustave Freivalt	1871	R	Br	Ba	1902	9/ 9/1964	Augusta Lysek	1869		1945
August Gritzon	1883	R		Ba	1891					
Frederick Gritzon	1861	G					Caroline	1863		1949
Carl G. Gross	1865	G		N	1892					
August Gross	1877	G		N	1893					
Carl Gustav Gross	1852	G		N	1892					
Charles Grosse	1875	G		N	1893	10/ 3/1968	Emily Dams	3/21/1884		12/22/1959
August Grosse	1878	G		N	1893	6/30/1940				
Edward Grosse	1851	G		N	1892	3/22/1936	Marie Dirk (Doerk)	4/301845		11/28/1932
Gustave Grosse	1872	G		N	1892	1954	Bertha Rosner	12/25/1881	R	1964

Immigrant	Birth	C	Exit	Entry Year	Death	Spouse	Birth	C	Death
Frederick Guzek	1822	G		Ba 1893	991917				
Jacob Guzek	1857	G		N 1888					
John Gusick	1880	R	Br	Ba 1893	1966	Julia	1889		1970
Adolph Heisel	1878	R		N 1898	6/15/1953				
Gustav Heisel	1869	R		N 1888	1954	Mollie	1874		1955
Gustav Heisel	1873	G		Ba 1891	1945	Wilhelmina Grosse	1880	G	19__
John Heisel	1823	G		N 1886	10/28/1905	Mollie			
Ludwig Heisel	1848	G		N 1889	4/18/1934	Augusta Rakowski	1855		1941
Ludwig Heisel	1871	G		N 1888	1940	Mina Keshenberg			8/10/1957
Otto Heisel	1883	R		N 1890					
Rhinehold Heisel	1878	G	H	N 1889		Bertha Broderick			
Frederick Jashinsky	1858	G		Ba 1893	5/ 4/1931	Augusta Czudnochowski			
Fred Jashinsky	1883	R		Ba 1894	5/ 3/1972	Minnie Kostreva	1884		6/25/1971
Gottlieb Jashinsky	1874	R		Ba 1892	1969	Martha Kobus			1917
Gottlieb Jashinsky	1863	G		Ba 1892	10/10/1930	Julia	1882		1969
Gustav Jashinsky	1887	R		Ba 1893	12/ 5/1969	Julia Kostreva	3/ 4/1881		11/22/1918
Gust Jevorutsky	1888	R	Br	N 1904					
John Jevorutsky	1890	R		Ba 1892	1960	Martha Shetteck	1893		1975
Adam Kalbus	1857	G		N 1892	1931	Charlotte	1868		19__
William Kalbus	1886	R		Ba 1891	1917	Frieda	1870		

Immigrant	Birth	C	Exit	Entry	Year	Death	Spouse	Birth	C	Death
Albert Kempka	1869	R		N	1904		Charlotte Duda	3/ 1/1869		11/ 9/1957
Alexander Kempka	1867	R		N	1886	4/23/1936	Fredericka Shevy	1/18/1878		8/10/1945
Charles Kempka	1862	G		Ba	1904	1915	Mary	1865		8/31/1935
Julius Kempke	1863	R		N		1932	Augusta	1866		1953
Julius Charles Kempke	1888	R		N	1908	7/28/1976	Pauline Kempky			
Samuel Kempky	1867	G		Ba	1892	10/28/1938	Louise Mosdzen	4/15/1865		2/10/1949
William Keshenberg	1886	G		N		2/12/1964	Mollie Kobus	1886		
Martin Kloss	1871	G		Ba	1897	11/25/1945	Caroline Mosdzen			6/26/1935
Emil Kobus	1884	R	Br	N	1892	10/28/1958	Elizabeth Schwittay	9/ 7/1888		9/ 4/1958
Emil J. Kobus	1891	R	Br	N	1900	7/ 4/1963	Minnie Bieber			2/ 8/1968
John Kobus	1846	G		Ba	1900					
John Kobus	1875	G		Ba	1900					
Michael Kobus	1869	G		Ba	1901	1938	Mollie Kalbus	4/ 4/1870	G	10/ 3/1956
Wilhelm Kobus	1849	G		N	1891	8/13/1918				
William Kobus	1882	R		Ba	1898		Jennie White			
William Konietzke	1877	R		Ba	1892					
Fred Kostreva	1882	R		Ba	1901	1/22/1959	Augusta Kalbus	1881		1954
John Kostreva	1885	R	Br	N	1901		Charlotte Jashinsky			12/ 5/1928
John Kostreva	1852	G		N	1892	7/28/1938	Laura			
John Kostreva	1849	G	Br	Ba	1891	9/ /1968	Gustie Schwittay	6/16/1880		5/20/1972

Immigrant	Birth	C	Exit	Entry	Year	Death	Spouse	Birth	C	Death
Gottlieb Kostreva	1849	G	Br	Ba	1891	10/26/1936	Fredericka Czudnochowsky	6/ 1/1846		10/ 5/1926
Gottlieb Kostreva	1862	G		N	1911					
Gottlieb Kostreva	1886	R				11/25/1967	Bertha Jashinsky	4/15/1887		3/23/1965
Fred Kostreva	1881	R	H	Ba	1896	1/ 8/1955	Minnie Jakowski	10/27/1884		4/15/1971
Samuel Kostreva	1899	R					Ruth	3/28/1913		5/31/1951
William Kostreva	1875	R		Ba	1904	1942	Mollie	9/25/1874		2/13/1963
Michael Kovalski	1845	G		N	1890					
Frederick Kovneski	1869	G		N	1900	8/22/1978	Gusta Tachick	1900		
Adam Krause	1854	G		N	1903					
Charles Krause	1861	G		Ba	1888		Louise Ewald			
Gustav Krause	1891		Br	Ba	1903	4/ 3/1952	Ida Salewski	1/11/1900		4/21/1977
Michael Krause	1866	G	H	N	1906	7/20/1932	Caroline	1869		1955
Samuel Krause	1865	G	H	Ba	1903	7/17/1949	Jennie Grossman	1867		1936
Saumel Krause	1884	R	Br	N	1901	5/24/1917	Lydia Wertelewski	2/ 1/1888	R	4/15/1965
Samuel Krause	1885	R	Br	N	1903		Minnie	3/23/1889		8/24/1905
William Krause	1856	G		N	1891					
Wilhelm Krause	1862	G		Ba	1891					
Wilhelm Leisner	1850	G		N	1890	4/ 3/1939	Edna Salewsky			
Gustav Lentz	1869	R					Lizzie	1874		1943
Gustav Lentz	1878	R		Ba	1887					

Immigrant	Birth	C	Exit	Entry	Year	Death	Spouse	Birth	C	Death
Michael Lentz	1878	R		Ba	1886					2/11/1944
Steve Lentz	1873	R	Br	Ba	1886	5/ 6/1949	Gustie Sheman			
Gottlieb Lentz	1843	G		Ba	1887	8/16/1939	Katherine			
Gustav Lentz	1857	G		Ba	1887		Katherine			
Adolph Mattrisch	18__	G		N	1887	6/ 5/1978	Caroline Leisner			6/13/1933
Gottlieb Mattrisch	1867	G		N	1887	1948	Amelia Heisel			6/15/1945
William Mattrisch	1853	G		N	1887					
William Mattrisch	1861	G		N	1887	9/14/1951	Mary Heisel	1863		1940
Adolph Matz (Mix)	1885	R			1890					
Ludwig Murock	1861	G	Br	Ba	1891		Minnie Shevy			1906
William Murrach	1858	G		N	1888	1942	Mary Shevy	1866		1935
William Murrach							Minnie White			
Carl Mursau	1882	R		N	1902	1947	Martha Czudnochowski			10/ 7/1975
Frederick Mursau	1868	R		N	1902	8/23/1937	Emily			
John Mursau	1841	G		N	1902		Jennie Goblicki			
Ludwig Mursau	1877	R		Ba	1901	1966	Martha	1892		1975
Michael Mursau	1872	R		N	1902	1944				
August Nasgovitz	1868	R		N	1892	7/21/1949	Martha Heisel	1877		10/31/1960
Karl Nasgovitz	1833	G		Ba	1891					
Ludwig Nasgovitz	1874	R		Ba	1891	11/ 5/1964	Minnie Kostreva	3/25/1877		1/ 6/1962

Immigrant	Birth	C	Exit	Entry	Year	Death	Spouse	Birth	C	Death
William Nasgovitz	1871	R		N	1892	1927	Augusta Patz	1883		
Albert Neshek	1890	R		N	1900	7/29/1976	Martha Salewski 1917/Amalia Patz			1964
August Neshek	1892	R		N	1900	7/29/1977	Laura Charnetski	1891		1965
Emil W. Neshek	1892	R	Br	Ba	1911		Mary Charnetski			
Fred Neshek	1875	R		Ba	1903	1938	Minnie Durki	1878		1/ 8/1978
John Neshek	1866	R		N	1900	5/ 4/1959	Louise Nasgovitz	1868		1951
Michael Neshek	1869	R		N	1900					
John Ollech	1871	R		Ba	1893	1925	Minnie Guseck	1868		1951
Fred Olshefski	1882	R		Ba	1892					
Frank Olshefski	1871	G	Br	N	1890		Lottie Shevy			
Michael Olshefski	1855	G		Ba	1891					
Adam Patz	1852	G		N	1889	1936	Regina Shevy	3/26/1860		8/ 8/1959
Gustav Patz	1904	R					Minnie Bedora	5/ /1886	R	1930
Herman Patz	1881	R		N	1888	5/13/1943				
John Patz	1871	R		N	1890	1947	Augusta Tibusch	4/ 1/1871		8/13/1975
John C. Patz	1884	R		N	1890	3/26/1973	Emily Tachick	6/ 2/1894		1977
Michael Patz	1866	G		Ba	1887	3/25/1977	Wilhelmina Ollech	4/12/1869		9/26/1934
William Patz	1855	G				1922	Bertha	1880		1960
Frederick Pelot	1878	R	Br	Ba	1893	1966	Bertha Shevy	1886		1964
Gottlieb Pelot	1838	G				1919				

Immigrant	Birth	C	Exit	Entry	Year	Death	Spouse	Birth	C	Death
Gustav Pelot	1864	G		N	1893		Minnie Gusick	3/ /1882	G	
Wilhelm Pelot	1875	R	Br	P	1886	9/22/1959	Caroline Nasgovitz	3/ 5/1865	G	7/ 5/1928
Charles Pillath	1873	R				8/18/1964	Mary Poppek	6/12/1868		8/25/1953
Fred Pillath	1877					11/ 3/1966				
Gottlieb Pillath	1839	G		Ba	1887	9/24/1919	Maria Badura	1/18/1839		1/23/1899
Michael Pillath	1869	R		Ba	1887	2/15/1926	Maria Tappek	1/ /1868	R	1953
Michael Rakowsky	1883	R	Br	N	1890					
Wilhelm Rakowsky	1873	R	Br	N	1890	1953	Maria Kupachsky			
Charles Rosner	1864	G		N	1892	1949	Caroline			1952
Chris Rosner		G					Maria Rakowsky Kupachsky Badora		R	
Louis Rosner	1872	R		Ba	1892					
August Salewsky	1869	G		Ba	1890		Augusta	1883		1928
Fred Salewski	1852	G		N	1892					
Frederick Salewski	1841	G		N	1892	1917	Louise	1843		1927
John Salewski	1866	G		N	1888	3/24/1935	Charlotte	1870		1964
August Schewe	1869	G	An	P		3/ 8/1944				
Carl Schivy	1860	G		Ba	1891	1937	Catherine Bertsch	1861	G	1929
Charles Schivy	1880	R		N	1890		Katherine Tocic			
Frederick Schivy	1826	G		N	1890	9/ 5/1901	Wilhelmina Goroncy	11/26/1827		9/27/1909
Gust Shivy							Bertha Salewski	4/19/1876		12/ 9/1946

Immigrant	Birth	C	Exit	Entry	Year	Death	Spouse	Birth	C	Death
John Shivy	1842	G		Ba	1892	2/12/1922	Amortha Ragowski	3/25/1842	G	12/ 4/1916
Carl Shevey	1822	G		Ba	1891					
Gustav Shevy	1875	R		Ba	1890	5/18/1959	Bertha Salewski 1946/Minnie Heisel			
Gustav Shevy	1882	R	Br	Ba		1962	Augusta Keshenberg	6/14/1890 (Div)		12/30/1958
Louis Shevy	1856	G			1888	1924	Caroline Murrach	5/19/1874		4/24/1961
Ludwig Shevy	1849	G		N	1888		Hattie Dorce			
Louis Sheavey							Anne	4/18/1864		4/ 9/1905
Michael Shevy	1847	G		N	1890	1935	Charlotte	1849		1920
Michael Shevy	1856	G	Br	Ba	1891	1/13/1936	Charlotte Tachick	7/21/1861		9/27/1940
Michael Shevy	1877	R		N	1889					
Michael Shevy	1888	R		N		7/1956	Mollie Tachick	11/ 3/1895		
Seferin Shevy	1888	R	An	Q-S	1908	3/ 2/1940	Ida Salewski	1/ 1/1897		4/ 8/1937
William Shevy	1879	R		Ba	1891	3/ 6/1966	Gustie Salewski	6/ 1/1884		10/ 9/1961
Albert E. Schwittay	1874	G		N	1890	1/19/1913	Gertrude			
Frederick Schwittay	1842	G		N	1889					
John Schwittay	1891	R		N	1892		Mary	1/25/1892		
Gottlieb Schwittay	1859	G		N	1888					
Samuel Schwittay	1881	R		N	1892					
Samuel Schwittay	1841	G		N	1891					
Theodore Schwittay	1882	R	H	N	1888	12/ 5/1976	Martha Jashinsky	1886		1958

Immigrant	Birth	C	Exit	Entry Year	Death	Spouse	Birth	C	Death
Michael Shetteck	1859	G		N	1892	1921	Louise	1856		1917
John Stank	1853	G		N	1890	2/22/1927	Minnie Charnetsky	9/ 7/1860		2/17/1945
Frederick Stank	1870	R		Ba	1892		Charlotte			
Frederick Stank							Caroline Krasta			
Gottlieb Stank	1873	R		Ba	1892					
Michael Stank	1868	R		N	1890	10/ 8/1958	Frieda Shevy	11/16/1877		10/20/1944
Samuel Stank	1866	R		Ba	1892	11/19/1947	Wilhelmina Kovalski			
William Stank	1866	G		N	1886	1965	Louisa Shevy	1861	R	2/ 3/1901
Adam Stankevitz	1840	G		Ba	1890	2/17/1915	Caroline Rhode			
Mathias Stankevitz	1852	G		N	1888	3/21/1948	Wilhelmina	5/15/1858		4/15/1927
Frederick Swenty	1825	G		N	1888		Regina Broderick			
William Swente	1861	G		N	1888		Jeanette Swenty	9/25/1872		2/22/1938
Frederick Suchalla	1882	G	An	N	1909	1958	Emily	1888		1965
Charles Tachick	1875	R		Ba	1891	10/21/1933	Augusta Swenty	10/25/1877	R	3/18/1956
Frederick Tachick	1868	R		Ba	1901	12/ 1/1933	Minnie Stank	12/13/1872	R	3/ 5/1943
John Tachick	1837	G		Ba	1891	1/21/1924	Louise Shevy			1959
John Tachick	1862	G		N	1888	2/ 4/1927	Caroline Bednarz	7/16/1873	R	3/ 8/1928
William Tachick	1864	G		Ba	1891	1894	Anna Nichols			
Alexander Trzaska	1858	R		N	1887					
Adolph Tuttas	1858	G		Ba	1892	7/23/1938	Caroline Sopher	10/22/1868		5/22/1913

Immigrant	Birth	C	Exit	Entry	Year	Death	Spouse	Birth	C	Death
Gust Tuttas	1883	R		Ba	1893	1925	Ida	1888		1967
Gust Victor Tuttas	1889	R	Br	Ba	1903		Lydia Murrach			
Henry Uhl	1848	G		N	1890	8/11/1924	Pauline Semrau	1853		1/ 2/1904
Julius Wardecke	1877	R	H	N	1908		Augusta			
John A. (Bialy) White	1862	G		Ba	1902	1920	Wilhelmina	1869		1962
Charles White	1872	R		Ba	1887	4/ 1/1948	Bertha Czudnochowski	4/14/1879		2/27/1938
Fred White	1872	R		Ba	1891	1942	Bertha Kobus	1883		1964
Frederick White	1871	R		Ba	1891					
Michael White	1841	G		Ba	1891					
John Wellskopf	1884	G	Br	N	1904	8/10/43	Martha Shevy	R		6/18/69
Gottlieb Wertelewski	1858	G		N	1888	2/15/1933	Wilhelmina Anuta (Div)	1868		7/ 5/1928
John B. Wertelewski	1860	G		N	1888	8/ 9/1911	Mary Anuta	11/ 1/1865		12/11/1946
Adam Will	1866	G		N	1888	7/21/1935	Louise Swenty	4/ 4/1868		8/21/1945
Carl Will	1866	G	H	N	1888	7/20/1958	Louise Gusick	2/ 1/1878		2/ 4/1968
Jacob Will	1854	G		Ba	1892					
Michael Will	1857	G		N	1890	11/22/1945	Wilhelmina	6/24/1864		9/ 4/1945
Tom Zysk	1873	R		N	1892	1920				

Note On Immigrant List

The compilation of the list of original naturalized immigrants was a most difficult undertaking. The Naturalization Records of both Marinette and Oconto Counties, Wisconsin were first examined. Because the information in the naturalization proceedings was incomplete, it was necessary to make up a complete list of the death records of those which were recorded in both counties. Many persons who have come here and lived here and are buried here are not found in the records in the court houses. Additionally, in order to assist in checking the names of the wives of the immigrants, a complete record was made of all of the marriages of the children of the East Prussians from Russia as well as those who came direct from Germany. All marriages from the 1890's through 1963 were copied and cross checked. The obituary files of the Marinette Daily Eagle Star were checked. In the early years almost no deaths were reported in the Eagle Star. I believe that the death of my Grandfather on March 3rd, 1907, was the first obituary to be found. "The Searchlight" a newspaper published by Albert E. Schwittay when he was a lawyer, District Attorney, Sheriff and Assemblyman from and for Marinette County was also examined for its entire existence. It is also on Microfilm and can be obtained from The Historical Society of Wisconsin. Interviews with some of the knowledgeable persons still living in the area and the solicitation of pictures and information brought some help. "THE TACHICK LEGACY" by Marilyn Tachick Asplund of Canada and Marjorie Tachick Johnson was most helpful as to that family. Barbara Jane Day provided help for the Bedora, Shevy, Pelot and Tachick families as well as the Ship's Roster of the Frederick Anutta Family. Researchers were employed in Chicago, in Washington and in Germany. A membership was taken in the Verein fuer Familienforschung in Germany and through them the STACJA NAUKOWA POLSKIEGO TOWARZYSTWA HISTORYCZNE-GO (Instytut Mazurski) in Olsztyn, (formerly Allenstein in East Prussia but now a part of Poland) has also helped. Two trips were made to Germany and the work of collecting information and records of our people has extended over most of my lifetime. We ask your indulgence if there are errors or omissions. Believe me, every resource has been examined where possible. I am satisfied that much information will come in after publication of this work and we will be grateful for all additional information and corrections. It is hoped that the efforts will be measureably appreciated. Consider the necessity of taking the inscriptions from the grave stones in both cemeteries in cold, windy and even rainy weather, only to find that even there there is no confirmation of available records in all cases. Limited space prevents setting forth all the information gathered.

Michael J. Anuta 1978

ORIGIN OF EAST PRUSSIAN NAMES

In a series of articles published in DAS OSTPREUSSENBLATT (Organ der Landmanschaft Ostpreussen) on July 7 through July 14th 1962, Ernest Hartman wrote about the "Herkunft Ospresussischer Familienamen" (Origin of East Prussian Family names). His research led him to the conclusion that the people who came to East Prussia were often called by the name of the town from which they came. For example, Lewaltski was a family who came from Lehwalde. Seminsky came from Seeman and Caldborsky came from Kaltenborn.

Names in the area influenced by the Lithuanians were changed from Aschmann to Aschmans, Peter to Petereit, Rose to Rossat. Schneider to Schneidereit, Sturm to Sturmat and Wald to Waldeit.

The French and French-Swiss Protestant Huguenots who fled to East Prussia and settled around Koenigsberg, Insterberg and Gumbinnen also had their names changed in the course of time. Chevallier became Schawaller, Guillet was changed to Gille, Pliquet to Plikert and Camplair to Kempler or Kempke. Additional research of family names and their gradual change or change to protect their origin, to a different name from their original name, will no doubt give greater light to names of families who have lived in this province of Germany.

NOBILITY

A number of the families of the East Prussians of this history were at least of minor nobility. The Czudnochowski (Czudnochowsky, Czudnochowsky, (latin) and similar spellings stem from the family of this name of nobility status going back to the 1600's according to the researcher in Germany. The Heisel, Sivi, (Shevy), Czak and a number of other families bore the prefix "von". Such titles were not used when the families moved to Russia or to the new world. Confirmations of titles are difficult if not impossible to obtain because of destruction of records in the wars and difficulty of access because of Soviet government policies.

The Prussian Kings usually restored the titles, both civil and military which had been held by the French Huguenots when in France when they settled in the domains of the Prussian Kings.

EPILOGUE

THE FINAL PILGRIMAGE

There is something emotionally moving in seeing a family burial plot with parents and children resting near each other. It is our living contact with eternity that carries us all along. Without these reminders of those who have gone, there would be less to refresh our memories of the gifts they have given to us of life, love or gracious charm and friendship. God's love embraces us all, when we abide in his love.

OLD TOWN CEMETARY NORTHWEST OF VILLAGE

New Baptist Cemetary acquired in 1910 north of the Village
of Pound on US 141

New Baptist Cemetary acquired in 1910 north of the Village of Pound

New Baptist Cemetary in Pound

New Baptist Cemetary in Pound

New Baptist Cemetary in Pound

BIBLIOGRAPHY

(1) GESCHICHTE OST und WESTPREUSSENS, Bruno Schumacher Holzner Verlag Wurzburg

(2) CARLYLE WORKS: FREDERICK THE GREAT, Thomas Carlyle

(3) OSTPREUSSEN Band 16 Der Reihe Die Deutschen Lands Umschau Verlag Wurzburg.

(4) CATHERINE THE GREAT, Haslip Putnam 1977

(5) 1968 Britannica

(6) FROM CATHERINE TO KRUSCHEV, Adam Giesinger

(7) THE EMIGRATION FROM GERMANY TO RUSSIA, 1763-1862 Karl Stump AHSGR

(8) WELTSGESCHICHTE F. Seckler Verlag von Carl Hirsch Konstanz

(9) HISTORY OF FRENCH PROTESTANT REFUGEES, Charles Weiss 1854

(10) THE CZARS GERMANS, Hattie Plum Williams AHSGR

(11) THE REFORMATION OF THE SIXTEEN CENTURY, Leonard W. Cowie, Putnam 1970

(12) THE PRUSSIANS, Jean Quatrafages

(13) THE HUGUENOTS, Otto Zoff Fischer 1972

(14) THE HUGUENOTS, Samuel Smiles, Genealogical Pub. Co. 1972

(15) THE HENDERSON MENNONITES, Voth

(16) JOURNEY ACROSS RUSSIA, McDowell & Conger, National Geographic Soc.

(17) EVOLUTION OF THE EARTH, 2nd Ed. Dott and Batten

(18) WITH FIRE AND SWORD, Sienkiewicz

(19) THE TRAIL OF THE HUGUENOTS, Reaman Gen Pub 1972

(20) FIRE AT PESHTIGO, Robert W. Wells Prentiss Hall 1968

(21) TOLSTOY, Henri Troyat

(22) GERMAN COLONISTS IN SOUTH RUSSIA, Keller

(23) THE GERMAN ELEMENT IN THE U.S., Faust

(24) RUSSIAN LANGUAGE SOURCES ON GERMAN COLONISTS, Virden & Long Work Paper 22 AHSGR

(25) MIDDLE EUOPEAN MIGRATIONS, Arthur Flegel AHSGR Work Paper 8

(26) THE BIBLE

(27) THE WHITE LAMB, Mela Meisner Lindsay

(28) GEOLOGY OF THE GREAT LAKES, J. L. Hough 1958 Ill. Univ. Press p 289

(29) CONTRIBUTION OF GERMAN RUSSIANS TO RUSSIAN PROTESTANTISM Dr. Albert W. Ward, Jr. Work Paper 12-1973 p 20 et seq.)

(30) SEVENTY CENTS FOR A LIFETIME OF FREEDOM, Lindsay, p 40 Work Book 13 AHSGR

(31) HANDBUCH DER PRESSE DER HEIMAT VERTRIEBENEN Dr. Paul O. Kurth 1953 Holzner Verlag Kitzingen-Main

(32) DIE DEUTSCHEN IN WOHLYNIEN Heinz Heckel z. St. Beuthen (Oberschlesien)

(33) POLAND, KEY TO EUROPE, R. L. Duel, A. Knopf Pub.

(34) THE TWELVE, Edgar Goodspeed p 199

(35) FRENCH BLOOD IN AMERICA Lucian J. Fosdick, Baker 1911

(36) GESCHICHTE DES PROTESTANTISMUS IM RUSSLAND Erik Amburger – Evangelisches verlagwerk Stuttgart.

(37) EAST WIND Maria Zeitner Like & Ruth Hunt, Zonderhaven Pub.

(38) DEI DEUTSCHEN WOHLNIER IN UEBERSEE, Deutsche Post aus dem Osten pp 179-181 by Adolph Ehrt and also (33) p 247 et seq.

(39) MARTRYDOM OF ST. ANDREW, Budge

(40) NEMETSKIAII KOLONI NA VOLHNI by A. I. Vitovich, from Istoricheskii vestnik IX September 1915 pp 884-892 Library of Congress) Translated by William Lewis, Colorado State Univ. Fort Collins Colo.

(41) OUTLINE OF HISTORY H. G. Wills p 750 et seq.

(42) KUECHE KOCHEN by American Society of Germans from Russia 631 D St., Lincoln, Nebr.

(43) "TRADITIONAL UKRAINIAN COOKERY" by Savella Stachishin, Trident Press Limited, Winnipeg, Can. 1967

(44) GEOLOGY OF GREAT LAKES, Jack L. Hough, Ill. Univ. Press. 1958

(45) CATHOLIC ENCYCLOPAEDIA Spellman McGraw Hill

(46) CANADA A TO Z by Robert S. Kane, Doubleday & Co. 1964

APPENDIX

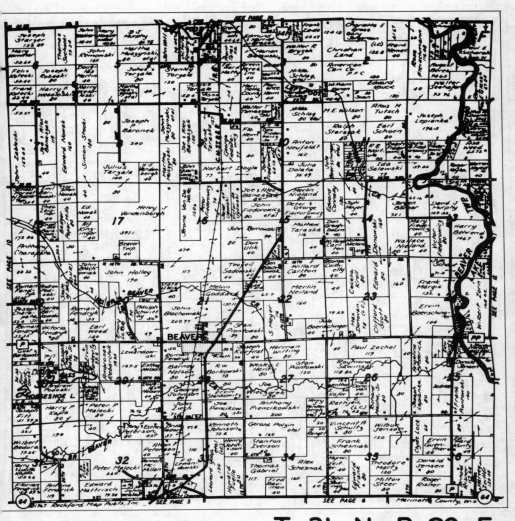

PARTS OF **BEAVER – LAKE**   **T. 31 N.– R. 20 E.**

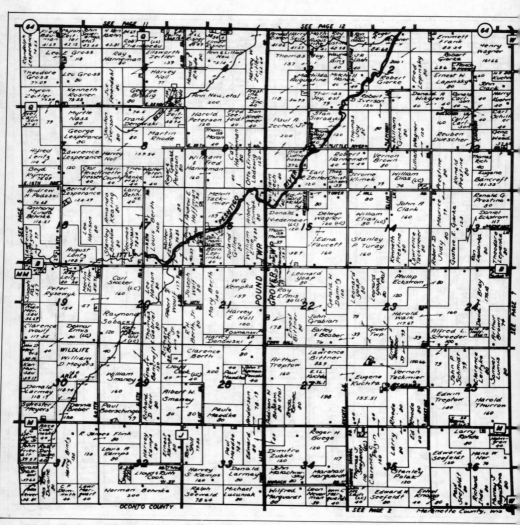

PART OF **GROVER – POUND**   **T. 30 N.– R. 21 E.**

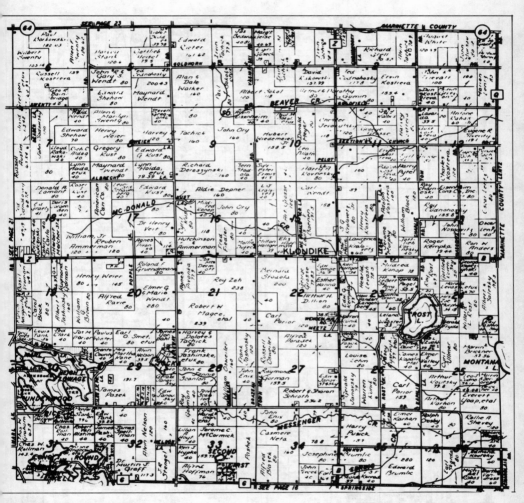

SOUTH PART **BRAZEAU** T. 30 N.–R. 19 E.

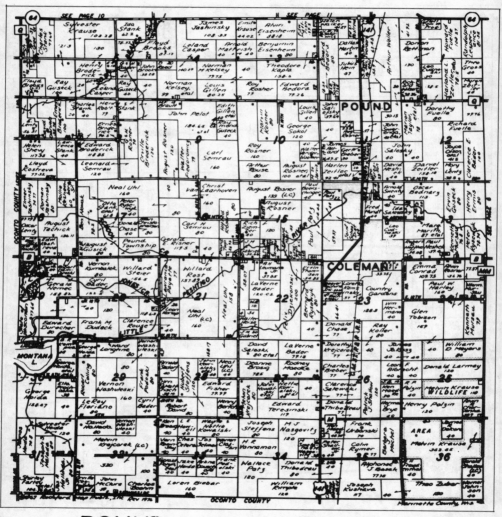

PART OF **POUND**

T. 30 N.-R. 20 E.

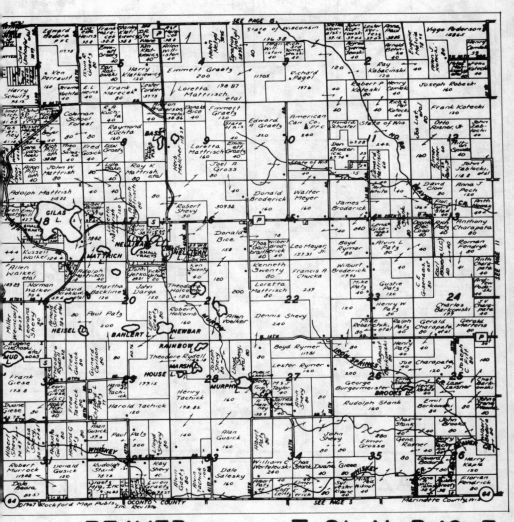

PART OF **BEAVER**   T. 31 N.–R. 19 E.

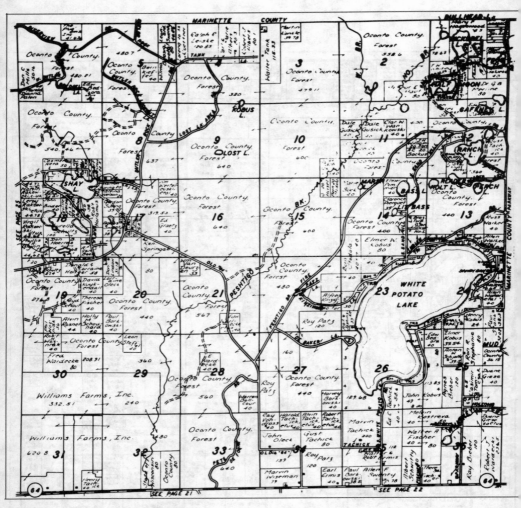

BRAZEAU　　　　　**T. 31 N.–R. 18 E.**

(Translation of Document shown on Page 38)

CONFIRMATION
BY
FREDERICK THE GREAT
OF
LAND GRANT AND INN KEEPING PRIVILEGES
In Rummy, Amts Mensguth
to
AMTS KRUEGER MICHAEL HANNUTTA
June 18th 1785

HIS ROYAL HIGHNESS OF PRUSSIA, our most gracious Lord and Sovereign, hereby confirms, ratifies and verifies, the lands privileges and properties described herein in his Majesty's Domain in the Jurisdiction of Rummy, Amts Mensuth, to

MICHAEL HANNUTTA

as left him by inheritance and the validity thereof in all points and clauses thereof and at the same time grants the lands and properties herein described with their acquirements and appurtenances, to the heirs and descendents and legitimate owners so long as this inheritance conyeyance manifests, for all time unto the holders thereof, providing the taxes assessed thereon shall be paid.

Signed June 18th 1785

SIGNATURE FRIEDRICH REX

CONFIRMATION ATTEST
For the inheritance Deed for
MICHAEL HANNUTTA in regard to his heirly
bequeathed freehold at Rummy, Mensguth
Jurisdiction (S) Blumenthal v. Gaudi

NOTE: The translation of the Michael Labusch document is much the same. Each document consists of upwords of a dozen pages.

THREE TREASURES FROM EAST PRUSSIA
Tuning Fork   Mortar and Pestal   Prayer-Song Book

INDEX

SUGGESTED READING

Emigration from Germany to Russia 1763-1860, Dr. Karl Stumpp, AHSGR

Pilgrims of the Earth, Richard D. Scheuerman, Galleon Press, 1976

The Black Sea Germans in the Dakotas, George Rath. Pine Hill Press, 1977

Russian-German Settlements in the U.S., Richard Sallet, N.D. Regional Studies, 1974

Pioneers on Two Continents, Theodore C. Wenzlaff, Service Press, Henderson Ne. 1974

The Pastor, Fred W. Gross, Dorrance, 1973

War and Peace, Tolstoy

Elizabeth and Catherine, Robert Coughlan, Time Inc. 1974

The Memoirs of Catherine the Great, Dominique Maroger, MacMillan

The Reformation of the Sixteenth Century, Leonard W. Cowie, Wayland, 1970

August 1914, Alexander Solzhenitsyn, 1972

The History of Wisconsin, Alice Smith (2 Vols.) Hist. Soc. of Wis., 1976

Les Actes des Colloques des Eglises Francaises et des Synodes des Eglises Etrangeres Refuges en Angletere, 1581-1654, Lymington London 1890

The High and the Mighty, Hans Brandenburg, (The emergence of the Evangelical Movement in Russia) Oxford Univ. Press 1977

The Fall of Eagles, C.L. Sulzberger, Crown Pub. 1977

Jesus spricht: Predigt die Heilsbotschaft der ganzen
Schöpfung! Wer dann glaubt und sich taufen läßt,
wird gerettet werden. Markus 16, 15. 16. (Menge)

1912 ❦ 1937

Festschrift zur Jubelfeier
des fünfundzwanzig=
jährigen Bestehens
der Baptistengemeinde
Ortelsburg
Evangelische Freikirche

Im Auftrage der Gemeinde herausgegeben
von Julius Labusch und Prediger Alfred Cierpke

Innenansicht der Kapelle

Festordnung zur Jubelfeier der Gemeinde

20.00 Uhr
Weihe- und Dankgottesdienst. Leitung: Prediger A. Cierpke

Am Festsonntag, den 5. September 1937

9.00—9.25 Uhr
Gebetsandacht. Leitung: Ältester W. Gallmeister sen.
9.30—10.45 Uhr
Festgottesdienst. Festpredigt: Prediger A. Pawlitzki, Lyck
11.00—12.00 Uhr
Feier des heiligen Abendmahls. Leitung: Prediger A. Cierpke
15.00—18.30 Uhr
Jubiläumsfest. Jubiläumspredigt: Prediger M. Morét,
Berlin-Spandau
Jubiläumsbericht: Fr. Ältester Julius Labusch
Kurze Grußreden: Vertreter der Stadt Ortelsburg, der Al-
lianz, des Bundes, der Vereinigung, der Nachbargemeinden
Grußreden i. A. sämtlicher Arbeitsgruppen der Gemeinde:
Ältester Fr. Hartwich und Diakon Johann Laskowski
Erfrischungspause
20.00—22.00 Uhr
Festabend. Leitung: Prediger A. Cierpke
„Bundesdienst ist Gemeindedienst"
Bundesältester Prediger P. Schmidt, Berlin
Gemeindegeschichte im Lichtbild
Erklärungen: Ältester A. Schulz

Nachklänge am Montag

15.00—16.30 Uhr
Gemeinschaftsstunde im Frauendienst
17.00—18.00 Uhr
Feierstunde der Sonntagsschule
20.00 Uhr
Gemeindeabend mit Austausch von Erinnerungen

Inhaltsverzeichnis

Vorwort

Ich wandte mich um, zu sehen nach der Stimme,
die mit mir redete. Und als ich mich wandte, sah
ich sieben goldene Leuchter und mitten unter den
sieben Leuchtern einen, der war eines Menschen
Sohn gleich. **Offb. 1, 12. 13.**

Groß und wunderbar ist die erste Erscheinung, die Johannes,
der Jünger Jesu, auf der Insel Patmos hat. Er sieht sieben
goldene Leuchter und Einen, der zwischen den Leuchtern wandelt.

Die Gemeinden Jesu sind goldene Leuchter.

Das sagt uns Offb. 1, 20. Das war auch unsere Erfahrung
sowohl beim Blättern in der Geschichte der Gemeinde Ortelsburg
als auch in der Mitarbeit und Beobachtung des Gemeindelebens.
Viele sehen die Gemeinde Jesu als eine geringe menschliche Organisation an. Der Herr sagt, sie sind mit Gold, dem edelsten
Metall dieser Erde, zu vergleichen und sind damit das Beste auf
der Welt. Geistreiche Menschen behaupten vielfach, nur ihnen sei
das Licht der Erkenntnis aufgegangen. Der Herr aber sagt von
den Gemeinden, daß sie Licht haben, denn sie sind mit den
Leuchtern zu vergleichen. (ὁ λύχνος = Leuchter, Leuchte, auch po-
etisch Fackel zum Unterschied von ὁ λαμπτήρ = Laterne, Lampe,
Kandelaber.) Es sind sieben goldene Leuchter. Sieben ist die
heilige Zahl, die Zahl der Vollendung. Drei ist die Zahl Gottes
und damit des Himmels, vier ist die Zahl der Erde. Himmel und
Erde gehören zusammen und begegnen und vereinigen sich in der
Gemeinde Jesu. Die Siebenzahl sagt uns, daß Gott alle Gemeinden sieht und ihm zuletzt nicht eine Gemeinde und nicht ein
Gläubiger fehlen wird.

**Unter ihnen wandelt auch in der Gegenwart
Jesus Christus.**

Die sieben goldenen Leuchter, die Johannes sah, waren herrlich.
Was aber ist ihre Herrlichkeit gegen die Herrlichkeit des Einen in
ihrer Mitte, von dem sie alle ihre Herrlichkeit haben!? Der Blick
des Jüngers Johannes haftet nicht mehr an den Leuchtern,
sondern an dieser gottmenschlichen Gestalt. „Menschensohn" nennt
er ihn. In der Beschreibung aber bezeichnet er ihn als Gottessohn.

Er trägt ein langes Gewand, Königsmantel und Priestergewand zugleich. Sein einst blutiges Haupt und wallendes Haar erstrahlt in vollkommener und fleckenloser Heiligkeit. Seine Augen, die einst um die heilige Stadt geweint haben, sind wie eine richtende Feuer= flamme. Die einst durchbohrten Füße leuchten wie Messing und durchschreiten jeden Gemeindegarten. Seine Heilandsstimme, die einst gerufen: „Kommt her, die ihr mühselig und beladen seid!", ist jetzt wie das Rauschen großer Wasser. Sieben Sterne, d. h. alle seine Boten, hält er in seiner rechten Hand, der Hand der Kraft. Sein Wort aber, das jetzt noch manchem Weltmenschen so ohnmächtig erscheint, wird zum zweiseitig scharf geschliffenen Schwert. Und doch leuchtet sein Angesicht all seinen Gläubigen freundlich wie die helle Sonne. Was einst Johannes bei diesem Gesicht erlebte — er fiel zu seinen Füßen als ein Toter —, muß jeder Sünder schon heute erleben. Dann macht er aber beim Ab= sterben der Sünde und der Welt die Erfahrung, die selig=froh schon Johannes gemacht hat. Der Herr legte seine rechte Hand auf ihn und sprach: „Fürchte dich nicht, ich bin der Erste und der Letzte und der Lebendige!" — So schreitet der Herr auch heute durch die Gemeinde Ortelsburg wie durch all seine Gemeinden. Fast ist es uns, als hörten wir seine Schritte und vernehmen deut= lich seine Stimme. Möge es für uns, für seine Gemeinde, zu aller Zeit heißen: „Jesus wandelte mit ihnen."

Vertrauensvoll lege ich diese Festschrift in die Hände unserer Geschwister und Freunde als erstes Zeitdokument der Gemeinde= geschichte der Gemeinde Ortelsburg. Der Herr Jesus wandelte mit der Gemeinde 25 Jahre lang. Mögen wir alle, die Brüder und die Schwestern, Freunde und Weltmenschen, besonders aber unsere Jugend und Kinder, das sehen und zur Anbetung kommen! —

Der Dank gehört zuerst dem erhöhten Haupt der Gemeinde, Jesu Christo, der uns solche Pfade geführt hat. Eine Reihe lieber Mitarbeiter, die an dieser Gemeindegeschichte mitgearbeitet haben, seien dankbar erwähnt. Die Vor= und Gemeindegeschichte hat der langjährige Älteste der Gemeinde, Br. Julius Labusch, in Ver= bindung mit mir geschrieben. Der gegenwärtige Älteste Br. Fried= rich Hartwich hat das Material mit durchgesehen und treu für= sorglich beraten. Br. Paul Zintarra hat das statistische Material geliefert. Schw. Edith Samorski und Schw. Hedwig Bollin haben sorgfältig und selbstlos die Schreibmaschinenarbeiten an= gefertigt. Ihnen allen sei an dieser Stelle herzlichst gedankt.

Möge diese Festschrift nicht einen Menschen, sondern den Herrn der Gemeinde, Jesum Christum, verherrlichen! Ihm sei Ehre in der Gemeinde in Zeit und Ewigkeit!

Alfred Cierpke.

I. Zur Gemeindegeschichte

1. Vorgeschichte

Die ersten Baptisten kamen in den Jahren 1869 bis 1871 nach
Ortelsburg. Es waren dieses die Familien Carl Werschkull und
Eduard Bollin. Ihnen folgten andere Familien. Durch gesegnete
Hausversammlungen schenkte der Herr Bekehrungen. Die regel=
mäßigen Hausandachten fanden insbesondere bei den Familien
Eduard Bollin in der Niederstraße und August Sarge in Beutner=
dorf statt. Unter den Männern, die mit ihnen dem Werke zum
Segen geworden sind, waren der langjährige Älteste Br. August
Sarge und Br. Jakob Samorski, beide 1883 getauft. Ihnen folgte
1891 Br. Wilhelm Gallmeister sen., den der Herr durch eine
gründliche Bekehrung seinem Werke schenkte. Die vorgenannten
fünf Brüder haben eine gründliche Pionierarbeit getan. In der
Gemeinde Rummy dienten der später nach Amerika ausgewanderte
Prediger Hein und seit 1871 Prediger F. W. Kottke. Diese ge=
segneten Zeugen ihres Herrn kamen öfters nach Ortelsburg und
hielten hier Versammlungen. Im Jahre 1888 wurde ein be=
sonderer Versammlungsraum im Hause der Geschw. Werschkull
in der Kaiserstraße erbaut, welcher der Gemeinde bis zum Jahre
1897 zur Verfügung stand, weil das Haus 1892 verkauft wurde.
Prediger Kottke verlegte am 1. Oktober 1894 seinen Wohn=
sitz von Rummy nach Ortelsburg, was für das hiesige Werk
ein großer Vorteil war. Im Jahre 1897 erbaute in dankens=
werter Weise Br. Jakob Samorski einen größeren Versamm=
lungsraum in der Königsberger Straße und vermietete ihn
der Gemeinde. So kam die Gemeinde wieder zu einem Heim. Das
Missionsgebiet der Gemeinde Rummy war so groß geworden, daß
sich die Gemeinde entschloß, in Br. Adolf Pawlitzki aus der
Stationsgemeinde Hirschberg i. Ostpr. im März 1899 einen
Missionsgehilfen anzustellen. Br. Pawlitzki nahm seinen Wohn=
sitz auch im zentral gelegenen Ortelsburg, nachdem er das Pre=
digerseminar in Hamburg von 1899 bis 1902 besucht hatte.

Das Werk des Herrn nahm zu. Der Wunsch, nun einen eigenen gottesdienstlichen Raum zu besitzen, wurde zum betenden Überlegen. Der Herr fügte es so, daß am 3. Mai 1903 der Grundstein zu der jetzigen Kapelle, mit einer Feier verbunden, gelegt wurde. Groß war die Freude, als am 10. Juli 1904 die fertige Kapelle feierlich ihrer Bestimmung übergeben wurde. Um das Grundstück und den Bau der Kapelle haben sich besonders die Brüder Jakob Samorski, Christian Kuczewski, Wilh. Gallmeister und Carl Werschkull verdient gemacht. Die Kapelle sollte nicht nur Ortelsburg, sondern der gesamten Gemeinde Rummy, deren Station Ortelsburg noch war, für größere Versammlungen zur Verfügung stehen. Die beiden Prediger Kottke und Pawlitzki haben sich gegenseitig gut ergänzt. Mit apostolischer Liebe und großem Zeugenmut hatte sich Br. Kottke dem weitverzweigten Werke gewidmet. Er war ein harmonischer Charakter. An der einmal erkannten Wahrheit, auch an der strengen Sitte, hielt er strikt fest. Alles, was weltlichen Charakter trug, wurde abgelehnt und bekämpft. Einrichtungen und Veranstaltungen — auch wenn sie noch so fromm schienen —, die aber mit der Heiligen Schrift nicht in Einklang zu bringen waren, mied er. Die teilweise gesetzliche Art hat der Gemeinde nicht geschadet, sie vielmehr vor Verweltlichung bewahrt. Daß in den Gemeindestunden über lange oder kurze Handschuhe, über Blumen am Hut, über paarweises Gehen zur Hochzeit und so viele äußerlichen Dinge debattiert wurde, mutet uns zwar seltsam an, zeugt aber von der Gewissenhaftigkeit, mit der das Leben bis in alle Einzelheiten, besonders der Gesinnung nach, unter Gottes Einfluß gestellt werden sollte. Br. Kottke hat z. B. eine Trauung abgelehnt, weil die Braut in einem Schleier erschien. Es war eben damals weltlich. Auch Trauringe wurden aus demselben Grunde nicht getragen. — Mit diesem treuen und biederen Gottesboten diente in jugendlicher Frische der Mann, der die jüngste Generation zu verstehen suchte und dem Evangelium die gesetzliche Schärfe zu nehmen bemüht war, aber doch die geistliche und schriftgemäße Tiefe, die sich durch erhöhte Geistesleistung kennzeichnet, gab. Es war Br. Pawlitzki, der seine Studienerfahrungen von Hamburg in die Praxis umzusetzen bemüht war. Für Br. Pawlitzki war es auch ein Vorteil, daß er die masurische Muttersprache des Südens unserer Provinz verstand. So konnte er hier durch zielbewußte Wirksamkeit und nüchterne Schriftauslegung eine Lebensarbeit tun und zu dem aus der

8

Prediger F. W. Kottke

Prediger M. Morét

Prediger U. Pawlitzki

Prediger U. Cierpke

Ältester A. Sarge

Ältester A. Meier

Ältester J. Labusch

Ältester Fr. Hartwich

Gemeindegeschichte Ortelsburg nicht fortzudenkenden Gottesmann
werden. Im Herbst 1907 verlegte Br. Kottke seinen Wohnsitz
nach Romanowen. Br. Pawlitzki war es fortan vorbehalten, die
vier Arbeitsplätze der Gemeinde Rummy, nämlich Rummy, Ortelsburg, Gr.-Schöndamerau und Olschöwken, und auch eine ganze
Anzahl kleinerer Predigtplätze allein zu bedienen. Zu dieser Zeit
half in der Gemeinde Br. Gustav Johannes Thiel im Missionsdienst. Br. Thiel war ein erfahrener Mann, schlicht und mit
Gottesfurcht erfüllt. Ehe er den Namen Gottes aussprach, machte
er jedesmal eine Ehrfurchtspause. Leider hat ihn sein leidender
Körper stark behindert. — Im Jahre 1909 erhielt die Gemeinde
Rummy nach zwölfjähriger Vorarbeit und der zunächst erteilten
Ablehnung des Gesuchs Korporationsrechte. Vor der Behörde
hatte die Gemeinde ihren Sitz in Ortelsburg. Die Gemeinde entwickelte sich im Frieden. Prediger A. Pawlitzki nahm zum 15. Mai
1911 nach neunjähriger gesegneter Tätigkeit in Ortelsburg einen
Ruf der Gemeinde Insterburg an. In dem Bemühen, wieder
einen geeigneten Missionsboten zu bekommen, wurde die Gemeinde
Ortelsburg auf Br. Maximo Morét aus Berlin aufmerksam gemacht, und sie berief ihn in den Missionsdienst. Br. Morét kam
Weihnachten 1911, ging jedoch mit Empfehlungen der Gemeinde
im nächsten Jahr zum Studium ins Predigerseminar nach Hamburg. Zu gleicher Zeit wählte die Gemeinde Rummy Br. Jersak
zu ihrem Prediger, der aber nur ganz kurze Zeit hier verblieb. —
Ein markanter Zeuge Gottes war zu jener Zeit der frühere Lehrer
Schallnaß, der sich nach seiner Abdankung ganz dem Predigtdienst
hingegeben hatte. Auch er diente des öfteren in Ortelsburg. Er
war es auch, der die Einweihung des Gemeindesaales bei Br.
Jakob Samorski leitete. Prediger Schallnaß vollzog auch die erste
Taufe nach der Gemeindegründung in Ortelsburg. — Im Laufe
der Jahre hatten sich die Mitglieder in Ortelsburg so vermehrt,
daß Bemühungen um einen eigenen Kassenhaushalt und eine
selbständige Gemeinde in die Wege geleitet werden konnten. —
Als Hilfsprediger der Gemeinde Rummy diente der jetzt 98 Jahre
alte Br. Ernst Porps, der auch ab und zu zur Evangeliumsverkün-
digung nach Ortelsburg kam. — Von der Selbständigwerdung
wollte zunächst die Muttergemeinde nichts wissen. Nach längeren
Verhandlungen, die im Auftrag der Ostpreußischen Vereinigung
Prediger Pawlitzki als Vorsitzender der Gemeindestunde und Br.
Julius Labusch als Schriftführer hatten, erklärte sich schließlich die

Gemeinde Rummy damit einverstanden, daß Ortelsburg, ihr ge=
segnetes Arbeitsfeld, eine selbständige Gemeinde wird. Die ent=
scheidende Gemeindestunde, in der die Mitglieder aus Ortelsburg,
Rohmanen, Schiemanen und Umgebung zwecks Gründung einer
selbständigen Gemeinde mit den Segenswünschen der Mutter=
gemeinde entlassen wurden, war am 7. Juli 1912 in Rummy. Am
18. August 1912 wurde alsdann die Gemeinde Ortelsburg mit
239 Mitgliedern gegründet. Ältester wurde Br. August Sarge,
Diakone wurden die Brüder Christ. Kuczewski und Friedr. Sarge. In
den Vorstand gewählt wurden die Brüder Wilhelm Brosch,
Wilhelm Gallmeister, Jakob Janowski, Karl Jaschinski, Julius
Labusch und Jakob Samorski. Die der Gemeinde gehörige Kapelle
war mit einer Hypothek von Rm. 12 000.— belastet. Doch konnte
der Zinsaufwand durch Mieten usw. gedeckt werden. Die Mitglieder
waren sich der Pflicht bewußt, für die Sache des Herrn Opfer zu
bringen.

2. Protokoll der Gemeindeversammlung

Rummy, den 7. Juli 1912.

Vorsitzender: Br. Pawlitzki, Insterburg.
Anwesend: Br. Wieczorek, Schwentainen, Mitglied des Ver=
einigungskomitees.
Protokollführer: Br. Labusch, Ortelsburg.

Seinerzeit hatten die Geschwister aus Ortelsburg erklärt,
aus dem Gemeindeverband der Baptistengemeinde Rummy=Or=
telsburg auszutreten, um sich als Baptistengemeinde Ortelsburg
zu organisieren. Nach einigen Verhandlungen und Belehrungen
auch durch das Vereinigungskomitee zogen die Geschwister aus
Ortelsburg diese ihre Erklärung zurück und reichten ein Gesuch
und Bitte um Entlassung aus der Gemeinde zwecks Konstituie=
rung als selbständige Gemeinde ein.

Nach einigen Erklärungen wird beantragt und gegen eine
Stimme beschlossen: Die Gemeindeversammlung erklärt sich im
Prinzip mit einer Trennung der Gemeinde einverstanden.

Es kommt nun darauf an, die Trennung so vorzunehmen, daß
beide Gemeinden, sowohl die Muttergemeinde als auch die Tochter=
gemeinde, lebensfähig sind und bleiben. Nach Meinung einiger
Brüder sollte die Trennung so geschehen, daß etwa Rohmanen,
Seedanzig, Schiemanen, Plohsen, Passenheim, Jedwabno zu

10

Ortelsburg gehören, und die Stationen Schöndamerau, Olschöw=
ken, Mensguth nebst den übrigen Stationen, als zur Gemeinde
Rummy gehörig, verbleiben.

Es wird beantragt und beschlossen, die Grenzen der beiden
Gemeinden in der angedeuteten Weise festzulegen und die Ge=
schwister der zuerst genannten Stationen zwecks Gründung als
selbständige Gemeinde zu entlassen. Sie gehören mit ihren
Pflichten und Rechten zu der bezeichneten Gemeinde, können aber
die Versammlungen dort besuchen, wo es ihnen passend erscheint.

Bezüglich der vermögensrechtlichen Auseinandersetzung wird
gegen einen anderen Antrag, eine Predigerwohnung für die Ge=
meinde Rummy als Gesamtgemeinde zu bauen, folgendes be=
schlossen:

Das Kapellengrundstück Ortelsburg wird ohne jegliche Ent=
schädigung der Gemeinde Ortelsburg überlassen. Die der Gemeinde
vermachten Legate, Rm. 1000.— von Br. Kolwe und Rm. 300.—
von Schw. Blanknagel, werden als Grundstock zum Bau einer
Predigerwohnung für die Gemeinde Rummy verwandt. Die neue
Gemeinde Ortelsburg zahlt zum Bau dieser Wohnung Rm. 1000.—
zu, und im Übrigen baut die Gemeinde Rummy die Prediger=
wohnung allein. Die vorhandene Taufwäsche bleibt gemeinsames
Eigentum der Korporationsgemeinde.

Ferner wird beschlossen: Die beiden Gemeinden bleiben als Kor=
porationsgemeinde eins. Der jeweilige Leiter der Gemeinde Or=
telsburg ist der 1. Vorsitzende, der jeweilige Leiter der Gemeinde
Rummy der 2. Vorsitzende der Korporationsgemeinde. Die Ge=
meinde Rummy hat das Recht, 2 Vorstandsmitglieder mehr als
die Gemeinde Ortelsburg für die Korporationsgemeinde zu stellen.

Die Geschwister wünschen ein brüderliches Zusammenwirken
der beiden Gemeinden, gegründet auf persönliches, herzliches und
geschwisterliches Verhältnis.

Die Geschwister aus Ortelsburg und Rummy bitten gegen=
seitig für alles Unliebsame, das in den in dieser Angelegenheit
gepflogenen Verhandlungen vorgekommen ist, um Verzeihung
und wünschen fortan mehr in ihrem Tun und Handeln Jesum zu
verherrlichen.

Br. Pawlitzki und Br. Wieczorek, Letzterer auch im Namen
seiner Gemeinde, wünschen den beiden Gemeinden Rummy und
Ortelsburg Gottes reichsten Segen.

gez.: A. Pawlitzki.   gez.: J. Labusch.

3. Gemeindegeschichte

Die neugegründete Gemeinde stand unter der Leitung ihres Ältesten Br. August Sarge. Ihm standen drei Diakone und sieben Vorstandsmitglieder zur Seite. An Arbeitsgruppen in der Gemeinde waren vorhanden: ein Gesangverein, ein Jugendverein und zwei Sonntagsschulen — eine in Ortelsburg und die andere in Gr.-Schiemanen. Die Gründung der Gemeinde war ordnungsmäßig geschehen, Missionseifer war da, nur der Hirte der Gemeinde fehlte. Da berief die Gemeinde für die beiden Ferienmonate Juli und August 1912 Br. G. Freutel vom Predigerseminar, der im Segen diente. In der masurischen Sprache dienten seinerzeit ab und zu die Brüder Frassa und Zagray. Zu ihrem Seelsorger berief die Gemeinde im Juli 1913 Br. Otto Schäfer, der seine Studien im Predigerseminar in Hamburg abgeschlossen hatte. Bis zu seinem Kommen diente hier der gesanglich und musikalisch begabte Br. Emil Janssen aus Oldenburg, der dann im Herbst 1913 zum Predigerseminar ging. Als ein Lied zur Predigereinführung fehlte, setzte er sich hin und komponierte eins. An seine Wirksamkeit denkt die Gemeinde mit Freuden zurück. Am 13. Januar 1913 wurde der Martha-Verein gegründet, der den Frauen Gelegenheit zur Gemeinschaft untereinander und zum Liebesdienst an Kranken und Alten bot. — Br. Schäfer ging mit großen Eifer ans Werk. Er war begabt und lieferte gute Predigten. Er ging jedoch schon im April 1914 nach Allenstein. Bis zu dieser Zeit war einer der treuesten Stützen der jungen Gemeinde der Schmiedemeister Br. August Sarge, der als Ältester ihr vorstand. Gleich nach seiner Bekehrung hatte er in Einfalt, aber wahrer Herzensfrömmigkeit anderen Leuten von dem Herrn Jesus erzählt. Seine jahrelang geübten Lesegottesdienste waren gern besucht. Eins seiner Lieblingslieder war: „Näher, mein Gott, zu dir." Als die verantwortungsvollen Gemeindeaufgaben über seine Kräfte gingen, trat er 1913 von seinem Posten als Ältester zurück, hat aber als ältester Diakon der Gemeinde bis zu seinem Heimgang am 29. November 1932 der Gemeinde treu gedient. An seine Stelle wurde Br. August Meier am 4. Dezember 1913 als Ältester gewählt. Zu Diakonen wurden die Brüder Christian Kuczewski und Fritz Sarge am gleichen Tage ernannt. — Die gesegnete Entwickelung des Werkes wurde durch den am 1. August 1914 ausgebrochenen Weltkrieg jäh unterbrochen. Unsere wehr-

12

pflichtigen Brüder mußten hier an der Grenze sofort zum Heeres=
dienst. Schwere Kriegserlebnisse erlebte unsere Stadt, als gleich
im ersten Kriegsmonat die Russen hier einzogen und große Ver=
wüstungen anrichteten. Die Zahl der in Ortelsburg verbliebenen
Geschwister war klein, doch bemühte man sich, das Werk des
Herrn zu fördern. Gesangverein, Jugendverein und Sonntags=
schule wurden wieder ins Leben gerufen. Regelmäßige Tauffeiern
bildeten die Frucht der neuen fleißigen Arbeit. Ein Höhepunkt war
der 8. Oktober 1916, an dem die Ordination von Prediger M.
Morét in Anwesenheit der Prediger Kottke und Wieczorek er=
folgte. Prediger Morét hatte seine volle Kraft dem Herrn zur
Verfügung gestellt. Die Predigten fanden guten Anklang. Es gab
gut besuchte Versammlungen. Im Kontakt mit den Geschwistern
versuchte Br. Morét viele zur Mitarbeit heranzuziehen. Selbst in
den Nachversammlungen bei Evangelisationen arbeiteten die Ge=
schwister praktisch mit. Die zarte Gesundheit hielt dem anstrengen=
den Dienst in der Gemeinde auf die Dauer doch nicht stand. In=
folge dauernder Krankheit gab Br. Morét seinen Dienst am
1. Oktober 1920 auf, um zunächst seine Gesundheit wieder her=
zustellen. Für die Gemeinde war es schwer, einen geeigneten
Prediger als Nachfolger zu finden. Das Suchen dauerte fast zwei
Jahre. Immer wieder kam die Gemeinde auf Br. Pawlitzki zu=
rück. Groß war deshalb die Freude, als Prediger Pawlitzki seinen
Dienst in Insterburg auf den wiederholten Ruf der Gemeinde
hin aufgab und zum 1. Juli 1922 wieder nach Ortelsburg kam.
Unter seiner zielsicheren Leitung, seinen nüchternen und tief=
gründigen Predigten und nicht zuletzt durch die treuen Haus=
besuche hat sich die Mitgliederzahl ständig vermehrt. Sie stieg
von 257 im Jahre 1922 auf 437 im Jahre 1935. — In Gr.=
Schiemanen, der größten Station, wurde im Jahre 1928 eine
Kapelle mit einem Kostenaufwand von Rm. 12 000.— erbaut.
Die Kapelle in Ortelsburg, in gotischem Kirchenstil erbaut, machte
auch in ihrer inneren Ausgestaltung einen kirchlichen Eindruck,
entsprach aber nicht den Ansprüchen, die im allgemeinen an eine
Baptistenkapelle gestellt werden. Die Gemeinde hat sich ent=
schlossen, durch einen inneren Umbau, nachdem bereits vorher
die Kanzel geändert worden war, den Raum freundlicher und
zweckmäßiger zu gestalten. Der Umbau geschah im Jahre 1929
von sachkundiger und außerordentlich geschickter Hand durch Br.
Johann Laskowski, während Br. Wilhelm Gallmeister jun. eine

13

schöne praktische Beleuchtungsanlage lieferte. Kostenaufwand: rund Rm. 12000.—. Nicht lange danach wurde das Kastellan= haus von den Brüdern Johann Laskowski und Albert Baron er= baut. Für diese praktischen Bauten ist die Gemeinde dankbar. Auch die Orgel, die bis dahin in den Kapellenraum hineingebaut war und den Platz für die Sänger stark beeinträchtigte, wurde in einen Vorbau eingebaut und bedeutend vergrößert, so daß sie jetzt einen schönen musikalischen Klangkörper darstellt. Um die neue Orgel hat sich unser Gesangsmeister Br. Julius Labusch sehr ge= müht. — Die auf dem Kapellengrundstück ruhenden Schulden sind, nachdem von der alten Schuld ein Teil infolge Geldentwer= tung herabgesetzt werden konnte, bis auf rund Rm. 5000.— be= glichen worden. Von Interesse dürfte es sein, daß während der Geldentwertung die Entschädigung des Predigers teilweise in Naturalien erfolgte. Die Gemeindekasse schloß im Jahre 1923 mit einem Betrag von Rm. 812 561 562 380 377.— ab. Das sind 812 Billionen, 561 Milliarden, 562 Millionen, 380 Tausend, 387 Mark. — Auch als Konferenzgemeinde wurde Ortelsburg mehrere Male in Anspruch genommen. So fanden — noch als Station der Gemeinde Rummy — eine Konferenz der Ost= preußischen Jünglingsvereinigung und eine Konferenz der Ost= preußischen Jungfrauenvereinigung statt. Als selbständige Ge= meinde hatte Ortelsburg im Jahre 1921 die letzte Ostpreußische Jünglings=Vereinigungskonferenz mit 100 Abgeordneten und Ostern 1922 die erste Ostpreußische Jugend=Vereinigungskonferenz mit 205 Abgeordneten. Einen guten Feriendienst im Juli und August des Jahres 1924 tat Br. Hermann Zart vom Prediger= seminar. Auch die Ostpreußische Gemeinde=Vereinigungskonferenz fand hier 1924 und 1931 statt. — Nach dreizehnjähriger ge= segneter Tätigkeit als Prediger und Seelsorger der Gemeinde nahm Br. A. Pawlitzki einen Ruf der Gemeinde Lyck zum 1. September 1935 an. Die Gemeinde hatte sich im Frieden stetig entwickelt und ließ ihren vielgeliebten Seelsorger ungern ziehen. Br. Pawlitzki hat hier in den fast 25 Jahren eine Lebensarbeit getan. — Die Gemeinde hatte zum 1. August des Jahres 1935 Br. Adolf Gärtner als jungen Prediger vom Predigerseminar gerufen, der ursprünglich neben Br. Pawlitzki sich besonders der Jugend widmen sollte. Nach einigen Wochen der Zusammenarbeit und einem fleißigen Jugenddienst hat Br. Gärtner den vollen Gemeindedienst dann bis zum 1. April 1936 getan und sich Mühe

14

gegeben, den vielen Anforderungen an ihn nachzukommen. Sein Vikariatsjahr neigte sich dem Ende zu. Da nahm er einen Ruf der Gemeinde Neustadt, O.-Schl., vom Bunde empfohlen, an.

Es hat sich als segensreich erwiesen, an die Seite der Prediger Älteste zu setzen, die verantwortlich mit ihnen zusammenarbeiten und ihre besten Stützen sind. Wir nannten schon den Namen des langjährigen ersten Ältesten der Gemeinde, Br. August Sarge sen. Als er zurücktrat, wurde am 4. Dezember 1913 Br. August Meier an seine Stelle gewählt, der seinen Dienst bis zum Kommen von Br. M. Morét im Jahre 1915 in Treue versehen hat. Br. Meier hat seine vielseitigen Gemeindeerfahrungen segensvoll für die Gemeinde Ortelsburg verwandt. Im Jahre 1920 wurde Br. Julius Labusch durch das Vertrauen der Gemeinde zum Ältesten gewählt. Er hat dieses Amt bis zum Jahre 1935 so verwaltet, daß die Gemeinde sein Lebenselement wurde und er mit Leib und Seele an ihr hing. Am 1. April 1935 übernahm Br. Friedrich Hartwich, vom Vertrauen der Gemeinde getragen, seinen Dienst als verantwortlicher Ältester. Mit Sorgfalt und Liebe hat sich Br. Hartwich diesem Dienst gewidmet und der Gemeinde Bestes gesucht, — zunächst an der Seite von Br. Pawlitzki und nach seinem Weggang in Verbindung mit Br. Gärtner. Auch der neue Prediger fand bald sein Vertrauen, nämlich Br. Alfred Cierpke, Königsberg-Tragheim, der zum 1. Juni 1936 berufen wurde. Nachdem Br. Cierpke bereits vor seinem Dienstantritt am 12. April 1936 13 Neubekehrte getauft hat, sind bis zum Jubiläum durch fünf weitere Taufen 70 neue Mitglieder der Gemeinde hinzugetan worden, was uns alle zur Dankbarkeit und Anbetung zwingt. Möge uns der Herr auch weiterhin solche Zunahmen schenken!

Die Gemeinde entwickelt sich in Frieden unter dem sichtbaren Segen des Herrn. Eine Baptistengemeinde sollte immer Missionsgemeinde sein, damit sich der Herr fruchtbar und segensvoll in ihr offenbare!

4. Stationen

Sie waren täglich und stets beieinander einmütig . . .
und brachen das Brot hin und her in den Häusern.

Apg. 2, 46.

Es gibt nur wenige Baptistengemeinden in unserem Bunde, die nicht Außenarbeitsfelder — wir nennen sie Stationen — haben. Sie werden zumeist von der Muttergemeinde sehr gepflegt, denn in ihnen herrscht dadurch, daß die Arbeit jung ist, ein frischer Missionsgeist. — Die Gemeinde Ortelsburg hat 4 Stationen: Gr.-Schiemanen, Passenheim, Plohsen und Rohmanen.

Gr.-Schiemanen.

Der Anfang der Missionsarbeit in Schiemanen reicht weit zurück. In den Jahren 1860 und 1861 kamen die Brüder Nasgowitz und Hein als Sendboten Jesu nach Jeschonowitz und Schiemanen. Als Frucht dieser Arbeit wurden folgende Geschwister getauft: Br. Wilhelm Tantius und seine Ehefrau Gottliebe am 5. Juli 1861 und Br. Johann Caika am 21. Juli 1861. Im Jahre 1863 kamen eine Reihe Geschwister dazu, denen der Herr das Herz auftat. Br. Tantius hat längere Zeit mit dem Wort gedient. Als Br. Kottke sein weitverzweigtes Gemeindegebiet bediente, waren Br. Para und Br. Johann Wittkowski Diakone in Gr.-Schiemanen. Bis zum Jahre 1906 war Gr.-Schiemanen Station der Gemeinde Kl.-Dankheim, von da ab Station der Gemeinde Rummy. Nach der Organisation von Ortelsburg als selbständige Gemeinde zählte Gr.-Schiemanen als Station von Ortelsburg. Das Werk entwickelte sich langsam, aber stetig. Es fand seinen besonderen Freudentag in der am 26. April 1928 erfolgten Grundsteinlegung zur Kapelle. Seit der Zeit befindet sich die Station in einem normalen Aufstieg. Leiter ist Br. Wilhelm Para. Ihm steht in der Sonntagsschule, die jahrelang Br. Fritz Goliath geleitet hat, jetzt Br. Gustav Grabosch I zur Seite.

Passenheim

In der heute 4000 Einwohner zählenden Stadt ist seit dem Jahre 1900 von unserer Seite aus Reichsgottesarbeit getan worden. Sie fand in der Wohnung von Bäckermeister Labusch statt, der später nach Westfalen zog. Seit dem Jahre 1920 fanden die Versammlungen zumeist bei Geschw. Suchalla, vorübergehend auch bei Geschw. Lubinetzki, statt. Der Missionswagen

Der Gemeinde=Brüderrat

Gesangchor

Frauengruppe

Gitarrengruppe

unseres Bundes war 1934 auch in Paffenheim und hatte gute Versammlungen. Das Werk fand hier wohl den härtesten Boden. Zu dieser Station gehören heute 20 Mitglieder. Leiter ist Br. Emil Suchalla. Die Sonntagsschule wird von den Schwestern Elise Rekewitz und Lydia Suchalla gepflegt. Die Versammlungen finden in einem dazu hergerichteten Zimmer statt.

Plohsen.

Obwohl die Entfernung von den Wohnungen der Geschwister von Plohsen und den Ortschaften um Plohsen herum fast die gleiche ist, finden dort seit einer Reihe von Jahren monatlich ein bis zwei Stubenversammlungen bei unseren Geschw. Gottlieb Nischik statt. Seit einem Jahr sind die Versammlungen regelmäßig sonntäglich und werden mit Liebe durch Br. Friedrich Latza vorbereitet. Eine kleine Sonntagsschule ist ins Leben gerufen worden und wird von Br. Emil Jortzik betreut. Auch in diesen kleinen Versammlungen offenbart sich der Herr.

Rohmanen.

In diesem langgestreckten Dorf fanden Versammlungen schon vor der Gründung unserer Gemeinde statt. Die Sendboten Gottes aus Rummy haben hier viele Stubenversammlungen gehalten, in denen Menschen zum Frieden mit Gott gekommen sind. Die Arbeit geschah zeitweilig auch in Arbeitsgemeinschaft mit der Station Gr.-Schöndamerau. Bei der Gründung der Gemeinde Ortelsburg wurde die Station übernommen. Die Versammlungen fanden in den vergangenen Jahren nur gelegentlich statt. Möge Gott diese Kleinarbeit segnen! Leiter ist Br. Jakob Janowski.

5. Erinnerungen an Ortelsburg

Da wird gar manche Zeit mit ihren Gnadenwundern in meinem Geiste wach. Stunden waren es, in denen verlorene Söhne zum Vaterhaus zurückkehrten und verirrte Töchter den Heimweg zu Christo fanden. Doch darüber wird von den himmlischen Registratoren für die Analen der oberen Welt Bericht geschrieben.

Zum Lob des Herrn will ich über göttliche Hilfe und Durchhilfe aus der Zeit etwas anführen, in die der Erwerb, die Sicherstellung und Erhaltung des Gemeindeeigentums fällt. Diese Dinge

liegen 15 bis 20 Jahre vor der Gründung der Gemeinde Ortels=
burg zurück, sind aber für die Gestaltung der Gemeinde von ent=
scheidender Bedeutung.

Meine annähernd 25 Jahre während Tätigkeit in Ortelsburg
setzt sich außer den über zweieinhalb Jahren des Helferdienstes
vor und während der Seminarzeit aus 9 Jahren nach der Se=
minarzeit — 1902 bis 1911 — und über dreizehn Jahren der
letzten Wirksamkeit zusammen. Diese Zeitspannen gegeneinander
gestellt, ergeben folgendes Bild: Die Zeit von 1902 bis 1911, in
der Ortelsburg Station der Gemeinde Rummy war, war für
Ortelsburg mit seinem Kapellenbau die Zeit des Wagens, des
Handelns, der Hetzarbeit und mancher dunkel heraufziehenden
Wolken und drohender Stürme, die aber von der Sonne des
Heils durchbrochen und von der Hand des göttlichen Helfers zer=
teilt wurden. Die letzten 13 Jahre der zweiten Dienstperiode
waren demgegenüber trotz des Baues der Kapelle in Gr.=
Schiemanen und des Umbaues der Kapelle in Ortelsburg eine
Zeit ruhiger Entwickelung und des gleichmäßigen Aufbaues der
Gemeinde. Denn da waren sach= und fachkundige Brüder da, die
solche Ausführungen auf ihren Schultern mitgetragen haben.

Nachdem die Erstlinge in Ortelsburg sich zunächst in Wohn=
zimmern versammelten und dann zur Station ausgebildet einen
Saal in der Kaiserstraße und später in Beutnerdorf innehatten,
wurde 1902 der Bauplatz erworben. Doch es war weder das
Kaufgeld noch ein Baufonds vorhanden. Da wurde es nach der
Rückkehr vom Seminar neben der Seelengewinnung meine Auf=
gabe, die Mittel für den Bau der Kapelle flüssig zu machen,
während der 62jährige Br. Kottke die Seelsorge übte.

Die erste Frage, bei der in guter Meinung verschiedene Auf=
fassungen zutage traten, war die Frage der Bauart. Die einen hielten
es für ratsam, zunächst ein Wohnhaus mit einem Versammlungs=
saal zu errichten und dann Gelder für eine später zu erbauende
Kapelle zu sammeln. Andere Brüder wollten eine neuzeitliche
Kapelle mit Prediger= und Kastellanwohnung erbaut haben. Bei
der Abstimmung entschied die Mehrheit für letzteres. Das erweckte
bei Ersteren Besorgnis und Befürchtung und führte zu dem un=
bedachten Ausspruch, daß die Kapelle doch zum Tanzsaal werde,
da es nicht möglich sein werde, ihre Kosten zu tragen.

Mit welchen Empfindungen des Gottvertrauens wir am
Pfingstdienstag, den 2. Juni 1903, den Grundstein legten, dafür

18

sprechen die Textworte: „Wir haben einen Gott, der da hilft"
(Pf. 68, 21) und: „Fürchte dich nicht, du kleine Herde" (Luk. 12, 32),
die wir der Feier voranstellten. Beide Schriftstellen, in den Steinen
vor dem Eingang der Kapelle eingemeißelt, sollen den nachkom=
menden Geschlechtern Kunde hiervon geben.

In diesem Gottvertrauen galt es zu handeln und Opfer zu
bringen. Durch Aufstellung von Listen wurden 6000 bis 7000
Mark innerhalb der Gemeinde gezeichnet. Mein geschätzter väter=
licher Bruder Kottke — mit dem wir über die Bauart nicht
gleicher Meinung waren — tat in aller Treue den Dienst an der
Gemeinde, während ich vom Herbst 1903 bis 1905 die meisten
Gemeinden in Ost= und Westpreußen und viele Gemeinden im
Bunde über Berlin hinaus bis nach Emden, dem Industriegebiet
und bis Frankfurt a. M. als Kollektant bereist habe. Etwa
Rm. 6800.— durfte ich für den Bau buchen und Rm. 6000.—
nach Abzug der Bahngelder an die Baukasse abführen.

Als am 10. Juli 1904 die Kapelle eingeweiht wurde, verschönte
auch schon die Orgel den Gemeindegesang. Diese wurde nicht aus
Baugeldern, sondern aus Extragaben und Sonderbeiträgen der
hierfür interessierten Geschwister beschafft. Der Versammlungs=
besuch nahm ständig zu. Er wies am Vormittag unter hundert
und am Nachmittag über hundert Besucher auf. Das war mir
eine besondere Freude.

Wie eine gewitterschwüle Wolke zog im Frühjahr 1907 die
Sorge um die Sicherstellung des Gemeindeeigentums herauf. Nur
einige Brüder, die als verantwortliche Dienstträger dastanden,
wußten um diese Not. Br. W. Gallmeister sen., einer der beiden
Namensträger der Kapelle, war nach Kl.=Heyde bei Deutsch=Eylau
verzogen. Durch wirtschaftliche Bedrängnis und die Verflochten=
heit der Umstände kam das Kapellengrundstück in Gefahr, un=
rechtmäßig belastet zu werden. Da galt es zu handeln. Br. Gall=
meister trug in vorbildlicher Weise Sorge um das Wohl der Ge=
meinde. In aller Stille wurde das Kapellengrundstück auf einen
anderen Bruder als Namensträger übertragen. Doch dieser Vor=
fall sowie auch der Grundbuchbesitz der Kapelle in Rummy, die
noch auf den Namen des Bruders Ferdinand Schimanski ein=
getragen war — der sich längst in einem Altersheim in Amerika
befand —, wurden Anlaß, mit allem Nachdruck die Rechtsfähigkeit
der Gemeinde zu erwerben.

Die Beschaffung der vielen Unterlagen hierfür war mühevoll

und zeitraubend. Nach einer fünf Monate langen Vorarbeit konnte das Gesuch am 19. August 1907 eingereicht werden. Leider wurde dieses zunächst vom zuständigen Ministerium mit der Begründung abgelehnt, daß die „dauernde Lebensfähigkeit der Gemeinde nicht gewährleistet" sei. Da gab es wiederholte Reisen zur Regierung und Klarlegungen über' die Dinge. Da soll es nicht unerwähnt bleiben, daß der zuständige Dezernent durch sein wohlwollendes Verhalten uns wertvolle Dienste geleistet hat. Das neu eingereichte Gesuch hatte vollen Erfolg, und nach zweieinhalb Jahre langen Bemühungen konnte die Kapelle in Ortelsburg am 15. Dezember 1909 auf den Namen der Korporationsgemeinde aufgelassen werden.

Im Herbst 1907 verließ mein väterlicher Freund Br. Kottke Ortelsburg und folgte, 67jährig, noch einem Ruf der Gemeinde Romanowen, der er noch über vier Jahre mit der Heilsbotschaft diente. So blieb ich aber auf dem weiten Missionsfeld Rummy-Ortelsburg allein und hatte auf den ländlichen Plätzen am Sonntag meistens viermal in der deutschen und masurischen Sprache zu predigen. Die Folge war, daß ich Anfang Mai 1910 ernstlich erkrankte und meine ersten Ferien, die vier Monate dauerten, nehmen mußte. Nach einem Ferienaufenthalt in Zippelsförde und einer weiteren Kur in Lippspringe konnte ich die Arbeit an der Gemeinde am 11. September wieder aufnehmen. Da ich mich aber den vielen Anforderungen auf dem verzweigten Gebiet mit der geschwächten Kraft nicht gewachsen sah, erkannte ich in dem Ruf der Gemeinde Insterburg die Wegweisung meines Herrn.

Mein Wechsel im Jahre 1911 und die Nachfolgerfrage bei der Berufung von zwei Brüdern wurden zum Anlaß, daß in der Gemeindeversammlung in Rummy am 7. Juli 1912, in der ich die Leitung hatte, Ortelsburg mit 239 Gliedern von Rummy als selbständige Gemeinde entlassen wurde. Wenn die Gemeinde heute mehr als doppelt so stark ist, dann ist es Gnade, für die dem Herrn alle Ehre gebührt. Möge die Gemeinde wachsen nach außen und nach innen und zunehmen an Jesusähnlichkeit!

Adolf Pawlitzki.

20

II. Die Arbeitsgruppen der Gemeinde

1. Der Gemeinde=Brüderrat

So habt nun acht auf euch selbst und auf die
ganze Herde! Apg. 20, 28.

Der Brüderrat, früher „Vorstand" genannt, ist das Verant=
wortung tragende Organ der Gemeinde. Alle Angelegenheiten der
Gemeinde werden hier gründlich und betend durchberaten und
beschlußreif gemacht. Aufnahmen und Wiederaufnahmen, Aus=
schlüsse und Überweisungen, Kassen= und Grundstücksangelegen=
heiten, besonders aber die Missionsziele der Gemeinde werden hier
durchgesprochen. In allen Dingen wird möglichste Einmütigkeit
erstrebt. Im Brüderrat werden die Beschlußvorschläge in das
Protokollbuch eingetragen. Das gesamte Protokoll wird dann in
der Gemeindestunde vom Schriftwart der Gemeinde vorgelesen,
vom Prediger eingehend erklärt und, falls sich kein Widerspruch
erhebt, angenommen. So ist es zu einer feinen, brüderlichen und
harmonischen Arbeit gekommen, die der Gemeinde zum Segen
gereicht. Die Leitung der Brüderratssitzungen und Gemeinde=
stunden hat der Prediger in Verbindung mit dem verantwort=
lichen Ältesten. Die Arbeit des Brüderrats ist in folgende Gebiete
aufgeteilt: Dem Prediger zur Seite steht der verantwortliche
Älteste Br. Friedrich Hartwich. Hier ist es ein Hand=in=Hand=
arbeiten, das oft täglichen Gedankenaustausch erfordert. Interne
Angelegenheiten werden dann ferner mit den Mitältesten Br.
Wilhelm Gallmeister sen. und Br. Artur Schulz besprochen.
Regelmäßig einmal im Monat kommt der Brüderrat zu Ge=
meinderatungen zusammen. Unsere Gemeindekasse ist seit fünf=
zehn Jahren in den guten und vertrauenswürdigen Händen des
Gemeinde=Hauptkassierers Br. Johann Laskowski. Ihm stehen
12 Unterkassierer, meist Brüder aus dem Brüderrat, zur Seite.
Diese besuchen die Mitglieder einmal monatlich und nehmen gern
die freiwilligen Missionsbeiträge entgegen. Diese Methode hat
sich sehr gut bewährt. Schriftwart der Gemeinde ist Br. Paul

Zintarra. Seine sorgfältige Feder führt das Mitgliederregister.
Ihm ist auch die Bearbeitung der Mitgliedscheine übertragen. Als
Grundstücksverwalter bemüht sich Br. Wilhelm Gallmeister jun.
Der eifrige Pfleger unserer Heidenmission ist Br. Fritz Dischereit.
Die Brüder Soldaten begrüßt besonders und betreut Br. Fritz
Wondollek. Vertrauensmann für die Sparkasse deutscher Bap-
tisten in Berlin ist Br. Johann Laskowski. Kassierer der Sterbe-
kasse der deutschen Baptisten in Berlin ist Br. Walter Cznottka.
Bei dieser Angelegenheit sei hier auch erwähnt, daß unsere
Kastellangeschwister Friedrich Kostrzewa und Frau zur Zufrieden-
heit in ihrem vielseitigen Dienst an der Gemeinde bemüht sind.

Der gegenwärtige Gemeindebrüderrat setzt sich aus folgenden
Brüdern zusammen:

Prediger: Alfred Cierpke.

Älteste: Friedrich Hartwich, Wilhelm Gallmeister sen., Artur
Schulz.

Diakone: Paul Biernath, Fritz Dischereit, Wilhelm Gallmeister
jun., Jakob Janowski, Johann Laskowski, Friedrich Latza,
August Meier, Wilhelm Para, August Sarge, Georg
Schlüter, Gerhard Welskopf, Fritz Wondollek, Paul Zintarra.

2. Predigthelfer

Darum, ihr lieben Brüder, seht unter euch nach
sieben Brüdern, die ein gut Gerücht haben und
voll Heiligen Geistes und Weisheit sind. Apg. 6, 3.

Als neutestamentliche Gemeinde glauben wir an das soge-
nannte „Allgemeine Priestertum" der Gläubigen und lehnen den
Unterschied von „Geistlichen" und „Laien" ab. Nach dem Neuen
Testament ist jeder Gläubige, der den Heiligen Geist besitzt, ein
Geistlicher und zum Zeugendienst für den Heiland berufen. Wir
erwarten daher von allen Gemeindegliedern, daß sie sich in diesem
Zeugendienst an der Welt fleißig üben und darin den Herrn durch
ein Leben des Dienstes und der Hingabe an Jesum verherrlichen.

In Verfolg dieser Linie hat die Gemeinde einige Brüder für
den regelmäßigen Dienst am Wort bei Abwesenheit des Predigers
im Gemeindeort und besonders auf den Stationen noch besonders
herausgestellt. Wir haben große Hochachtung vor diesen Brüdern,
die neben ihrem Beruf sich für diesen besonderen Dienst rüsten
und der Gemeinde unentgeltlich zur Verfügung stellen.

Gegenwärtig dienen folgende Brüder in der Wortverkündigung: Fritz Dischereit, Wilhelm Gallmeister sen., Gustav Grabosch I, Friedrich Hartwich, Julius Labusch, Friedrich Latza, August Meier, Wilhelm Para, Artur Schulz und Fritz Wondollek.

3. Gesangchöre

> Der Herr hat mir ein neues Lied in meinen
> Mund gegeben, zu loben unseren Gott. Ps. 40, 4.

Wie fast bei allen Baptistengemeinden nahm die Frage des Chorgesanges in unserer Gemeinde einen wichtigen Platz ein. Schon in den ersten Anfängen der Station Ortelsburg versuchten die Geschwister, auch durch Gesang zu wirken. Infolge der geringen Anzahl und oft des Fehlens geeigneter Leiter war es jedoch keine ständige Einrichtung. Erst vom Jahre 1899 ab besteht hier ununterbrochen ein Gemischter Chor. Während der letzten Jahre wurde auch ein Männerchor, überwiegend aus den Brüdern des Gemischten Chors, sowie eine Gitarrengruppe gebildet. Außer der Verschönerung der Gottesdienste fanden jährlich wiederholt Gesangsgottesdienste statt. Der Chor gehört dem Christlichen Sängerbund an, dessen Untergliederung die Ostmärkische Sänger= vereinigung ist, der auch der Sängerkreis Ortelsburg mit Um= gebung angehört. Wiederholt nahm der Chor an besonderen Gesangsveranstaltungen teil, z. B. an den Vereinigungs=Sänger= festen und auch an dem fünfzigjährigen Bundes=Jubiläumsfest. Sich anfangs auf die Wiedergabe einfachster Lieder aus dem „Evangeliums=Sänger" und ähnlichen Notenbüchern beschränkend, hat sich der Chorgesang im Laufe der Jahre sehr gut herausgebildet, so daß in letzter Zeit auch schwierigere Sachen zum Vortrag gebracht werden konnten. So wurden in einer Anzahl von größeren Gesangsgottesdiensten in Ortelsburg und in den um= liegenden Gemeinden unter Zusammenschluß einer Anzahl von Chören der anliegenden Baptistengemeinden „Die Himmel er= zählen..." von Haydn und „Das große Halleluja" von Händel vorgetragen. Im März dieses Jahres veranstaltete der Chor ein WHW.=Fest, an welchem u. a. die beiden genannten Stücke nur mit eigenen gesanglichen Kräften unter Hinzuziehung von Musikern des Jäger=Bataillons gebracht wurden, das sowohl als Veranstaltung als auch in finanzieller Hinsicht ein sehr guter Er= folg war. Die Sänger wollen, ihren Aufgaben entsprechend, den

Herrn loben, den Geschwistern zur Freude und in Liedern das Evangelium verkündend, auch weiter ihren Dienst treu erfüllen. Bei besonderen festlichen Anlässen wirkt die Gitarrengruppe des Gesangschors mit. Die Lieder, um ein Beispiel herauszugreifen, eine Viertelstunde vor Anfang der Evangelisationsversammlung gesungen, tragen viel zur Stille und wirksamen Aufnahme des Wortes Gottes bei.

Der Gesangchor wurde von dem jungen, gesanglich begabten Br. Julius Labusch gegründet und jahrzehntelang geleitet. Heute leitet sein Bruder Paul Labusch verantwortlich den Chor. Beide Brüder wechseln sich jedoch ab und arbeiten vorbildlich Hand in Hand. Leiterinnen der Gitarrengruppe sind die Schwestern Dora Koch und Irmgard Salewski. Als Organisten betätigen sich die Brüder Heinz Welskopf und Wilhelm Gallmeister jun. und die Schwestern Dora Koch und Irmgard Cierpke.

4. Frauendienst

Dient dem Herrn mit Freuden.   Ps. 100, 2.

Nach dem Vorbild anderer Gemeinden wurde am 15. Januar 1913 ein Marthaverein gegründet. Die Schwestern halten regelmäßig ihre Zusammenkünfte, fertigen Handarbeiten an und versuchen, dieselben in den jährlich wiederkehrenden besonderen Veranstaltungen zu verkaufen. Diese Veranstaltungen sind auch Gelegenheiten zu gemütlichen, zwanglosen Feiern. Neben der Bestreitung der Ausgaben für mancherlei Liebesdienste haben die Schwestern jährlich nicht unwesentliche Beträge für besondere Anschaffungen in der Kapelle oder als Hilfe für Sonntagsschule oder Gemeindekasse geleistet. Die Zusammenkünfte dienen auch erbaulichen Zwecken. Aber auch für größere Veranstaltungen der Gemeinde war die Frauengruppe eine nicht zu entbehrende Einrichtung. Im stillen wirkend hat die Frauengruppe gewiß viel Segen gestiftet. Wir sind unseren Schwestern für ihre Tätigkeit sehr dankbar.

Als letzte Leiterin des Frauendienstes sei die Predigerfrau Schw. Rosa Pawlitzki genannt. Unter ihrer umsichtigen Leitung hat sich die Frauengruppe nach der missionarischen Seite hin besonders gut entwickelt. Im gleichen Sinne arbeitet gegenwärtig unsere Schw. Wilhelmine Sarge.

Gemeindejugend

Bibelklasse

Religionsunterricht

Sonntagsschulhelfer

Sonntagsschule

Außenansicht der Kapelle

5. Jugendgruppe

> Wie wird ein Jüngling (eine Jungfrau) seinen
> (ihren) Weg unsträflich gehen? Wenn er (sie)
> sich hält nach deinen Worten.   Pf. 119, 9.

Besondere Jugendarbeit ist in unserer Gemeindegeschichte des deutschen Baptismus erst seit ungefähr 50 Jahren getan worden. Da die Gemeinde Ortelsburg erst 25 Jahre alt ist, hat sie immer Jugendarbeit gehabt. Schon vor der Gemeindegründung, etwa seit 1908, finden wir Spuren dieser Arbeit. Jungfrauen und Jünglinge kamen getrennt zusammen. Br. Julius Labusch hat sich jahrelang darum gemüht, nachdem er selbst es war, der in weitschauender Weise sich um unseren Nachwuchs dadurch gekümmert hat, daß er besonders Jugendstunden organisierte. Alle jungen Prediger standen mitten in der Jugendarbeit. Hier sei besonders der Name M. Morét genannt. In vorbildlicher Jugendarbeit hat sich in den Jahren von 1919 bis 1932 Br. Johann Laskowski, dann Br. Gerhard Meier und zuletzt Prediger Adolf Gärtner der Jugend gewidmet. Gegenwärtig liegt die Jugendarbeit in den Händen von Prediger A. Cierpke. — Die Arbeit bestand in der Ausarbeitung von biblischen Themen, in der Traktat= und Schriftenmission, in der Verteilung von „Friedensboten", besonders auch am Totensonntag, und in der individuellen Förderung der Jugendlichen, besonders nach der geistlichen Seite. Nicht unerwähnt sei die Soldatenmission während der Kriegszeit und in der Nachkriegszeit.

An dieser Stelle denken wir auch mit Freuden an die Jungschararbeit in der Nachkriegszeit zurück. Unter den Mädchen arbeiteten Schw. Helene Pawlitzki und Schw. Hedwig Bollin, unter den Knaben Br. Gerhard Welskopf. Die Arbeit war fruchtbar und segensreich. Sie ist heute unter den Kindern von zehn bis vierzehn Jahren in den Bibelscharen neu aufgenommen worden.

6. Religionsunterricht

> Weil du von Kind auf die Heilige Schrift weißt,
> kann dich dieselbe unterweisen zur Seligkeit durch
> den Glauben an Christum Jesum.   2. Tim. 3, 15.

Die biblische Unterweisung unserer Kinder nach einem bestimmten Lehrplan sehen wir als eine hohe Aufgabe und Gewissenspflicht an. Im Anschluß an die Unterweisung im Elternhaus und den regelmäßigen Unterricht in der Sonntagsschule nehmen wir die Kinder im Alter von zwölf bis vierzehn Jahren für zwei volle Jahre in besonderen Bibel- und Glaubensunterricht. Als Leitfaden dienen: F. W. Herrmann, „Religionsunterricht" und „Glaubensbekenntnis und Verfassung der Gemeinden gläubig getaufter Christen". Gegenwärtig nehmen 35 Kinder an dem Unterricht teil. Leiter ist Prediger Cierpke.

7. Sonntagsschule und Bibelklasse

Lasset die Kindlein zu mir kommen und wehret
ihnen nicht, denn solcher ist das Reich Gottes.
Mark. 10, 14.

Sonntagsschulen waren vielfach die ersten Anfänge in der Reichsgottesarbeit unserer Gemeinden. Die Arbeit an den Kindern ist eine der fruchtbarsten im Reiche Gottes. Deshalb sind unsere Sonntagsschulen zumeist älter als unsere Gemeinden. Sie waren Stubensonntagsschulen, in denen sich Lehrer und Schüler unter den Augen des Heilands ganz nahe kamen. — Aus ältester Zeit der Reichsgottesarbeit in Ortelsburg ist der Name des Br. Wilh. Brosch, der in den Jahren 1890 bis 1906 die Kinder zuerst in der Kaiserstraße, dann in der Königsberger Straße und zuletzt in der neuerbauten Kapelle unterrichtete, dankbar zu nennen. Eine Zeitlang hat sie auch Br. Johann Beier in seiner Wohnung gehabt. Schon damals gab es Weihnachten 100 Kinder. Es waren dann Br. Julius Labusch und Br. Christian Kuczewski lange Jahre Sonntagsschulleiter. Seit dem Jahre 1918 hat der lebhafte, alle Kinderherzen erobernde Br. Artur Schulz die Sonntagsschule geleitet. Seit dem Jahre 1936 hat Br. Schulz die Knabenbibelklasse als fördernde Bibelarbeit an den heranwachsenden Knaben übernommen, während ihn der aus Westfalen zugezogene Br. Otto Przygodda in der Sonntagsschulleitung abgelöst hat. Br. Przygodda arbeitet mit Sorgfalt und Liebe. Ihm stehen folgende Mitarbeiterinnen zur Seite: die Schwestern Hedwig Bollin, Elfriede Cierpke, Berta Lazarus, Lotte Pawlitzki, Erna Moschkelewski, Edith Samorski, Traute Samorski, Erna Sarge, Frieda Schlüter, ferner als Mitarbeiter die Brüder: August Meier, Heinrich Nowak, Karl Pech und Gerhard Welskopf. Mögen wir die Sonntagsschularbeit stets mit Heilandsaugen anschauen!

26

8. Bibelgruppen

Ich habe keine größere Freude denn die, daß ich höre meine Kinder in der Wahrheit wandeln.

3. Joh. 4.

Um der Eigenart der oft krisenhaft im Entwickelungsalter stehenden jungen Menschen zu dienen und ihnen von einer ganz praktischen Seite echtes Christentum zu zeigen, haben wir die frühere „Jungschararbeit" wieder aufgenommen und zu einer Knabenbibelgruppe und Mädchenbibelgruppe zusammengeschlossen. Hier lernen sie Gotteserkenntnis und Menschenkenntnis auf Grund der Heiligen Schrift, hier lernen sie frohe und christliche Jugend= lieder, hier üben sie praktischen Liebesdienst an Alten und Kranken. Schon früh sollen unsere Kinder für ganz praktisches Christentum, für ein Christentum der Tat, erzogen werden.

Die Gründung der Knabenbibelgruppe erfolgte am Montag, den 21. Juni 1937. Anwesend sind durchschnittlich 10 Knaben. Leiter sind die Brüder Friedrich Görtz und Helmut Brosch.

Die Mädchenbibelgruppe wurde am Donnerstag, den 24. Juni 1937, gegründet. Leiterinen sind die Schwestern Edith Samorski und Elfriede Cierpke. Anwesend sind durchschnittlich 20 Mädchen.

9. Schriftenmissionsgruppe

Laß dein Brot über das Wasser fahren, so wirst du es finden nach langer Zeit. Pred. 11, 1.

Das gedruckte Wort reicht weiter als das gesprochene. Das hatten unsere Väter schon früh erkannt. Oncken stattete die jungen aus Hamburg reisenden Handwerker mit Traktaten aus und sandte sie so mit dem gedruckten Wort Gottes in die Heimat. So wurde das Wort des mündlichen Zeugnisses unterstützt durch gedrucktes Evangelium. Wir sind bemüht, die Zeitschriften unseres Verlagshauses nicht nur selbst zu lesen, sondern auch möglichst weit zu verbreiten. Unser rühriger Zeitschriftenwart ist Br. Georg Schlüter. Er hat sein Amt von dem langjährigen treuen Br. Michael Faber, der verstorben ist, übernommen. Gegen= wärtig haben wir folgende Verbreitungszahlen:

„Der Wahrheitszeuge"	68	„Der Friedensbote"	171
„Der Morgenstern"	87	„Der Jungbrunnen"	20
„Der Hilfsbote"	2	„Der Frauendienst"	25

Zurzeit findet ein durch die ganze Gemeinde durchgeführter Friedensboten=Werbefeldzug statt, für den wir uns 500 neue Abonnenten zu werben zum Ziel gesetzt haben.

Einen wichtigen Zweig der Schriftenmission bildet die Kalendermission. Wenn wir daran denken, daß die Mühe, einen Kalender unterzubringen, nicht groß ist und das Wort Gottes und eine kleine Auslegung desselben ein ganzes Jahr lang die Leser bewußt unter den Einfluß Gottes stellt, dann lohnt sich die Arbeit immer. Das Jahr 1936 war in der Gemeindegeschichte darin das erfolgreichste. Dadurch, daß wir die ganze Gemeinde für diesen Dienst aufgerufen haben, ist es möglich geworden, im vergangenen Jahr 1335 Kalender unterzubringen gegenüber 370 im Jahre 1935. Das sind fast 1000 Kalender mehr. Der Herr segne darin alle Bemühungen fernerhin!

10. Büchertisch

Suchet in dem Buche des Herrn und leset...,
denn Gottes Geist ist es, der es zusammenbringt.
Jes. 34, 16.

Ein christliches Buch kann ein Freund im Leben werden. Bücher können besonders die Jugend dazu führen, christlichen Idealen nachzustreben und bibelfeste Menschen zu werden. Um den manchmal schnellen Bedarf an Bibeln, Testamenten, Liederbüchern und christlichen Büchern nachzukommen, hat die Gemeinde am 1. Oktober 1936 einen kleinen Büchertisch eingerichtet. Diese Einrichtung hat sich sehr gut bewährt. Der Zweck ist ein rein missionarischer. Bücherwarte sind die Brüder Gerhard Hartwich und Gunhard Geschke.

III. Anhang

1. Kurzgefaßte Chronologie

1869: Die ersten Baptisten in Ortelsburg.
Br. Carl Werschkull sen. kommt als Polier zum Bau des Amtsgerichts nach Ortelsburg.

1871: Br. Eduard Bollin aus Jablonken kommt nach Ortelsburg gezogen. Dienstantritt des Predigers F. W. Kottke in Rummy.

1881: Beginn der regelmäßigen Hausandachten. Die Brüder Prediger Hein und Kottke leiten vornehmlich die Versammlungen.

1883: Es werden getauft: 8. Juli Br. Jakob Samorski, 3. Oktober Br. August Sarge sen.

1888: Eigener Versammlungsraum bei Geschw. Werschkull, Kaiserstraße.

1891: 16. August: Br. Wilhelm Gallmeister sen. wird von Br. Kottke getauft.

1897: Br. Jakob Samorski baut und vermietet der Gemeinde einen größeren Versammlungsraum an der Chaussee nach Mensguth, jetzt Königsberger Straße.

1898: März: Br. Adolf Pawlitzki von der Gemeinde Osterode, Station Hirsch= berg, wird von der Gemeinde Rummy für den Missionsdienst berufen.

1899: September bis Juni 1902 besucht Br. A. Pawlitzki das Prediger= seminar in Hamburg.

1902: 1. Juli: Br. Pawlitzki wird Prediger der Gemeinde Rummy.

1903: 3. Mai: Grundsteinlegung zur Kapelle in Ortelsburg.

1904: 10. Juli: Kapelleneinweihung in Ortelsburg.

1907: Herbst: Prediger Kottke folgt einem Ruf der Gemeinde Romanowen. Prediger Thiel dient aushilfsweise in Ortelsburg.

1909: Die Gemeinde erhält nach langen Bemühungen Korporationsrechte und hat vor der Behörde ihren Sitz in Ortelsburg.

1911: 15. Mai: Prediger Pawlitzki folgt einem Ruf der Gemeinde Insterburg. Weihnachten: Br. Maximo Morét, Berlin, wird für den Missions= dienst berufen und besucht von 1912 bis 1915 das Predigerseminar in Hamburg.
Die Gemeinde Rummy beruft Br. Jersak zum Prediger. Dieser bleibt aber nur ganz kurze Zeit. In Ortelsburg dient von Zeit zu Zeit Br. Porps von Rummy.

1912: 7. Juli: Entlassung der Stationsgemeinde Ortelsburg in der Gemeinde= stunde in Rummy zur selbständigen Gemeinde.

Juli bis August: Br. G. Freutel vom Predigerseminar dient in seinen Ferien in Ortelsburg.

18. August: Die Gemeinde Ortelsburg wird mit 237 Mitgliedern gegründet.

1913: Juli: Br. Otto Schäfer vom Predigerseminar in Hamburg wird von der Gemeinde als Prediger berufen.

1914: Prediger O. Schäfer folgt einem Ruf der Gemeinde Allenstein.

Juli bis August: Br. M. Morét dient während seiner Seminarferien in der Gemeinde Ortelsburg.

Der Weltkrieg bricht aus, und Br. Morét muß mit den Geschwistern vor den hereinbrechenden Russen fliehen.

1915: November: Br. M. Morét wird nach seinem Studium in Hamburg-Horn als Prediger der Gemeinde berufen.

Die Kapelle dient noch einige Zeit als Reservelazarett für Leichtverwundete.

1916: 8. Oktober: Ordination von Prediger M. Morét in Ortelsburg.

1920: 1. Oktober: Krankheitshalber gibt Br. M. Morét seinen Dienst an der Gemeinde auf und folgt nach seiner Wiederherstellung einem Ruf der Gemeinde Kiel II.

1921: Ostern: Konferenz der Ostpreußischen Jünglingsvereinigung in Ortelsburg.

1922: 1. Ostpreußische Jugend-Vereinigungskonferenz in Ortelsburg.

1. Juli: Prediger A. Pawlitzki, Insterburg, folgt einem Ruf der Gemeinde als Prediger.

1923: Br. Hermann Zart vom Predigerseminar dient Juli und August in Ortelsburg.

1924: Ostpreußische Gemeinde-Vereinigungskonferenz in Ortelsburg.

1928: Einweihung der neuen Kapelle in Gr.-Schiemanen.

1929: Umbau der Kapelle in Ortelsburg mit Einbau der neuen Orgel.

1930: 1. Dezember: Prediger F. W. Kottke heimgegangen.

1931: Ostpreußische Gemeinde-Vereinigungskonferenz in Ortelsburg.

1935: 1. August: Br. Adolf Gärtner vom Predigerseminar kommt als Vikar nach Ortelsburg.

1. September: Prediger Adolf Pawlitzki folgt einem Ruf der Gemeinde Lyck.

1936: 1. April: Prediger A. Gärtner folgt einem Ruf der Gemeinde Neustadt, O.-Schl.

1. Juni: Prediger Alfred Cierpke von der Gemeinde Königsberg-Tragheim wird zum Prediger der Gemeinde Ortelsburg berufen.

2. Übersicht über die jährliche Mitgliederbewegung

Jahresanfang	Mitgliederzahl Anf. des Jahres	Zunahme durch				Abnahme durch						Reine Zunahme	Reine Abnahme	Ganze Mitgliederzahl	Ende des Jahres
		Taufen	Zeugnis	Wiederaufnahme	Summa	Gestorben	Entlassen	Ausgewandert	Gestrichen	Ausgeschlossen	Summa				
1912 18.8.	239					4	7	1	1	2	15	—	15	224	1912
1913	224	11	8		19	2	15	3	1	5	26	—	7	217	1913
1914	217	5	5	1	11	3	11	—	—	6	20	—	9	208	1914
1915	208	1	4	—	5	3	5	—	—	—	8	—	3	205	1915
1916	205	11	5	1	17	—	—	—	—	1	1	16	—	221	1916
1917	221	19	2	2	23	1	4	—	—	—	5	18	—	239	1917
1918	239	5	9	2	16	3	13	—	—	—	16	—	—	239	1918
1919	239	8	16	—	24	5	10	—	5	—	20	4	—	243	1919
1920	243	21	13	3	37	6	37	—	—	2	45	—	8	235	1920
1921	235	18	21	2	41	7	11	—	—	1	19	22	—	257	1921
1922	257	23	32	1	56	3	31	2	3	3	42	14	—	271	1922
1923	271	20	10	3	33	1	5	—	1	2	9	24	—	295	1923
1924	295	45	3	4	52	7	15	2	—	1	25	27	—	322	1924
1925	322	16	31	4	51	2	27	1	—	2	32	19	—	341	1925
1926	341	30	19	2	51	1	19	1	1	9	31	20	—	361	1926
1927	361	15	9	1	25	4	10	2	—	3	19	6	—	367	1927
1928	367	31	9	3	43	3	28	—	1	3	35	8	—	375	1928
1929	375	21	13	2	36	3	23	2	—	3	31	5	—	380	1929
1930	380	23	13	1	37	4	20	—	1	5	30	7	—	387	1930
1931	387	14	15	5	34	3	10	—	—	4	17	17	—	404	1931
1932	404	5	15	1	21	4	9	—	1	5	19	2	—	406	1932
1933	406	27	10	2	39	8	10	—	1	4	23	16	—	422	1933
1934	422	19	23	2	44	5	20	—	—	2?	2?	15	—	437	1934
1935	437	8	32	3	43	5	24	—	1	4	34	9	—	446	1935
1936	446	18	27	3	48	3	20	—	—	3	26	22	—	468	1936
1937	468	65	11	12	88	3	8	—	2	3	16	72	—	540	Juli 1937

3. Gebet aus der Didache

(Lehre der zwölf Apostel.)

Entstanden etwa 90 bis 150 n. Chr.

Gedenke, Herr, deiner Gemeinde,
sie zu retten von allem Bösen,
und sie zu vollenden in deiner Liebe,
und führe sie von den vier Winden zuhauf,
sie, die Geheiligte, in dein Reich,
das du ihr bereitet hast.
Denn dein ist die Kraft und die Herrlichkeit
in Ewigkeit.
Kommen möge die Gnade,
und vergehen möge diese Welt.
Hosianna Gott!
Ist jemand heilig, so trete er hinzu;
wer es nicht ist, der tue Buße.
Maran atha! Der Herr kommt!
Amen.

2407 37 500   Druck von J. G. Oncken Nachf., Kasse